12-14-05

My dearest husband

How I love you—so very much! You are my rock in troubled times always turning our[illegible] back to the One who[illegible] forgive my short comings[illegible] love me always, as[illegible] you.

Always, Forever

Aurelia

The Miracle of the Seventh Day

The Miracle of the Seventh Day

A Guide to the Spiritual Meaning, Significance, and Weekly Practice of the Jewish Sabbath

Rabbi Adin Steinsaltz

An Arthur Kurzweil Book

JOSSEY-BASS
A Wiley Imprint
www.josseybass.com

Published by Jossey-Bass
A Wiley Imprint
989 Market Street, San Francisco, CA 94103-1741 www.josseybass.com

First Jossey-Bass / John Wiley and Sons edition published 2003. Originally published as *A Song for the Sabbath Day: Prayers, Hymns, and Blessings for the Shabbat and Festival Table, With English Translation and Transliteration. Introductions and Commentaries by Rabbi Adin Even-Israel Steinsaltz,* by The Israel Institute for Talmudic Publications, Jerusalem, copyright © 1999.

Jossey-Bass books and products are available through most bookstores. To contact Jossey-Bass directly call our Customer Care Department within the U.S. at 800-956-7739, outside the U.S. at 317-572-3986 or fax 317-572-4002.

Jossey-Bass also publishes its books in a variety of electronic formats. Some content that appears in print may not be available in electronic books.

Typesetting by Ari Davidow

Library of Congress Cataloging-in-Publication Data
Siddur. Sabbath. English & Hebrew. Selections.
[Song for the Sabbath day]
Miracle of the seventh day : a guide to the spiritual meaning, significance, and weekly practice of the Jewish Sabbath / by Adin Even-Israel Steinsaltz.
p. cm.
Originally published under title: A song for the Sabbath day.
ISBN 0-7879-6545-6 (alk. paper)
1. Sabbath—Liturgy—Texts. 2. Hymns, Hebrew—Texts. 3. Benediction—Judaism—Texts. 4. Judaism—Liturgy—Texts. 5. Sabbath—Prayer-books and devotions. 6. Grace at meals—Judaism—Texts. 7. Sabbath—Liturgy. I. Steinsaltz, Adin. II. Title.

BM675.S3Z5586 2003
296.4'5—dc21

2002043312

Printed in the United States of America

FIRST EDITION

HB Printing 10 9 8 7 6 5 4 3 2

Contents

The Departure of Shabbat 135

Grace after Meals 177

Acknowledgments

Hebrew editing and proofreading: Rabbi Yehonatan Eliav, Meir Hanegbi, Yehudit Shabtai

English translations, editing, and proofreading: Rabbi Jonathan Chipman, Yehudit Shabtai

The *Zemirot* were translated by:

Jonathan Wittenberg: *Menuḥah ve'Simḥah, Mah Yedidut, Yah Ribbon, Tzamah Nafshi, Yom Zeh le'Yisrael, Yah Ekhsof, Yom Shabbaton, Ki Eshmerah Shabbat, Dror Yikra, El Mistatter, Yedid Nefesh, Ha'Mavdil, Elohim Yisadenu, Eli Ḥish, Adir Ayom ve'Nora, Ḥaddesh Sesoni*

Tuvia Natkin: *Kol Mekaddesh, Yom Shabbat Kodesh Hu, Tzur mi'Shelo, Ḥai Adonai, Barukh Adonai Yom Yom, Barukh El Elyon, Yom Zeh Mekhubbad, Shimru Shabtotai, Shabbat ha'Yom l'Adonai, Be'Motzaei Yom Menuḥah, Agil ve'Esmaḥ, Ish Ḥasid Hayah, Amar Adonai le'Yaakov, Eliyahu ha'Navi, Ribbon ha'Olamim*

In honor of Lotte and Ludwig Bravmann

by their family and friends
on the occasion of their fiftieth wedding anniversary,
19 Adar 5759

Introduction

This book is intended for use as a companion at the Sabbath table. It is designed both for those who know very little and for those well versed in the laws and customs of Shabbat. For those with little knowledge, it may serve as a guidebook to assist them in following or conducting a Shabbat meal, complete with blessings before and after the meal and hymns sung at the table. For those already knowledgeable, the book will shed new light upon the significance of various elements of the Sabbath and provide further insight into the history and development of the prayers and traditions of the day.

The observance of the Sabbath is one of the most important precepts of Judaism. The holiness of the day and the commandments to remember and honor it are stressed throughout the sources, from the description of the Creation, in which Shabbat plays a central role, to the Ten Commandments, the Latter Prophets, and subsequent Jewish literature of every age and locale.

"Thou shalt not labor on the Sabbath" is repeated several times throughout Scripture, and the basic view of the Sabbath as a day of rest appears very simple. But in practice, the Jewish Sabbath is unique. Indeed, a comparison with the Christian and Muslim variations of it—not to mention the modern secular "weekend"—only underlines this uniqueness. Shabbat is not merely a day when one refrains from work, nor is it merely the day when it is customary to attend public prayer. It is a day when one enters a completely different sphere.

The rabbinic sayings comparing Shabbat to the World to Come are more than mere figures of speech. People work in physical and spiritual ways to repair the reality of the world, and this may be considered the meaning of the weekday. But, on the seventh day, there is a cessation of all work, and a heavenly delight is manifested. The week is thus devoted to an awakening process from below; it is as though the Shabbat is the hidden purpose of labor—a purpose that is revealed only on the seventh day. As it is written: "And it shall come to pass that every new moon and every Shabbat, shall all flesh come to bow down before Me" (Isaiah 66:23).

Shabbat means putting aside creative activity in order to concern oneself completely with personal reflection and matters of the spirit, free of struggle and tension. The key element in Shabbat observance is a kind of passivity: refraining from "work." Yet, over a period of three thousand years, the Jewish people have developed a tradition that transforms what might otherwise be a day of mere inactivity into one of joy and inner peace—"a day of rest and holiness," in the words of the liturgy. This tradition is one of the hallmarks of Jewish culture as a whole.

The fact that we, and we alone, celebrate Shabbat is an expression of God's special affection for us, a "sign" and token of that love. Therefore, throughout the prayers recited on this day we say—regarding the Sabbath, and the Sabbath only—"in love." It is this unique aspect of Shabbat, in fact, that places it above all the Festival days in the Jewish calendar. Festival days are, in essence, connected to the Jewish people, commemorating specific miraculous events that befell us. The Almighty joins us, so to speak, in the celebrations and joy of these days, thus making them "the festivals of the Lord" (Leviticus 23:4)—times in which we convene and meet with the Almighty.

Shabbat, in its essence, is not connected to the Jewish people: Shabbat preceded the Jewish people. It is the day of rest and elevation of the Almighty Himself, after having completed Creation. Yet, because of His love for us, God has given us a special gift: an invitation to share His own day with Him. This is the significance of the verse: "It is a sign between Me and the children of Israel for all time, for in six days the Lord made the heavens and the Earth, and on the seventh day He ceased from work and rested"

(Exodus 31:17). The essence of Shabbat is really a trickle, an infiltration, of the next world into this world. It is a percolation and diffusion of an existing Divine Reality.

Approached from a distance, the body of Shabbat prohibitions can appear to be an endless maze of details: "don't do," "don't move," "don't touch." Yet, for all the elaboration these prohibitions have received, the principles underlying them are quite simple. The key formula here is, "Thou shalt not do any manner of *melakhah*." The concept of *melakhah* is understood both in the simple sense of "work," which is its plain meaning—labor that entails excessive effort or activity for which payment is rendered, for example.

However, there is also a more complex sense of *melakhah* that flows from the context in which it first appears: the story of the Sabbath of Creation. This definition of labor is based to a large extent on the concept of *imitatio Dei*. In this case, the term has the meaning of an act of physical creation. Just as God ceased from His labor—creation of the world—on the Sabbath, so the children of Israel are called upon to refrain from creative work on this day. What is decisive is not the degree of effort involved, or whether the action receives monetary compensation, but rather, whether it results in the appearance of something new in the physical world. Thus, relatively effortless activities such as writing and profitless activities such as landscaping one's yard become forbidden. Similarly, it is not permitted to kindle or handle fire on Shabbat—a fact that has always been of great practical significance. Not only is smoking prohibited; so also is operating a vehicle or tool requiring internal combustion.

Of course, no single definition could cover all the complex issues likely to arise from the prohibition of labor. Instead, the rabbis chose an elemental model for those actions forbidden on the Sabbath: the work of construction of the Tabernacle in the desert, explicitly prohibited by the Torah. A large part of the legal, or halakhic, discussion in the Talmud on forbidden and permitted acts on the Sabbath is an elaboration and expansion of this basic model and the derivation of practical conclusions from it.

Over and above the basic prohibitions, a set of secondary restrictions was enacted by the rabbinical authorities down through the ages. A few of these laws were in effect as early as the period of the First Temple. These secondary restrictions are known as *shevut* prohibitions. In most cases, they are intended as a hedge around the more fundamental prohibitions, designed to prevent certain habitual activities from leading to Shabbat violations. Such activities include commerce, playing musical instruments, taking drugs (unless they are vital to health), riding animals (a prohibition also based on the positive biblical injunction to allow animals to rest on Shabbat), and handling *muktseh* objects. The notion of *muktseh* is a complex one in halakhah, but basically it refers to the handling of objects connected to activities that are forbidden on the Sabbath. These include raw materials such as stone, soil, and wood not prepared specifically for use on Shabbat, and especially money.

While the heart of Shabbat observance is refraining rather than doing, one cannot underestimate the positive dimension of the "culture" of Shabbat. It is this dimension that makes it, in the words of the liturgy, "a day of joy and rest, quiet and security," a day of holiness, a day when one acquires a *neshamah yeteirah,* an "extra soul." To a certain extent, the meaning of Shabbat (and this is what distinguishes it from imitations adopted by other peoples) lies in the fact that it is not a day of gloom, hedged in by strict prohibitions.

On the contrary, festivity is of the essence. Even one who is newly bereaved or has a fresh memory of some other personal catastrophe must stop mourning when Shabbat arrives. The *neshamah yeteirah* each Jew is said to acquire on Shabbat is really an augmented ability to rejoice in tranquility, to accept life with a feeling of wholeness and contentment. Shabbat is a time to disengage oneself from workaday affairs—even reading, speaking, and thinking about them are forbidden. Even when it comes to spiritual matters, vexation and anxious self-analysis should be avoided. The holiness of the day must be sought in a spirit of pleasure, relaxation, and ease.

The phrase "Call the Sabbath a delight" (Isaiah 58:13) inspired several customs included within the generic term *oneg Shabbat,* "Sabbath delight." They include, for example, the three Sabbath festive meals, the injunction to wear festive garments in honor of the Sabbath, and so on. Thus, before Shabbat begins, candles are lit, preferably on or near the dinner table. This practice was also originally part of the *oneg Shabbat,* a way of insuring that the Sabbath meal would be eaten in the light. It also adds a festive quality to the day. Every Jew is obliged to light candles, but over the centuries the tradition arose that it should be done, wherever possible, by the woman of the house. (There is also a beautiful custom according to which each woman and girl in the family lights her own Shabbat candles.) The connection between the night of Shabbat and the woman's role is a deep and ancient one, of which the candle-lighting is but one part.

The Shabbat mealtimes—to which this book is largely devoted—fulfill an important role in the course and customs of the day, both because they are mandatory and because they are surrounded by ceremonies of blessings, study, and song.

Unlike weekday meals, those eaten on Shabbat are not for physical sustenance alone, but serve to fill the mitzvah of Sabbath joy. We are called upon to observe the sanctity of Shabbat by refraining from work and devoting the day to heavenly matters, and by honoring it through physical pleasures. Therefore, the pleasures of the body, which on weekdays are merely a permissible option, have, on Shabbat, an aspect of a commandment. It is a mitzvah to eat three Shabbat meals: Friday evening, Shabbat lunch, and a third meal in the late afternoon of Shabbat. These are "sacred meals," both in their ceremonial character and in their deeper meaning, meals in which the Jewish family, as a religious (not merely social) unit, communes with the sanctity of the day. Indeed, the Shabbat meal may be compared to the Seder meal of Passover: not simply a festive meal, but a meal that is, itself, a form of Divine service.

The Shabbat meal is therefore accompanied by a great variety of special customs, as well as by words of Torah and prayer. The actual customs vary largely from place to place. Already at the time of our sages, it was a habit to eat special foods on Shabbat, and so it is to this day. Every community and congregation has its special Shabbat dishes that are inseparably intertwined with the very substance of these meals. However, halakhically speaking, there is only one binding law on Shabbat meals: that of the "double-bread"—that is, at each Shabbat meal there should be at least two loaves of bread, in remembrance of the double portion of manna that came down from Heaven in the desert on Fridays (Exodus 16). An ancient custom, mentioned in the Talmud, is to eat fish during Shabbat meals. Special care is also taken everywhere to eat (or drink) something warm (ḥamin) on Shabbat—although the prohibition against cooking requires that the ḥamin must be prepared before the Sabbath. Eating the ḥamin is a rebuke against the strictures of the Samaritans and the Karaites, who forbade eating warm food on the Sabbath.

The Torah exhortation "Remember the Sabbath day to sanctify it," which was originally a general injunction to mark the commencement of the Sabbath by word and deed, was also stylized into benedictions and prayers. The first two of the three meals begin with Kiddush ("sanctification"), a special benediction usually said over a cup of wine (or spirits or grape juice in the case of people who do not tolerate alcohol well). After *netilat yadayim* (ritual hand washing), the meal itself begins. In most Jewish communities it is customary to sing *zemirot,* special Sabbath hymns, at the table. The effect is to reinforce the sense of togetherness and spirituality appropriate to the Sabbath table.

The manifestations of *oneg Shabbat* (it was even said that "sleep is a delight on the Sabbath") also include spiritual aspects. The sages introduced the reading of a portion of the Torah, which came to be known as *parashat hashavua* (the portion of the week), on Sabbath morning and during the afternoon Minḥa service. In the Talmudic era, scholars preached on Shabbat afternoon.

In general, Shabbat should be devoted as much as possible to holy activities, especially prayer and study, which we may feel we do not have time for during the week. Thus, one who finds it inconvenient for one reason or another to attend public prayer during the week should make a special effort to do so on Shabbat. While the mitzvot, or commandments, of Shabbat also apply to isolated individuals, it is desirable to foster collective—familial and communal—observance of them. In addition, certain aspects of public worship, such as the ceremonial reading of the Torah, cannot be done on one's own. It is also appropriate to devote a certain amount of time each Shabbat to Torah study, if possible in communal and family settings. One may not be able to cover much ground in a once-a-week session, but the fulfillment of the mitzvah consists of setting aside a significant block of time for spiritual nourishment rather than achieving any particular intellectual goal.

At the end of Shabbat, we make Havdalah, which, in a sense, is parallel to the Kiddush with which we usher in the Shabbat. In essence, the commandment to remember the Shabbat is fulfilled not just on Shabbat, but on each day of the week. Just as our sages instituted the Kiddush to fulfill the commandment "Remember the Sabbath day, to sanctify it," so was the Havdalah (literally, "separation") instituted for the very same purpose: to underscore the sanctity and uniqueness of the Shabbat by making a distinction and separation between Shabbat and the weekdays. The texts, prayers, and songs of the end of Shabbat, as well as the *Melaveh Malkah* meal (a special meal held after the conclusion of Shabbat), all have the same purpose: to escort the Shabbat out with much ceremony, just as we greet her upon her arrival. *Melaveh Malkah* literally means "one who escorts the queen."

Thus, Shabbat is not only the sum or storehouse of the week, but also the source of blessing, the fountainhead from which all reality issues. This double function of end and beginning is actually a circular process; the week cannot start again without going through the Shabbat. In spite of being a halt and a summation, Shabbat is also a renewal; it provides the energy to continue. In this respect, then, the Shabbat is of the next world, with its paradisiacal power to keep supplying the life-replenishing delight of existence.

There is an ancient *piyyut* (liturgical poem), entitled *la'El asher Shavat* ("To the Almighty who Rested"), which is recited in the Shabbat morning prayer:

> To the Almighty God who rested from all His work, [who] on the seventh day was elevated and sat upon His Throne of Glory. He garbed the day of rest in beauty, He called the Shabbat day a delight. This is the glory of the seventh day, that on it the Almighty God rested from all His work. The seventh day offers praise and proclaims, "A Psalm, a Song of the Shabbat day—it is good to praise the Lord" (Psalms 92:1-2). Therefore, let all His creatures glorify and bless Almighty God; let them offer praise, honor, grandeur and glory to Almighty God, the King, Creator of all, who, in His holiness, gives His people Israel the heritage of rest on the holy Shabbat day.

This *piyyut*—conveying, as it were, the words of the Shabbat itself, mentions some of the praises of Shabbat. These praises are the essential things that may be said about Shabbat: it is a day of holiness, in which the Almighty, having descended, so to speak, to our world and created it during six days, once more ascends in His splendor and sits on His Throne of Glory. It is also a day of rest; but since it was given a special crown of glory, it is not merely a time of rest from hard labor, but rather a day that is "honored more than every other." And since "He called the Shabbat a delight," there is a special commandment to enjoy the Shabbat both in spirit and in body.

While we keep the Shabbat because we identify with the Almighty, we also want to express our feelings about this love-gift of Shabbat. Hence our response, "It is good to praise the Lord." That is why we sing songs of thanksgiving on Shabbat—to express our gratitude for this gift.

Out of all this emerges the song of the Shabbat day, which is a double, triple, and fourfold song: a song of gratitude for the rest, for the holiness, and for the gift of Shabbat—as well as a song of hope for the future, for the day "which will be entirely Shabbat and rest."

Shabbat Eve

Candle Lighting

The lighting of candles fulfills a part of the commandment to enjoy the Shabbat and festivals—which includes illuminating the home during mealtime—and is also a sign of respect for the sanctity of those days.

Even though this obligation applies to all those eating at a given place, the commandment to light candles is incumbent first and foremost upon the woman of the house, and a man does not light if his wife is present. The woman takes upon herself the sanctity of the Shabbat through the act of lighting candles. Today, it is increasingly common for girls also to light one candle and to recite the blessing over it.

Shabbat candles must be lit before sundown. The generally accepted procedure is for the woman to light the candles, cover her eyes with the palms of her hands, recite the blessing, and then gaze at the candles. It is customary for women to recite a personal prayer after lighting the candles (see page 13).

ברכות הדלקת הנרות
Candle Lighting Blessings

בָּרוּךְ אַתָּה יְיָ, אֱלֹהֵינוּ מֶלֶךְ הָעוֹלָם, אֲשֶׁר קִדְּשָׁנוּ
בְּמִצְוֹתָיו וְצִוָּנוּ לְהַדְלִיק נֵר שֶׁל שַׁבָּת.

Barukh attah Adonai, Eloheinu melekh ha'olam, asher kiddeshanu be'mitzvotav ve'tzizanu lehadlik ner shel Shabbat.

Blessed are You, Lord our God, King of the universe, who has sanctified us with His commandments and commanded us to kindle the light of Shabbat.

On a Festival day that falls on Shabbat:

בָּרוּךְ אַתָּה יְיָ, אֱלֹהֵינוּ מֶלֶךְ הָעוֹלָם, אֲשֶׁר קִדְּשָׁנוּ
בְּמִצְוֹתָיו וְצִוָּנוּ לְהַדְלִיק נֵר שֶׁל שַׁבָּת וְשֶׁל יוֹם טוֹב.

Barukh attah Adonai, Eloheinu melekh ha'olam, asher kiddeshanu be'mitzvotav ve'tzizanu lehadlik ner shel Shabbat ve'shel yom tov.

Blessed are You, Lord our God, King of the universe, who has sanctified us with His commandments and commanded us to kindle the Shabbat and Festival light.

On Festival days (except the seventh and eighth night of Pesaḥ) one adds:

בָּרוּךְ אַתָּה יְיָ, אֱלֹהֵינוּ מֶלֶךְ הָעוֹלָם, שֶׁהֶחֱיָנוּ וְקִיְּמָנוּ
וְהִגִּיעָנוּ לַזְּמַן הַזֶּה.

Barukh attah Adonai, Eloheinu melekh ha'olam, she'heḥeyanu ve'kiyyemanu ve'higgianu la'zman ha'zeh.

Blessed are You, Lord our God, King of the universe, who has granted us life, sustained us, and enabled us to reach this season.

תפילה לאשה אחר הדלקת הנרות

Prayer for Women after Lighting the Candles

יְהִי רָצוֹן מִלְּפָנֶיךָ יְיָ אֱלֹהַי וֵאלֹהֵי אֲבוֹתַי, שֶׁתְּחוֹנֵן אוֹתִי (וְאֶת אִישִׁי וְאֶת בָּנַי וְאֶת אָבִי וְאֶת אִמִּי) וְאֶת כָּל קְרוֹבַי, וְתִתֵּן לָנוּ וּלְכָל יִשְׂרָאֵל חַיִּים טוֹבִים וַאֲרֻכִּים, וְתִזְכְּרֵנוּ בְּזִכְרוֹן טוֹבָה וּבְרָכָה, וְתִפְקְדֵנוּ בִּפְקֻדַּת יְשׁוּעָה וְרַחֲמִים, וּתְבָרְכֵנוּ בְּרָכוֹת גְּדוֹלוֹת, וְתַשְׁלִים בָּתֵּינוּ, וְתַשְׁכֵּן שְׁכִינָתְךָ בֵּינֵינוּ. וְזַכֵּנִי לְגַדֵּל בָּנִים וּבְנֵי בָנִים חֲכָמִים וּנְבוֹנִים, אוֹהֲבֵי יְיָ, יִרְאֵי אֱלֹהִים, אַנְשֵׁי אֱמֶת, זֶרַע קֹדֶשׁ, בַּיְיָ דְּבֵקִים, וּמְאִירִים אֶת הָעוֹלָם בַּתּוֹרָה וּבְמַעֲשִׂים טוֹבִים וּבְכָל מְלֶאכֶת עֲבוֹדַת הַבּוֹרֵא. אָנָּא שְׁמַע אֶת תְּחִנָּתִי בָּעֵת הַזֹּאת, בִּזְכוּת

May it be Your will, O Lord God and God of my fathers, to show grace to me (and to my husband and to my children and to my father and mother) and to all those close to me, and grant me and all of Israel a good and long life. And remember us for goodness and for blessing, and visit us with salvation and mercy, and bless us with great blessings, and bring peace to our homes, and let your Shekhinah rest among us. And allow us to raise wise and understanding children, who love and fear God—offspring of truth, a holy seed, who will be attached to God and enlighten the

entire world with Torah and with good deeds, and labor in the service of the Creator. Heed my petition at this hour, through the merit of Sarah, Rivkah, Raḥel, and Leah our mothers. And give light to our candle so that it may not be extinguished forever, and show us the light of Your face, and let us be saved. Amen.

שָׂרָה וְרִבְקָה וְרָחֵל וְלֵאָה אִמּוֹתֵינוּ,
וְהָאֵר נֵרֵנוּ שֶׁלֹּא יִכְבֶּה לְעוֹלָם וָעֶד,
וְהָאֵר פָּנֶיךָ וְנִוָּשֵׁעָה. אָמֵן:

Order of Shabbat Eve

Each of the three parts of Shabbat—Friday evening, Shabbat day, and the late afternoon—manifests a different level of Shabbat. This is expressed both in the prayers for the Shabbat, and in the meals and other customs of the day.

Shabbat eve is both a climax and a final stage of the transition to all that the day signifies, both as the conclusion of the week and at a higher level of existence, beyond the six days of action; it is beyond time.

The beginning of Shabbat is thus, on the one hand, a kind of culmination of the six days that precede it, a seventh level including the other six within itself. On the other hand, it is a period that leads toward a higher level: that revealed on the Shabbat day, of the Sabbath as a day of a different kind, as having an essence beyond the six days of work.

This level of the Sabbath evening is bound up with the divine manifestation of the Shekhinah. The Shekhinah has a double aspect: it is the source of power for all lower entities; and it is also the totality, the vessel that absorbs all that is done in the world. The Shekhinah is called in Kabbalah "Kingdom," and is thus mentioned, explicitly and poetically, in the Shabbat songs. This is the essence of Shabbat eve as well: in one sense, it is the summing up and culmination of the previous week, but in another, it is also the beginning of the manifestation of the Shabbat itself, as the "crown" of the week.

The Shekhinah, which represents the divine power manifested in the infinite facets and variety of reality, has seventy names. Each name expresses another aspect, another face of this all-inclusive Presence; the multiplicity of names expresses the multiplicity of forms and shapes of Divine revelation in the world. The number seventy is thus the key to unfolding the ritual of the evening, devoted to the revelation of the Shekhinah.

Since Shabbat eve involves a particular manifestation of the Shekhinah, the prayers and customs of this evening emphasize the symbol of the Shekhinah, which is depicted, in the words of the prophets and elsewhere, as a feminine form: a queen, a bride, a wife. Consequently, the symbols and contents of Shabbat eve are always oriented to the female, whether as wife or as mother, whether in *Kabbalat Shabbat* and the ensuing evening prayers in the synagogue or within the home and the Jewish family.

On entering a Jewish home on the eve of the Sabbath, one sees, more than on any other day, how a dwelling may be made into a sanctuary: the table, with the loaves of Shabbat bread, recalls the Holy Temple with its shewbread, while the burning candles placed opposite it are reminiscent of the Temple menorah.

The candles lit by the woman of the house emphasize the light of the Shabbat, the sanctification of the home with the coming of the day, and the special role of the woman on this level of Shabbat evening. The two loaves of challah, special Shabbat bread, covered with a cloth, recall the manna, the bread from heaven resting between two layers of dew, which on Shabbat eve came down in double portion.

On returning from the synagogue on the eve of Shabbat, one enters the home and says in a loud and joyous voice, *Shabbat Shalom* (or "Good Shabbos"), as if one is receiving the Sabbath bride cheerfully. Besides the obvious intention to greet the members of the household who were not in the synagogue, there is also a kabbalistic sense of inviting the home to welcome the Shabbat sanctity. After everyone has been greeted, the ceremony of the meal itself begins.

ברכת הילדים
Blessing the Children

It is customary on the Shabbat eve to bless one's children. In some places, the custom is to bring the children before the rabbi for a blessing. Otherwise, the blessing is recited at home (some say it after *Shalom Aleikhem;* others, after Kiddush). The custom is to place both hands on the head of the child and to recite the text of the traditional blessing, adding one's own words of blessing as one sees fit. In some communities, the children then kiss their parents' hands.

For a daughter:

יְשִׂימֵךְ אֱלֹהִים כְּשָׂרָה
רִבְקָה רָחֵל וְלֵאָה.

Yesimekh Elohim ke'Sarah,
Rivkah, Raḥel, ve'Leah.

May God make you as Sarah,
Rivkah, Raḥel, and Leah.

For a son:

יְשִׂימְךָ אֱלֹהִים כְּאֶפְרַיִם
וְכִמְנַשֶּׁה.

Yesimkha Elohim ke'Efrayim
vekhi'Menasheh.

May God make you as
Ephraim and Menasheh.

יְבָרֶכְךָ יְיָ וְיִשְׁמְרֶךָ,

Yevarekhekha Adonai ve'Yishmerekha

May the Lord bless you and guard you,

יָאֵר יְיָ פָּנָיו אֵלֶיךָ וִיחֻנֶּךָּ,

Yaer Adonai panav elekha vi'yḥunnekka,

May the Lord make His countenance shine upon you and be gracious to you,

יִשָּׂא יְיָ פָּנָיו אֵלֶיךָ וְיָשֵׂם לְךָ שָׁלוֹם.

Yissa Adonai panav elekha ve'yasem lekha shalom.

May the Lord turn His countenance toward you and grant you peace.

שלום עליכם
Shalom Aleikhem

This liturgical poem is based on the Talmud (*Shabbat* 119b). The Talmud tells us that as we leave the synagogue on Shabbat eve, we are accompanied by two ministering angels. When these angels find our home is fully and peacefully ready for the Shabbat meal, they bless us. This poem, which appeared in print for the first time some 450 years ago, welcomes the angels and asks for their blessing.

שָׁלוֹם עֲלֵיכֶם מַלְאֲכֵי הַשָּׁרֵת, מַלְאֲכֵי עֶלְיוֹן,
מִמֶּלֶךְ מַלְכֵי הַמְּלָכִים הַקָּדוֹשׁ בָּרוּךְ הוּא.

Shalom aleikhem malakhei ha'sharet, malakhei elyon,
mi'melekh malkhei ha'melakhim, ha'Kadosh, barukh hu.

Peace unto you, ministering angels, messengers of the Most High, of the supreme King of kings, the Holy One, blessed be He.

Three times

בּוֹאֲכֶם לְשָׁלוֹם מַלְאֲכֵי הַשָּׁלוֹם, מַלְאֲכֵי עֶלְיוֹן,
מִמֶּלֶךְ מַלְכֵי הַמְּלָכִים הַקָּדוֹשׁ בָּרוּךְ הוּא.

Boakhem le'shalom, malakhei ha'shalom, malakhei elyon,
mi'melekh malkhei ha'melakhim, ha'Kadosh, barukh hu.

May your coming be in peace, angels of peace, messengers of the Most High, of the supreme King of kings, the Holy One, blessed be He.

Three times

בָּרְכוּנִי לְשָׁלוֹם מַלְאֲכֵי הַשָּׁלוֹם, מַלְאֲכֵי עֶלְיוֹן,
מִמֶּלֶךְ מַלְכֵי הַמְּלָכִים הַקָּדוֹשׁ בָּרוּךְ הוּא.

Barkhuni le'shalom, malakhei ha'shalom, malakhei elyon,
mi'melekh malkhei ha'melakhim, ha'Kadosh, barukh hu.

Bless me with peace, angels of peace, messengers of the Most High, of the supreme King of kings, the Holy One, blessed be He.

Three times

צֵאתְכֶם לְשָׁלוֹם מַלְאֲכֵי הַשָּׁרֵת, מַלְאֲכֵי עֶלְיוֹן,
מִמֶּלֶךְ מַלְכֵי הַמְּלָכִים הַקָּדוֹשׁ בָּרוּךְ הוּא.

Tzetkhem le'shalom, malakhei ha'shalom, malakhei elyon,
mi'melekh malkhei ha'melakhim, ha'Kadosh barukh hu.

May your departure be in peace, angels of peace, messengers of the Most High, of the supreme King of kings, the Holy One, blessed be He.

Three times

כִּי מַלְאָכָיו יְצַוֶּה לָּךְ לִשְׁמָרְךָ בְּכָל דְּרָכֶיךָ. יְיָ יִשְׁמָר
צֵאתְךָ וּבוֹאֶךָ מֵעַתָּה וְעַד עוֹלָם.

Ki malakhav yetzavveh lakh, lishmorkha be'khol derakhekha.
Adonai yishmor tzetkha u'voekha me'attah ve'ad 'olam.

For He will instruct His angels in your behalf, to guard you in all your ways [Psalms 91:11]. The Lord will guard your going and your coming from now and for all time [Psalms 121:8].

רבון כל העולמים

Ribbon Kol ha'Olamim

It is not known who composed this prayer, only that it was first printed in the same Siddur in which *Shalom Aleikhem* first appeared.

רִבּוֹן כָּל הָעוֹלָמִים אֲדוֹן כָּל הַנְּשָׁמוֹת,
אֲדוֹן הַשָּׁלוֹם, מֶלֶךְ אַבִּיר, מֶלֶךְ בָּרוּךְ
מֶלֶךְ גָּדוֹל, מֶלֶךְ דּוֹבֵר שָׁלוֹם, מֶלֶךְ
הָדוּר, מֶלֶךְ וָתִיק, מֶלֶךְ זָךְ, מֶלֶךְ חֵי
הָעוֹלָמִים, מֶלֶךְ טוֹב וּמֵטִיב, מֶלֶךְ
יָחִיד וּמְיוּחָד, מֶלֶךְ כַּבִּיר, מֶלֶךְ לוֹבֵשׁ
רַחֲמִים, מֶלֶךְ מַלְכֵי הַמְּלָכִים, מֶלֶךְ
סוֹמֵךְ נוֹפְלִים, מֶלֶךְ עֹשֶׂה מַעֲשֵׂה
בְרֵאשִׁית, מֶלֶךְ פּוֹדֶה וּמַצִּיל, מֶלֶךְ צַח
וְאָדוֹם, מֶלֶךְ קָדוֹשׁ, מֶלֶךְ רָם וְנִשָּׂא,
מֶלֶךְ שׁוֹמֵעַ תְּפִלָּה, מֶלֶךְ תָּמִים דַּרְכּוֹ.
מוֹדֶה אֲנִי לְפָנֶיךָ יְיָ אֱלֹהַי וֵאלֹהֵי
אֲבוֹתַי, עַל כָּל הַחֶסֶד אֲשֶׁר עָשִׂיתָ

Master of all worlds, Lord of all souls, Sovereign of peace; mighty King; blessed King; boundless King; King declaring peace; radiant King; ancient King; King of purity; King, the life of the universe; King of goodness; King, singular and unique; powerful King; compassionate King; King of the kings of kings; exalted King; King who supports the fallen; King who effects creation; King who redeems and rescues; King who is fair and ruddy; holy King; lofty, sublime King; King who hears prayers; King whose path is virtuous. I offer thanks to You, Lord my

God and God of my fathers, for all the kindness You have done, and will do, for me, together with all my family, and with all the people of the covenant. And blessed are Your holy pure angels who also carry out Your will. Sovereign of peace, King to whom peace belongs, bless me with peace, and remember me, my entire family, and all of Your people, the House of Israel, for good life and peace. King, exalted above all the Heavenly Hosts, who formed us and all of creation, I pray before Your radiant Presence: Grant me and my family the merit to find grace and understanding in Your eyes, and in the eyes of all the descendants of Adam and Eve, and in the eyes of all who see us, to perform Your service. Let us be worthy to welcome Your Shabbat with great joy, prosperity, and honor; and without transgressions. Remove from me, my family, and from all of Your people, the House of Israel, all manner of illness and suffering; all poverty, privation, and want. And give us the yearning to serve You truthfully, in awe and love. And let us be deserving of honor in Your eyes, and in the eyes of all who see us, for You are the King of

עִמָּדִי, וַאֲשֶׁר אַתָּה עָתִיד לַעֲשׂוֹת עִמִּי
וְעִם כָּל בְּנֵי בֵיתִי וְעִם כָּל בְּרִיּוֹתֶיךָ בְּנֵי
בְרִיתִי. וּבְרוּכִים הֵם מַלְאָכֶיךָ הַקְּדוֹשִׁים
וְהַטְּהוֹרִים שֶׁעוֹשִׂים רְצוֹנֶךָ. אֲדוֹן
הַשָּׁלוֹם, מֶלֶךְ שֶׁהַשָּׁלוֹם שֶׁלּוֹ, בָּרְכֵנִי
בַּשָּׁלוֹם, וְתִפְקוֹד אוֹתִי וְאֶת כָּל בְּנֵי
בֵיתִי וְכָל עַמְּךָ בֵּית יִשְׂרָאֵל לְחַיִּים
טוֹבִים וּלְשָׁלוֹם. מֶלֶךְ עֶלְיוֹן עַל כָּל
צְבָא מָרוֹם, יוֹצְרֵנוּ יוֹצֵר בְּרֵאשִׁית,
אֲחַלֶּה פָּנֶיךָ הַמְּאִירִים, שֶׁתְּזַכֶּה
אוֹתִי וְאֶת כָּל בְּנֵי בֵיתִי לִמְצֹא חֵן
וְשֵׂכֶל טוֹב בְּעֵינֶיךָ וּבְעֵינֵי כָל בְּנֵי אָדָם
וְחַוָּה וּבְעֵינֵי כָּל רוֹאֵינוּ לַעֲבוֹדָתֶךָ.
וְזַכֵּנוּ לְקַבֵּל שַׁבָּתוֹת מִתּוֹךְ רוֹב שִׂמְחָה
וּמִתּוֹךְ עֹשֶׁר וְכָבוֹד וּמִתּוֹךְ מִעוּט עֲוֹנוֹת.
וְהָסֵר מִמֶּנִּי וּמִכָּל בְּנֵי בֵיתִי וּמִכָּל עַמְּךָ
בֵּית יִשְׂרָאֵל כָּל מִינֵי חוֹלִי וְכָל מִינֵי
מַדְוֶה וְכָל מִינֵי דַלּוּת וַעֲנִיּוּת וְאֶבְיוֹנוּת,
וְתֵן בָּנוּ יֵצֶר טוֹב לְעָבְדְּךָ בֶּאֱמֶת וּבְיִרְאָה
וּבְאַהֲבָה, וְנִהְיֶה מְכֻבָּדִים בְּעֵינֶיךָ
וּבְעֵינֵי כָל רוֹאֵינוּ, כִּי אַתָּה הוּא מֶלֶךְ
הַכָּבוֹד, כִּי לְךָ נָאֶה כִּי לְךָ יָאֶה. אָנָּא מֶלֶךְ
מַלְכֵי הַמְּלָכִים, צַוֵּה לְמַלְאָכֶיךָ מַלְאֲכֵי
הַשָּׁרֵת מְשָׁרְתֵי שֶׁיִּפְקְדוּנִי בְּרַחֲמִים
וִיבָרְכוּנִי בְּבוֹאָם לְבֵיתִי בְּיוֹם קָדְשֵׁנוּ. כִּי
הִדְלַקְתִּי נֵרוֹתַי וְהִצַּעְתִּי מִטָּתִי וְהֶחֱלַפְתִּי
שִׂמְלוֹתַי לִכְבוֹד יוֹם הַשַּׁבָּת, וּבָאתִי

לְבֵיתְךָ לְהַפִּיל תְּחִנָּתִי לְפָנֶיךָ שֶׁתַּעֲבִיר
אַנְחָתִי. וְאָעִיד אֲשֶׁר בָּרָאתָ בְּשִׁשָּׁה
יָמִים כָּל הַיְּצוּר, וְאֶשְׁנֶה, וַאֲשַׁלֵּשׁ עוֹד
לְהָעִיד עַל כּוֹסִי בְּתוֹךְ שִׂמְחָתִי, כַּאֲשֶׁר
צִוִּיתַנִי לְזָכְרוֹ, וּלְהִתְעַנֵּג בְּיֶתֶר נִשְׁמָתִי
אֲשֶׁר נָתַתָּ בִּי. בּוֹ אֶשְׁבּוֹת כַּאֲשֶׁר צִוִּיתַנִי
לְשָׁרְתֶךָ, וְכֵן אַגִּיד גְּדֻלָּתְךָ בְּרִנָּה. וְשִׁוִּיתִי
יְיָ לִקְרָאתִי, שֶׁתְּרַחֲמֵנִי עוֹד בְּגָלוּתִי,
לְגָאֳלֵנִי, וּלְעוֹרֵר לִבִּי לְאַהֲבָתֶךָ, וְאָז
אֶשְׁמוֹר פִּקּוּדֶיךָ וְחֻקֶּיךָ בְּלִי עֶצֶב, וְאֶתְפַּלֵּל
כַּדָּת כָּרָאוּי וּכְנָכוֹן. מַלְאֲכֵי הַשָּׁלוֹם,
בּוֹאֲכֶם לְשָׁלוֹם, בָּרְכוּנִי לְשָׁלוֹם, וְאִמְרוּ
בָּרוּךְ לְשֻׁלְחָנִי הֶעָרוּךְ, וְצֵאתְכֶם לְשָׁלוֹם
מֵעַתָּה וְעַד עוֹלָם. אָמֵן סֶלָה.

honor; it befits You; for You it is seemly. Please, King of kings, direct Your angels, ministering angels of the Most High, to remember me with compassion, and bless me when they enter my home on our holy day. For I have lit my candles, prepared my bed, and changed my garments to honor the day of Shabbat. And I have come to Your house, setting before You my plea to banish my sighs; and I asserted that You created the universe in six days. I confirmed [this] a second time, and will do so again, joyfully, over my cup, as You have commanded me, to remember [Shabbat]; and to take delight in the additional soul you have bestowed within me. [On Shabbat] I shall rest—as You have commanded me—to serve You; and so, too, I shall tell of Your greatness with jubilant singing. I have set God before me—that You may yet have compassion on me in my exile, to redeem me, and to arouse my heart to Your love. And then I shall guard Your commandments and Your decrees without sadness; and I will pray properly, as is right and just. Angels of peace, enter in peace, bless me with peace; say "Blessed" over my readied table. And may your parting be in peace, from now to eternity. Amen, Selah.

אשת חיל

Eshet Ḥayil—Introduction

Eshet Ḥayil ("A Woman of Valor") is a hymn of praise to the good wife, the mother and woman of the house. Structured as an alphabetical acrostic, it is taken from the concluding section of the Book of Proverbs (31:10–31). In this context, the hymn bears a double meaning: as praise for the woman, and as glorification of the Shekhinah, which is, in a sense, the mother, the real housekeeper of the world.

The Woman of Valor celebrated here is not just a pale stereotype; she is a personality of great power, delineated in strong, clear lines. She is an energetic person, active in a great variety of spheres inside and outside the home, in relation to her husband and in relation to others. The real meaning of *Eshet Ḥayil* lies in her ability to realize her potential in every realm, bringing to fruition her own hopes and dreams and those of others.

Thus, rather than being a mere abstract collection of virtues, conjured out of thin air or mere theorizing, the Woman of Valor is a figure who exists in the real world. She is based upon real personalities in Jewish history, and to a large extent, upon Ruth. It is of Ruth that the verse says, "[Those who sit in] the gate of my people know you are a woman of valor [*eshet ḥayil*]" (Ruth 3:11); moreover, Ruth has the same combination of qualities: dedication, self-sacrifice, piety, modesty, industry, and initiative.

Indeed, the Woman of Valor never remained a merely literary figure; throughout the generations she shaped the personalities of real Jewish wives and mothers. Multitudes of Jewish women in every time and place put this ideal into practice to one degree or another, and it is to them that the House of Israel owes its strength and its very survival.

But all this is only the literal, surface level of the hymn. There are other levels of meaning that raise the figure of the Woman of Valor to another plane. The sages saw her as a metaphor for practical, applied knowledge, and her husband as a symbol of pure knowledge. The Woman of Valor is thus transformed into a metaphor, an idea, since practical wisdom, concerned with the affairs and needs of this world, is not opposed to abstract wisdom, but rather complements it. How so? While applying itself successfully in the material world, practical wisdom does not drown in materiality. It also contains other virtues: kindness, mercy, consideration, and faithfulness.

The Woman of Valor is also a metaphor for the soul. As such, she is the creative, motivating, constructive force that harnesses the powers of the body in the quest for human perfection. In another view, the Woman of Valor represents the wisdom of the Torah, both in relation to her husband (God) and in the transformative action that the Torah has upon the mundane.

At the highest, most theological level of interpretation, the Woman of Valor stands for the Shekhinah, the immanent reality of God in the world, while her husband symbolizes the transcendent essence of God. The Shekhinah, the cosmic mother, appears and acts in the world in the guise of the Congregation of Israel. But here she is not a tragic figure (such as Rachel weeping for her children in Jeremiah 31:14, or a wife forlorn and forsaken in Isaiah 54:6), nor is she associated with opposition or fear. Rather, she is a light filled with grace that illuminates the world from within. True, this world is not yet a perfect world that is all Sabbath; still, the Woman of Valor acts from within to change it, to draw reality toward its true purpose.

The paean to the Woman of Valor is unending, because its field of reference is ever wider and ever expanding. It begins with real women close at hand, expanding to encompass various historical personages, as well as the myriad unknown and unsung heroines of the past. The poem ascends from the concrete woman of flesh and blood to the level of abstract thought, of wisdom and Torah, and from this world to transcendent spiritual realms.

This song of praise, on all its levels, is sung on Shabbat eve, when we attempt to uncover the Shekhinah within the real, concrete woman; when practical wisdom is meant to be a manifestation rather than a concealing of the soul; when the Torah is the model within which human wisdom and the indwelling of the Shekhinah intermix;

when Shabbat (which is itself a bride and queen) becomes the model for the unification of the material and the spiritual, of the pleasures of the body and the ascent of the soul, at one and the same time and place.

אשת חיל (משלי לא, י־לא)
Eshet Ḥayil (Proverbs 31:10–31)

Who can find a woman of valor? Her value far exceeds that of gems.	אֵשֶׁת חַיִל מִי יִמְצָא, וְרָחֹק מִפְּנִינִים מִכְרָהּ. *Eshet ḥayil mi yimtza, ve'raḥok mi'pninim mikhrah.*
The heart of her husband trusts in her; he lacks no gain.	בָּטַח בָּהּ לֵב בַּעְלָהּ, וְשָׁלָל לֹא יֶחְסָר. *Bataḥ bah lev baalah, ve'shalal lo yeḥsar.*
She treats him with goodness, never with evil, all the days of her life.	גְּמָלַתְהוּ טוֹב וְלֹא רָע כֹּל יְמֵי חַיֶּיהָ. *Gmalat'hu tov ve'lo ra kol yemei ḥayyehah.*
She seeks out wool and flax, and works willingly with her hands.	דָּרְשָׁה צֶמֶר וּפִשְׁתִּים, וַתַּעַשׂ בְּחֵפֶץ כַּפֶּיהָ. *Darsha tzemer u'fishtim, va'taas be'ḥefetz kappehah.*

She is like the merchant ships; she brings her food from afar.

הָיְתָה כָּאֳנִיּוֹת סוֹחֵר, מִמֶּרְחָק
תָּבִיא לַחְמָהּ.

Hayta ke'oniyot soḥer, mi'merḥak
tavi laḥmah.

She rises while it is still night, gives food to her household, and sets out the tasks for her maids.

וַתָּקָם בְּעוֹד לַיְלָה, וַתִּתֵּן טֶרֶף
לְבֵיתָהּ וְחֹק לְנַעֲרֹתֶיהָ.

Va'takam be'od laila, va'titten teref
le'veitah ve'ḥok le'naarotehah.

She considers a field and buys it; from her earnings she plants a vineyard.

זָמְמָה שָׂדֶה וַתִּקָּחֵהוּ,
מִפְּרִי כַּפֶּיהָ נָטְעָה כָּרֶם.

Zamema sadeh va'tikkaḥehu,
mi'pri khapehha natah karem.

She girds her loins with strength, and flexes her arms.

חָגְרָה בְעוֹז מָתְנֶיהָ,
וַתְּאַמֵּץ זְרוֹעֹתֶיהָ.

Ḥagrah ve'oz motnehah,
va'teammetz zrootehah.

She realizes that her enterprise is profitable; her lamp does not go out at night.

טָעֲמָה כִּי טוֹב סַחְרָהּ, לֹא יִכְבֶּה
בַּלַּיְלָה נֵרָהּ.

Taamah ki tov saḥrah, lo yikhbeh
ba'laylah nerah.

She puts her hands on the spindle, and her palms grasp the distaff.

יָדֶיהָ שִׁלְּחָה בַכִּישׁוֹר,
וְכַפֶּיהָ תָּמְכוּ פָּלֶךְ.

Yadehah shillḥah va'kishor,
ve'khapehah tamkhu falekh.

She holds out her hand to the poor, and extends her hands to the destitute.

כַּפָּהּ פָּרְשָׂה לֶעָנִי, וְיָדֶיהָ
שִׁלְּחָה לָאֶבְיוֹן.

Kappah parsah le'ani, ve'yadehah
shillḥah la'evyon.

She does not fear for her household in the frost, for her entire household is clothed [warmly] in scarlet.

לֹא תִירָא לְבֵיתָהּ מִשָּׁלֶג, כִּי
כָל בֵּיתָהּ לָבֻשׁ שָׁנִים.

Lo tira le'veitah mi'shaleg, ki
khol beitah lavush shanim.

She makes her own tapestries; her garments are of fine linen and purple.

מַרְבַדִּים עָשְׂתָה לָּהּ, שֵׁשׁ
וְאַרְגָּמָן לְבוּשָׁהּ.

Marvadim astah lah, shesh
ve'argaman levushah.

Her husband is well-known at the gates, as he sits with the elders of the land.

נוֹדָע בַּשְּׁעָרִים בַּעְלָהּ, בְּשִׁבְתּוֹ
עִם זִקְנֵי אָרֶץ.

Noda' ba'shearim balah, beshivto
im ziknei aretz.

She makes linens and sells [them]; she provides the merchants with girdles.

סָדִין עָשְׂתָה וַתִּמְכֹּר, וַחֲגוֹר
נָתְנָה לַכְּנַעֲנִי.

Sadin astah vatimkor, va'ḥagor
natnah la'knaani.

Strength and dignity are her garb; she looks smilingly toward the future.

עֹז וְהָדָר לְבוּשָׁהּ, וַתִּשְׂחַק
לְיוֹם אַחֲרוֹן.

Oz ve'hadar levushah, va'tisḥak
le'yom aḥaron.

She opens her mouth with wisdom, and the teaching of kindness is on her tongue.

פִּיהָ פָּתְחָה בְחָכְמָה, וְתוֹרַת
חֶסֶד עַל לְשׁוֹנָהּ.

Pihah pathah ve'hokhmah, ve'torat
hesed al leshonah.

She watches the conduct of her household, and does not eat the bread of idleness.

צוֹפִיָּה הֲלִיכוֹת בֵּיתָהּ, וְלֶחֶם
עַצְלוּת לֹא תֹאכֵל.

Tzofiyyah halikhot beitah, ve'lehem
atzlut lo tokhel.

Her children rise and acclaim her also, her husband and he praises her:

קָמוּ בָנֶיהָ וַיְאַשְּׁרוּהָ,
בַּעְלָהּ וַיְהַלְלָהּ.

Kamu vanehah va'yashruhah,
baalah va'yehalelah.

"Many daughters have done worthily, but you surpass them all."

רַבּוֹת בָּנוֹת עָשׂוּ חָיִל, וְאַתְּ
עָלִית עַל כֻּלָּנָה.

Rabbot banot asu hayil, ve'at
alit al kullana.

Charm is deceptive and beauty is naught; a God-fearing woman is the one to be praised.

שֶׁקֶר הַחֵן וְהֶבֶל הַיֹּפִי,
אִשָּׁה יִרְאַת יְיָ הִיא תִתְהַלָּל.

Sheker ha'hen ve'hevel ha'yofi,
ishah yirat Adonai hi tit'hallal.

Give her praise for her accomplishments, and let her deeds laud her at the gates.

תְּנוּ לָהּ מִפְּרִי יָדֶיהָ,
וִיהַלְלוּהָ בַשְּׁעָרִים מַעֲשֶׂיהָ.

Tenu lah mi'peri yadehah,
vi'yhaleluha va'she'arim maasehah.

אתקינו סעודתא
Atkinu Seudata

This text, based upon kabbalistic notions elaborated in the Zohar (*Yitro* II:88b) prepares and invites us to the Shabbat meal. It is recited, with certain variations, before each of the three Shabbat meals. The Shabbat meal itself is a mitzvah, in which we see ourselves feasting at the table of the King. We hope that this meal will bring us to higher faith and give us joyous inspiration.

The phrase *Ḥakal Tappuḥin Kaddishin* ("Holy Apple Orchard") is the term used by the Zohar to refer to the Shekhinah, the form in which the Divinity is manifested on Shabbat eve. This phrase is taken from the biblical words "like the fragrance of the field which God has blessed" (Genesis 27:27). The first meal of the Shabbat day is, then, connected with the level of the Shekhinah, while the two other levels of holiness revealed on the Sabbath day—which in kabbalistic sources are called *Zeir Anpin* and *Attika Kaddisha*—are manifested through it, poetically, as the guests of the Shekhinah.

Prepare the meal of perfect faith,	אַתְקִינוּ סְעוּדָתָא דִּמְהֵימְנוּתָא שְׁלֵמָתָא, *Atkinu seudata di'meheimenuta shlemata,*
Which is the delight of the holy King;	חֶדְוָתָא דְּמַלְכָּא קַדִּישָׁא. *Ḥedvata de'malka kaddisha.*
Prepare the meal of the King.	אַתְקִינוּ סְעוּדָתָא דְּמַלְכָּא. *Atkinu seudata de'malka.*
This is the meal of the holy *Ḥakal Tappuḥin,*	דָּא הִיא סְעוּדָתָא דַּחֲקַל תַּפּוּחִין קַדִּישִׁין, *Da hi seudata da'ḥakal tappuḥin kaddishin,*

And *Zeir Anpin* and the holy Ancient One

וּזְעֵיר אַנְפִּין וְעַתִּיקָא קַדִּישָׁא

U'zeir anpin ve'attika kaddisha

Come to join her in the meal.

אַתְיָן לְסַעֲדָא בַּהֲדָהּ.

Atyan le'saada ba'hadah.

אזמר בשבחין
Azammer bi'Shvaḥin

Throughout the Jewish world, it is customary to follow *Atkinu* with this hymn, one of the three hymns composed by The Holy Ari for the three Sabbath meals. These hymns, written in Aramaic, describe the esoteric meanings of the Sabbath and its respective meals, and the connections woven on this day between humans and the upper worlds.

I will cut away [the forces of evil] with songs of praise, in order to enter the holy gates of *Ḥakal Tappuḥin*.

אֲזַמֵּר בִּשְׁבָחִין לְמֵיעַל גּוֹ פִּתְחִין,

Azammer bi'shvaḥin le'meial go pitḥin,

דְּבַחֲקַל תַּפּוּחִין דְּאִנּוּן קַדִּישִׁין.

Deva'ḥakal tappuḥin de'innun kaddishin.

We invite her [the Shekhinah] to the festive table, with the beautiful candelabrum shining on our heads.

נְזַמִּין לַהּ הַשְׁתָּא בִּפְתוֹרָא חַדְתָּא,

Nezammin lah hashta bi'fetora ḥadta,

וּבִמְנַרְתָּא טַבְתָּא דְּנַהֲרָא עַל רֵישִׁין.

Uvi'mnarta tavta de'nahara al reishin.

The Holy Ari: initials for *ha'Elohi* [or: *ha'Ashkenazi*] *Rabbi Yitzḥak* (the Divine [or: the Ashkenazic] Rabbi Isaac), i.e., Rabbi Isaac ben Shlomo Luria, who lived in Jerusalem and in Safed some 450 years ago. He was among the greatest kabbalists of all times. His *piyyutim* for the three Shabbat meals are among the few of his writings that have come down to us.

Between right and left the Bride approaches, adorned in ornaments, jewels, and robes.

יְמִינָא וּשְׂמָאלָא, וּבֵינַיְהוּ כַּלָּה,
Yemina u'smala, u'veinaihu kallah,

בְּקִשּׁוּטִין אָזְלָא, וּמָאנִין וּלְבוּשִׁין.
Be'kishutin azla, u'manin u'lvushin.

Her husband embraces her; through this gathering which brings her joy, the [forces of evil] will be utterly crushed.

יְחַבֵּק לָהּ בַּעְלָהּ, וּבִיסוֹדָא דִּילָהּ,
Yeḥabbek lah baalah, uvi'ysoda di'lah,

דְּעָבֵד נַיְחָא לָהּ, יְהֵא כַּתִּישׁ כַּתִּישִׁין.
De'avid naiḥa lah, yehe kattish kattishin.

They cry and despair, yet they are made null and void; but the faces [of Israel] are renewed, souls and spirits too.

צְוָחִין אַף עָקְתִין בְּטֵלִין וּשְׁבִיתִין,
Tzevaḥin af aktin beteilin u'shvitin,

בְּרַם אַנְפִּין חַדְתִּין וְרוּחִין עִם נַפְשִׁין.
Beram anpin ḥadtin ve'ruḥin im nafshin.

[The Shabbat soul] brings her great joy, double in measure, bestowing upon her light and abundant blessing.

חֲדוּ סַגִּי יֵיתֵי, וְעַל חֲדָא תַּרְתֵּי,
Ḥadu saggi yeytei, ve'al ḥada tartei,

נְהוֹרָא לָהּ יִמְטֵי, וּבִרְכָאָן דִּנְפִישִׁין.
Nehora lah yimtei, u'virkhaan di'nfishin.

Bridesmen, go forth and make preparation of delicacies of many kinds, fish as well as fowl.

קְרִיבוּ שׁוּשְׁבִינִין, עֲבִידוּ תִּקּוּנִין,
Krivu shushvinin, avidu tikkunin,

לְאַפָּשָׁא זִינִין, וְנוּנִין עִם רַחֲשִׁין.
Le'appasha zinin, ve'nunin im rahsḥin.

It is to form new souls and spirits, [to fathom] the thirty-two paths [of wisdom] and the three branches [of Scripture].

לְמֶעְבַּד נִשְׁמָתִין וְרוּחִין חַדְתִּין,
Le'mebad nishmatin ve'ruḥin ḥadtin,

בְּתַרְתֵּין וּתְלָתִין וּבִתְלָתָא שִׁבְשִׁין.
Be'tartein u'tlatin uvi'tlata shivshin.

She has seventy crowns; the supernal King becomes crowned with most sacred [songs of praise].

וְעִטּוּרִין שַׁבְעִין לַהּ, וּמַלְכָּא דִלְעֵלָּא,
Ve'itturin shavin lah, u'malka dileilla,

דְּיִתְעַטֵּר כֹּלָּא בְּקַדִּישׁ קַדִּישִׁין.
De'yitatter kola be'kaddish kaddishin.

[The Shabbat] is engraved and inscribed within all worlds [which were brought forth by] the "Ancient of Days" through combining [the four pristine elements].

רְשִׁימִין וּסְתִימִין, בְּגוֹ כָּל עָלְמִין,
Reshimin u'stimin, be'go kol almin,

בְּרַם עַתִּיק יוֹמִין, הֲלָא בַּטִּישׁ בַּטִּישִׁין.
Be'ram attik yomin, hala battish battishin.

May it be His will that His presence rest upon His people, who will delight for the sake of His Name in sweet things and honey.

יְהֵא רַעֲוָא קַמֵּיהּ דְּיִשְׁרֵי עַל עַמֵּיהּ,
Yehei raava kammeh de'yishrei al ammeh,

דְּיִתְעַנַּג לִשְׁמֵיהּ בִּמְתִיקִין וְדוּבְשִׁין.
De'yitannag li'shmeh bi'mtikin ve'duvshin.

I place to the south the mystical candelabrum; I set in the north the table with the loaves;

אֲסַדֵּר לִדְרוֹמָא מְנַרְתָּא דִּסְתִימָא,
Asadder li'droma menarta di'stima,

וְשֻׁלְחָן עִם נַהֲמָא בִּצְפוֹנָא אַרְשִׁין.
Ve'shulḥan im nahama bi'tzfona arshin.

With wine in the goblet and boughs of myrtle for the Bride and Groom, to invigorate the weak.

בְּחַמְרָא גוֹ כָסָא, וּמְדָאנֵי אַסָּא,
Be'ḥamra go khasa, u'medanei assa,

לְאָרוּס וַאֲרוּסָה, לְהִתַּקְפָא חַלָּשִׁין.
Le'arus va'arusa, le'hittakfa ḥallashin.

We fashion for them crowns from precious words; seventy crowns which transcend the fifty [gates].

נְעַטֵּר לְהוֹן כִּתְרִין בְּמִלִּין יַקִּירִין,
Neatter lehon kitrin be'millin yakkirin,

בְּשַׁבְעִין עִטּוּרִין דְּעַל גַּבֵּי חַמְשִׁין.
Be'shavin itturin de'al gabbei ḥamshin.

May the Shekhinah be surrounded by the six loaves on each side [of the table]; and may they correspond to the two sets of six loaves and the other articles [of the Temple].

שְׁכִינְתָּא תִּתְעַטָּר בְּשִׁית נַהֲמֵי לִסְטָר,
Shekhinta tit'attar be'shit nahamei li'star,

בְּוָוִין תִּתְקַטָּר, וְזִינִין דִּכְנִישִׁין.
Be'vavin titkattar, vezinin di'khnishin.

The impure powers who are far from holiness, the angels of destruction who oppress [us] and all those confined [in Purgatory] rest and have respite [on Shabbat].

שְׁבִיתִין וּשְׁבִיקִין, מְסָאֲבִין דִּרְחִיקִין,
Shvitin u'shvikin, mesaavin di'rḥikin,

חֲבִילִין דִּמְעִיקִין, וְכָל זִינֵי חַרְשִׁין.
Ḥavilin di'mikin, ve'khol zinei ḥarshin.

To slice the challah,the size of an olive or of an egg, [interpreting] the two *yuds* either according to its simple or phonetic reading.

לְמִבְצַע עַל רִפְתָּא, כְּזֵיתָא וּכְבֵיעָתָא,
Le'mivtza al rifta, ke'zeita ukhe'veiata,

תְּרֵין יוּדִין נַקְטָא, סְתִימִין וּפְרִישִׁין.
Trein yudin nakta, setimin u'ferishin.

Olives [have within them] pure oil, which when pressed in a millstone, flows in a stream; so the bread contains within it divine secrets.

מְשַׁח זֵיתָא דַּכְיָא דְּטַחֲנִין רֵיחַיָּא,
Meshaḥ zeita dakhya de'taḥanin reiḥayya,

וְנַגְדִּין נַחֲלַיָּא בְּגַוָּהּ בִּלְחִישִׁין.
Ve'nagdin naḥalaya be'gavvah bi'lḥishin.

Let us discuss secrets of Torah, which are not revealed; hidden and concealed.

הֲלָא נֵימָא רָזִין, וּמִלִּין דִּגְנִיזִין,
Hala neima razin, u'millin di'gnizin,

דְּלֵיתְהוֹן מִתְחַזִּין, טְמִירִין וּכְבִישִׁין.
De'leithon mitḥazzin, tmirin u'khvishin.

May the Bride be crowned with supernal mysteries at this joyous feast of the holy angels.

אִתְעַטְּרַת כַּלָּה בְּרָזִין דִּלְעֵלָּא,
Itattrat kallah be'razin dileila,

בְּגוֹ הַאי הִלּוּלָא דְּעִירִין קַדִּישִׁין.
Be'go hai hillula de'irin kaddishin.

ויהא רעוא
Vi'Yhei Raava

This prayer is taken from the book *Shaar ha'Kavvanot,* by Rabbi Ḥayyim Vital, the greatest disciple of The Holy Ari.

May it be the will of the most holy Ancient One,

וִיהֵא רַעֲוָא מִן קֳדָם עַתִּיקָא
קַדִּישָׁא דְכָל קַדִּישִׁין,

Vi'yhei raava min kodam attika
kaddisha de'khol kaddishin,

The most hidden and most concealed of all,

טְמִירָא דְּכָל טְמִירִין, סְתִימָא דְכֹלָּא.

Tmira de'khol tmirin, stima de'kholla,

That He bring down the supernal dew

דְיִתְמַשֵּׁךְ טַלָּא עִלָּאָה מִינֵּהּ,

De'yitmashekh talla illaa minneh,

To fill the head of the *Zeir Anpin,*

לְמַלְיָא רֵישֵׁיהּ דִּזְעֵיר אַנְפִּין,

Le'malya resheh di'zeir anpin,

And to irrigate the Holy Apple Orchard

וּלְהַטִּיל לַחֲקַל תַּפּוּחִין קַדִּישִׁין

U'lehattil la'ḥakal tappuḥin kaddishin

With the light of His face, with will and joy of all.

בִּנְהִירוּ דְאַנְפִּין, בְּרַעֲוָא וּבְחֶדְוָתָא דְכֹלָּא.

Bi'nhiru de'anpin, be'raava uve'ḥedvata de'kholla.

And may it be drawn down from before the most holy Ancient One,

וְיִתְמַשֵּׁךְ מִן קֳדָם עַתִּיקָא
קַדִּישָׁא דְכָל קַדִּישִׁין,

Ve'yitmashekh min kodam attika
kaddisha de'khol kaddishin,

The most hidden and concealed of all,

טְמִירָא דְּכָל טְמִירִין, סְתִימָא דְּכֹלָּא,
Tmira de'khol tmirin, stima de'kholla,

Will and mercy, grace and loving-kindness,

רְעוּתָא וְרַחֲמֵי, חִנָּא וְחִסְדָּא,
Re'uta ve'raḥamei, ḥinna ve'ḥisda,

With the supernal illumination of will and joy,

בִּנְהִירוּ עִלָּאָה, בִּרְעוּתָא וְחֶדְוָתָא,
Bi'nhiru illaa, bi'ruta ve'ḥedvata,

Upon me and all the members of my household and all those that are with me,

עָלַי, וְעַל כָּל בְּנֵי בֵיתִי, וְעַל כָּל הַנִּלְוִים אֵלַי,
Alai, ve'al kol bnei veiti, ve'al kol ha'nilvim elai,

And upon all His people Israel.

וְעַל כָּל בְּנֵי יִשְׂרָאֵל עַמֵּיהּ.
Ve'al kol bnei Yisrael ammeh.

And may He save us from all troubles that come to the world,

וְיִפְרְקִינָנָא מִכָּל עַקְתִין בִּישִׁין
דְּיֵיתוּן לְעָלְמָא,
Ve'yifrekinana mi'kol aktin bishin
de'yeytun le'alma,

And prepare and give us food and livelihood,

וְיַזְמִין וְיִתְיַהֵב לָנָא מְזוֹנָא
וּפַרְנָסָתָא טַבְתָּא,
Ve'yazmin ve'yityahev lana mezona
u'farnasata tavta,

Without trouble and oppression,

בְּלִי צָרָה וְעַקְתָא,
Bli tzara ve'akta,

From the sign upon which all food is dependent.

מִמַּזָּלָא דְּכָל מְזוֹנָא בֵּיהּ תַּלְיָא.
Mi'mazzala de'khol mezona beih talya.

And save us from the evil eye

וִישֵׁזְבִינָנָא מֵעֵינָא בִּישָׁא,

Vi'shezvinana me'eina bisha,

And from the sword of the destroying angel, and from the judgement of *Gehinnom*

וּמֵחַרְבָּא דְּמַלְאַךְ הַמָּוֶת,
וּמִדִּינָהּ שֶׁל גֵּיהִנֹּם,

Ume'ḥarba de'malakh ha'mavet,
umi'dinah shel gehinnom,

And bring upon us and all our souls grace and mercy,

וְיֵיתֵי לָנָא וּלְכָל נַפְשָׁתָנָא
חִנָּא וְחִסְדָּא,

Ve'yeytei lana ule'khol nafshatana
ḥinna ve'ḥisda,

And long life and food, with generosity and kindness before Him.

וְחַיֵּי אֲרִיכֵי וּמְזוֹנֵי רְוִיחֵי,
וְרַחֲמֵי מִן קֳדָמֵיהּ.

Ve'ḥayyey arikhei u'mezonei reviḥei,
ve'raḥamei min kodameih.

Amen, so may it be His will. Amen and Amen.

אָמֵן כֵּן יְהִי רָצוֹן, אָמֵן וְאָמֵן.

Amen ken yehi ratzon, amen ve'amen.

Kiddush for Shabbat Eve

From the time the Shabbat begins until one makes Kiddush, it is forbidden to eat or drink anything. The table on which the festive meal is to be served should be prepared while it is still daytime. It is customary to have the two loaves of challah on the table, covered over, during the Kiddush ceremony. Kiddush must be made in the room where the meal is to be eaten. It is highly recommended to make this Kiddush over red wine.

Just before the Kiddush ceremony, one pours the wine from the bottle into a cup; the pouring of the wine must be with the intention of doing it for the sake of fulfilling the commandment of Kiddush. In an emergency where no wine is available, one may make Kiddush over bread, and instead of saying "who creates the fruit of the vine," one says "who brings forth bread from the earth." In such a case, one must ritually wash the hands (see "Washing of Hands") before making Kiddush, so that one can immediately eat of the bread.

From the halakhic perspective, the recitation of Kiddush fulfills the fourth of the Ten Commandments: "Remember the Sabbath day, to sanctify it" (Exodus 20:8) On the most basic level, this mitzvah is carried out merely by making an explicit declaration, at Shabbat's beginning, that Shabbat has arrived, and that we are taking its holiness upon ourselves. The wording of the Kiddush emphasizes the sanctity of Shabbat—the distinction between the weekdays and Shabbat—and, in the spiritual sense, prepares the individual for the transition from the hustle and bustle of the weekday world to the Sabbath, the day of sacredness and rest. The Kiddush is thus the most significant act of preparing the home for Sabbath, and is performed with great ceremoniousness and solemnity.

There needs to be an act of separation, of sanctification, at the very beginning of Shabbat, emphasizing the difference between the working days and the day of holiness, and enabling the soul to move into a state of inner tranquillity and spiritual receptivity. To be sure, the sanctity of Shabbat is already mentioned in the evening prayer. But there is a general principle in Judaism that, insofar as possible, abstract events or psychological processes need to be connected with definite actions. Hence, the Kiddush is connected with the drinking of wine.

Wine was chosen because of its unique nature, being associated with joy and festivity that reach to the depths of the soul ("For it is man's nature to be greatly aroused by it [wine]" [*Sefer ha'Ḥinukh*]). Wine "cheers God and man" (Judges 9:13), serving both as a component of human pleasure and as a libation poured over the sacrificial altar. The connection of ceremony and wine thus adds a further emphasis: it is a statement that the commandment is performed not only out of obedient acceptance of the yoke, but willingly and with heartfelt joy.

The wine cup must hold at least a *reviit* (three or, according to other opinions, five fluid ounces) of wine, and must be in perfect condition, without a chip or crack in its brim. It is customary to use a special decorative cup for the Kiddush ceremony. Before Kiddush, the wine cup, even though it is clean, must be rinsed out, both inside and out, as a sign of respect for the commandment. The wine is poured so that it fills the cup to the brim, as a sign of blessing.

The Kiddush cup symbolizes the Shekhinah—the vessel through which blessing comes—while wine symbolizes the bounty and plentitude coming from supernal sources.

Since wine, especially red wine, expresses the aspect of severity and judgment, a few drops of water—symbolic of grace and love—are added to the cup to create the proper mixture or harmony between benevolence and strictness. The cup is then placed on the palm of the right hand so that it is supported by the upturned fingers; it is reminiscent, in the language of the Zohar, of a five-petalled rose. For one of the symbols of *Malkhut* (God's kingdom) is the rose. And the cup of wine, thus expressing also the Shekhinah, stands in the center of the palm and is held by the petal fingers of the rose. Just before Kiddush, it is customary to gaze at the Shabbat candles, and then at the cup of wine.

It is customary in most Jewish communities for the Shabbat-eve Kiddush to be recited with all those present standing, because reciting the verses of *Vayekhulu* is like bearing testimony, and, according to Jewish law, witnesses must stand while testifying. By reciting *Vayekhulu,* a person attests that Heaven and earth were created by God, which is also the very basis and foundation for the sanctification of the Shabbat and for its observance. As the Torah clearly states, "It is a sign between Me and the children of Israel for all time, for in six days the Lord made heaven and earth, and on the seventh day He ceased from work and rested (Exodus 31:17)." Another reason for standing is that the Kiddush itself is a blessing over a commandment, and it is the custom to stand while reciting such benedictions.

After the recital of the Kiddush the one who has performed the ceremony drinks from the cup, thereby participating in that communion of the physical with the spiritual that is the essence of all ritual. While drinking the wine, all the participants sit down, to make the drinking a part of the meal (there are, however, those who drink the wine while still standing). The person who recites the Kiddush must drink a significant quantity, not just a sip. (Some drink at least a mouthful; others drink most of the wine in the cup, even if it is a big one.) According to the formal requirements of the halakhah, only the one reciting Kiddush needs to drink at least a mouthful; however, it is customary for all those present to taste of the Kiddush wine. The Kiddush cup is handed around, or the wine in it is poured out for each of the participants at the meal. If there are cups already filled with wine in front of them, they may drink from these cups, although it is specially commendable to drink from the cup of blessing. However, one who participates in the ceremony and has listened to the benediction fulfills the obligation even without drinking from the wine.

In the Kiddush itself there are two distinct sections, separated from each other by the blessing over wine. In the more precise versions, there are exactly thirty-five words in each of these halves, together making seventy, the mystical number of Shabbat night. Seventy also represents a multiple of two significant numbers: seven, which is the number of the seventh day, and ten, which alludes to the Divine revelation, which transcends reality.

Kiddush begins with the first mention of Shabbat in the Torah, at the end of the story of Creation (Genesis 2:1–3). This section, known as *Vayekhulu,* is preceded by the last two Hebrew words of the previous verse, "the sixth day," because, among other reasons, the first letters of these two words, together with those of the first two words of the next verse, form the Ineffable Name of God—the Tetragrammaton. This passage speaks of Shabbat from the transcendent viewpoint of God, as the goal and completion of Creation, of ceasing from the labors of Creation and returning power to the Creator, so to speak, to the source of things, to their nature and essence. This section stands by itself.

The second section of the Kiddush is preceded by the blessing over wine. This blessing is introduced by a call in Aramaic—*Savri (maranan ve'rabborai)* ("Attention friends")—asking all those present to prepare themselves to listen attentively to the blessing, which is the main part of the Kiddush.

The second section is the Kiddush text coined by the sages. While the first section depicted the Divine aspect of Shabbat, this section expresses the sanctity of Shabbat from the point of the Jewish people; it expresses all those elements that constitute the nature of Shabbat and the special relationship between Shabbat and the people of Israel.

This part begins with the customary opening for the blessing over any mitzvah: "Blessed are You, Lord our God, King of the Universe, who has hallowed us with His commandments." That is, the mitzvah is the way to acquire holiness and, moreover, is itself an act of holiness. Through it we are sanctified to the Holy One, since at the time of the mitzvah act we are together, and in unity with Him.

The prayer then goes on to speak of the chosenness of Israel. And being closer, Israel, more than all other nations, must carry on with and participate in the act of Creation, both by activity during the six days of the week and by rest and holiness on the Sabbath day.

The Exodus from Egypt is also mentioned here, because the Sabbath day—the day of rest from toil—is associated with the Exodus. Israel, a slave people, came to enjoy redemption and liberation, becoming a free nation able to cease from work and to rest at certain times. In an inner sense, the Exodus from Egypt symbolizes Israel's chosenness, its liberation from the travails and chains of the world, and its ascent to the service of God: "For to Me are the children of Israel servants" (Leviticus 25:55), and only the servant of the Lord is free (as in one of Rabbi Yehudah Halevi's poems). All these ideas are embodied in Shabbat, when we rest, like God, from all labors of the physical world and ascend above the practical world.

Immediately following Kiddush, the ritual washing of hands is performed in preparation for the festive meal (except in a few communities where the Kiddush is itself preceded by the handwashing). Care should be taken not to allow too great a period of time elapse between the Kiddush and the ritual handwashing.

קידוש לליל שבת
Kiddush for Shabbat Eve

Some people recite the following formula before the Kiddush (as well as before the blessing related to the fulfillment of some other commandments):

לְשֵׁם יִחוּד קוּדְשָׁא בְּרִיךְ הוּא וּשְׁכִינְתֵּיהּ, בִּדְחִילוּ וּרְחִימוּ,

Le'shem yiḥud Kudsha, brikh hu u'Shkhinteh, bi'dḥilu u'reḥimu,

הֲרֵינִי מוּכָן וּמְזֻמָּן לְקַיֵּם מִצְוַת עֲשֵׂה לְקַדֵּשׁ עַל הַיַּיִן,

hareini mukhan u'mezumman lekayyem mitzvat aseh lekaddesh al ha'yayin

כִּדְכְתִיב: זָכוֹר וְשָׁמוֹר, זָכְרֵהוּ עַל הַיַּיִן.

kedi'khtiv: zakhor ve'shamor—zokhrehu al ha'yayin.

For the sake of the union of the Holy One, blessed be He, with His Shekhinah, with awe and love, I am ready and prepared to perform the commandment to sanctify [the Shabbat] over wine, as it says: "remember" and "observe," remember it [the Shabbat] over wine.

In a whisper:

וַיְהִי עֶרֶב וַיְהִי בֹקֶר

Va'yhi erev va'yhi voker,

Aloud:

יוֹם הַשִּׁשִּׁי. וַיְכֻלּוּ הַשָּׁמַיִם וְהָאָרֶץ וְכָל צְבָאָם. וַיְכַל

yom ha'shishi. Va'yekhulu ha'shamayim veha'aretz ve'khol tzevaam. Va'yekhal

אֱלֹהִים בַּיּוֹם הַשְּׁבִיעִי מְלַאכְתּוֹ אֲשֶׁר עָשָׂה. וַיִּשְׁבֹּת בַּיּוֹם הַשְּׁבִיעִי מִכָּל

Elohim ba'yom ha'shvii melakhto asher asah. Va'yishbot ba'yom ha'shvii mi'kol

מְלַאכְתּוֹ אֲשֶׁר עָשָׂה. וַיְבָרֶךְ אֱלֹהִים אֶת יוֹם הַשְּׁבִיעִי וַיְקַדֵּשׁ אֹתוֹ,

melakhto asher asah. Va'yevarekh Elohim et yom ha'shvii va'ykaddesh oto,

כִּי בוֹ שָׁבַת מִכָּל מְלַאכְתּוֹ אֲשֶׁר בָּרָא אֱלֹהִים לַעֲשׂוֹת.

ki vo shavat mi'kol melakhto asher bara Elohim laasot.

סַבְרִי מָרָנָן וְרַבָּנָן וְרַבּוֹתַי:

Savri maranan ve'rabbanan ve'rabbotai:

בָּרוּךְ אַתָּה יְיָ, אֱלֹהֵינוּ מֶלֶךְ הָעוֹלָם, בּוֹרֵא פְּרִי הַגָּפֶן.

Barukh attah Adonai, Eloheinu melekh ha'olam, bore' pri ha'gafen.

בָּרוּךְ אַתָּה יְיָ, אֱלֹהֵינוּ מֶלֶךְ הָעוֹלָם, אֲשֶׁר קִדְּשָׁנוּ בְּמִצְוֹתָיו

Barukh attah Adonai, Eloheinu melekh ha'olam, asher kiddshanu be'mitzvotav

וְרָצָה בָנוּ, וְשַׁבַּת קָדְשׁוֹ בְּאַהֲבָה וּבְרָצוֹן הִנְחִילָנוּ, זִכָּרוֹן

ve'ratzah vanu, ve'shabbat kodso be'ahavah uve'ratzon hinhilanu, zikkaron

לְמַעֲשֵׂה בְרֵאשִׁית. (כִּי הוּא יוֹם) תְּחִלָּה לְמִקְרָאֵי קֹדֶשׁ, זֵכֶר לִיצִיאַת מִצְרָיִם.

le'maaseh vereshit. (Ki hu yom) tehillah le'mikraei kodesh, zekher li'ytziat mitzrayim.

(כִּי בָנוּ בָחַרְתָּ וְאוֹתָנוּ קִדַּשְׁתָּ מִכָּל הָעַמִּים,) וְשַׁבַּת קָדְשְׁךָ

(Ki vanu vakharta ve'otanu kiddashta mi'kol ha'amim,) ve'Shabbat kodshekha

בְּאַהֲבָה וּבְרָצוֹן הִנְחַלְתָּנוּ. בָּרוּךְ אַתָּה יְיָ, מְקַדֵּשׁ הַשַּׁבָּת.

be'ahavah uve'ratzon hinhaltanu. Barukh attah Adonai, mekaddesh ha'Shabbat.

On the Shabbat of Ḥol ha'Moed Sukkot, one immediately adds:

בָּרוּךְ אַתָּה יְיָ, אֱלֹהֵינוּ מֶלֶךְ הָעוֹלָם, אֲשֶׁר קִדְּשָׁנוּ
בְּמִצְוֹתָיו וְצִוָּנוּ לֵישֵׁב בַּסֻּכָּה.

Barukh attah Adonai, Eloheinu melekh ha'olam, asher kiddshanu be'mitzvotav ve'tzivanu leishev ba'sukkah.

Translation of the Kiddush Text

And there was evening and there was morning, the sixth day. And the heavens and the earth and all their hosts were completed. And God finished by the Seventh Day His work which He had done, and He rested on the Seventh Day from all His work which He had done. And God blessed the Seventh Day and made it holy, for on it He rested from all His work which God created to function [Genesis 1:31-2:3].

Attention, friends!

Blessed are You, Lord our God, King of the universe, who creates the fruit of the vine.

Blessed are You, Lord our God, King of the universe, who has hallowed us with His commandments, has desired us, and has given us, in love and goodwill, His holy Shabbat as a heritage, in remembrance of the work of Creation; (for it is) the first of the holy festivals, commemorating the Exodus from Egypt. (For You have chosen us and sanctified us from among all the nations,) and with love and goodwill given us Your holy Shabbat as a heritage. Blessed are You, Lord, who hallows the Shabbat.

On the Shabbat of Ḥol ha'Moed Sukkot, one immediately adds:

Blessed are You, Lord our God, King of the universe, who has hallowed us with His commandments, and has commanded us to dwell in the sukkah.

Notes to the Kiddush

Vayekhulu—And [the heavens and the earth and all the hosts] were completed: The recitation of *Vayekhulu* is an act of witness: we testify to the creation of heaven and earth by God—the basis and the foundation of the sanctity of Shabbat and its observance. It is stated elsewhere in the Torah, "It is a sign between Me and the children of Israel for all time, for in six days the Lord made the heavens and the earth, and on the seventh day He ceased from work and rested" (Exodus 31:17).

Our sages dealt extensively with the exact meaning of the word *Vayekhulu*. Most of them understood it to be different from the similar word, *vayekhal,* found in the next verse, which means that God "ended" or "finished." Here the term means that everything has come to a state of completion, the perfection of its essential nature—that of being a perfected whole.

The heavens and the earth all their hosts: This means the entire universe, upper and lower worlds, and all the creatures of every kind that inhabit them ("their hosts").

And God finished by the Seventh Day His work which He had done: Our sages questioned the phrase "And on the seventh day God ended His work," because He ended His work not on the seventh day but at the end of the sixth day. The simplest way of interpreting this is that God ceased His work on the seventh day. Some sages (such as Rashi), however, explain this to refer to the seventh day itself. Shabbat and its repose are, then, in themselves, the culmination of the world's creation. They are the ultimate perfection, which had been lacking in the world and was achieved through this day of rest and repose.

And He rested on the Seventh Day from all His work which He had done: This seems to be a repetition of the previous line, but the terms "finished" (*va'yekhal*) and "rested" (*va'yishbot*) are not identical in meaning. Finishing work carries the negative connotation of a cessation or refraining from activity that has already been finished, while the second term implies resting in the positive sense of a state of leisure. There are, in fact, two separate Torah commandments regarding Shabbat: the negative commandment of refraining from work, and the positive commandment of resting.

And God blessed the Seventh Day and made it holy: Blessing and holiness are not visible phenomena. The continuous course of the physical world does not cease its progress on Shabbat. The blessing of the seventh day lies in the transformation of Shabbat into a fount of blessing from which all the other days of the week are blessed. Even though it may seem that it is Shabbat that receives the benefits of the labor done on the other days, in essence it is not only the conclusion of the world's creation, but also its very objective, for whose sake the world was created.

And made it holy: The holiness of this day lies in its having been sanctified as a holy day since the time of Creation ("the holy one of the Lord" [see Isaiah 58:13])—a holiness that was revealed to Israel at Mount Sinai as a specific commandment.

For on it He rested from all His work: This is the reason for the blessing, since rest and repose were created on Shabbat as the ultimate purpose of work.

Which God created to function: The previous line speaks of all His work that He "had done" (*asah*), while here it speaks of all His work that "God created to function" (*bara laasot*). One of the Aramaic translations of the Torah, the *Targum Yerushalmi* says, "that God created and will do hereafter"—that is, all future creations (as "the new heavens and the new earth which I make" [Isaiah 66:22]). Another reading is that creative activity and the ability to alter the state of the world were granted to us by God. Human beings became, so to speak, God's partners in Creation. We must therefore work toward improving and reshaping the world.

Blessed are You, Lord our God, King of the universe, who has hallowed us with His commandments, has desired us: This indicates God's pleasure and satisfaction with us, as in the verse "For the Lord desires His people" (Psalms 149:4).

And has given us, in love and goodwill, His holy Shabbat as a heritage: The concepts "love" and "goodwill" are mentioned in all of the Shabbat prayers and blessings. They express the idea that the gift of the Shabbat to the people of Israel is an expression of God's love. Our sages say, "The Holy One, blessed be He, said to Moses: 'I have a precious gift in My treasure house, called the Sabbath, and I desire to give it to Israel'" (*Shabbat* 10b). It is as though Shabbat is kept as a secret treasure by God, and He is now sharing this secret with the children of Israel alone, for "it is a sign between Me and the children of Israel" (Exodus 31:13).

As a heritage: The gift of Shabbat was not just for one generation, but is a heritage to all following generations. As it says, "And the children of Israel shall observe the Shabbat, establishing the Shabbat throughout their generations as an everlasting covenant" (Exodus 31:16).

In remembrance of the work of Creation: As stated in the Ten Commandments, "Remember the Shabbat day to sanctify it.... For in six days the Lord made the heavens and earth ... and rested on the seventh day" (Exodus 20:8, 11).

The first of the holy festivals: The Shabbat is the first of all the festivals, both because it was sanctified since the time of Creation and because it is the first to be mentioned among the festivals (see Leviticus 23:2–3).

Commemorating the Exodus from Egypt: As explained in the Ten Commandments, as they appear in Deuteronomy (5:15): "And remember that you were a slave in the land of Egypt, and that the Lord your God brought you out of there; ... therefore the Lord your God commanded you to keep the Shabbat day." Biblical commentators have already explained that, as Creator of the world, God is also its Lord and Master.

The Exodus from Egypt is a sign of His providence and rule over the world, and proof of His creation of the world.

For You have chosen us: As it says elsewhere, "The Lord did not set His love upon you, nor choose you, because you were more in number, … but because the Lord loved you" (Deuteronomy 7:7–8).

And sanctified us from among all the nations: As it says in this verse: "Verily, my Sabbaths you shall keep … that you may know that I am the Lord who sanctifies you" (Exodus 31:13).

And with love and goodwill given us Your holy Shabbat as a heritage: This choice and this sanctification are expressed in the gift of Shabbat, which is a sign of the covenant of love between God and Israel.

Blessed are You, Lord, who hallows the Shabbat: This blessing concludes the Kiddush. Unlike the holiness of the festivals, the holiness of Shabbat is not dependent upon the people of Israel; rather, it is God Himself who sanctifies it. This blessing is phrased in the present tense, because Shabbat was sanctified not only at the time of Creation; rather, the continued manifestation and influence of this holiness appears and emanates anew on every Shabbat.

The First Shabbat Meal

נטילת ידיים
Washing of Hands

After the Kiddush, the ritual washing of hands is done, and the following blessing recited:

בָּרוּךְ אַתָּה יְיָ, אֱלֹהֵינוּ מֶלֶךְ הָעוֹלָם, אֲשֶׁר קִדְּשָׁנוּ
בְּמִצְוֹתָיו וְצִוָּנוּ עַל נְטִילַת יָדָיִם.

Barukh attah Adonai, Eloheinu melekh ha'olam, asher kiddshanu be'mitzvotav ve'tzivvanu al netilat yadayim.

Blessed are You, Lord our God, King of the universe, who has sanctified us with His commandments, and commanded us concerning the washing of the hands.

ברכת המוציא
Blessing over Bread

Before bread is broken, the following blessing is recited:

בָּרוּךְ אַתָּה יְיָ, אֱלֹהֵינוּ מֶלֶךְ הָעוֹלָם, הַמּוֹצִיא לֶחֶם מִן הָאָרֶץ.

Barukh attah Adonai, Eloheinu melekh ha'olam, ha'motzi leḥem min ha'aretz.

Blessed are You, Lord our God, King of the universe, who brings forth bread from the earth.

The bread is dipped in salt. At mealtimes, the table should always have a salt container on it, just as salt had to be on the holy altar of the Temple. Then, the first Shabbat meal is held.

Shabbat Meals—General Notes

The table itself, on any day of the week, is considered an altar, as every act of eating, even on weekdays, should have an aspect of sacrifice. The relationship between the person, the food, and the intention with which it is eaten connects the physical world and the spiritual world, just like the tie created when offering a sacrifice on the altar.

On the other days of the week, the act of eating with such purpose involves a certain inner struggle: the pleasure derived from the food should not take the place of the intent to elevate and connect. The Shabbat meals, however, are themselves acts of sacrifice and of holiness, and the enjoyment derived from the act of eating is itself a mitzvah—that of *oneg Shabbat,* of experiencing enjoyment on and from Shabbat. Thus, participating in the Shabbat meal is a symbolic partaking of the feast of the King, the Holy One, blessed be He, in which the soul, the body, and the world are united in holiness.

While on weekdays the custom was to eat only two main meals, the rabbis decreed that on Shabbat we must eat three meals. The Shabbat meal is accompanied by many special customs, as well as words of Torah and prayer. The customs themselves vary greatly from place to place. Even in rabbinic times it was the custom to eat special foods on Shabbat, a practice continued to this day. Each community and congregation has its own special Shabbat dishes.

However, strictly speaking there is only one binding halakhic rule governing the Shabbat meals: at each Shabbat meal there must be at least two loaves of bread (known as *Leḥem Mishneh*), in remembrance of the double portion of manna that came down from Heaven in the desert on Fridays (Exodus 16).

There is a kabbalistic custom to have twelve loaves on the table at every Shabbat meal (like the shewbread, which was laid out every Shabbat on the Temple's golden table); few people, however, actually practice this custom. (Some explain the special shape of the challah—the braided Shabbat bread—of the Ashkenazic communities as an attempt to create six small loaves within each loaf, making twelve loaves in each pair of *Leḥem Mishneh*).

The basis of each of the Shabbat meals must be bread, of which at least an olive-size piece (some thirty grams—that is, one ounce) should be eaten. There are those who follow the Talmudic custom (*Shabbat* 33b) of bringing two bunches of myrtle, or other fragrant branches, to each meal, and reciting the blessing for fragrances over them. Another ancient custom, also mentioned in the Talmud (*Shabbat* 118b), is to eat fish during Shabbat meals. Special care is taken everywhere to eat or drink something warm (*ḥamin*) on Shabbat, in demonstration against the strictures of the Samaritans and the Karaites, who prohibited this.

זמירות לליל שבת
Zemirot *for Shabbat Eve*

It is a universal custom to sing *zemirot* in honor of Shabbat, either during the course of the meal or immediately before or after. Although there is a certain order in which the *zemirot* are sung by some, there is no fixed rule about this; some families sing more *zemirot,* and others fewer, depending upon the time available and the musical talents of the household members.

כל מקדש שביעי
Kol Mekaddesh Shvii

This *piyyut* was composed by an author named Moshe, whose name is concealed in the second word of each of the first three lines; in the subsequent verses, the lines are

Maḥzor Vitry is a halakhic work containing the liturgical cycle of the entire year, composed nearly nine hundred years ago in the French city of Vitry by Rabbi Simḥah ben Shmuel, a disciple of Rashi.

arranged in alphabetical order, the last line in each verse quoting a whole or a part of a biblical verse. This *piyyut* first appeared in *Maḥzor Vitry.*

Everyone who sanctifies the seventh day properly,

כָּל מְקַדֵּשׁ שְׁבִיעִי כָּרָאוּי לוֹ,
Kol mekaddesh shvii ka'rauy lo,

And who protects Shabbat from desecration;

כָּל שׁוֹמֵר שַׁבָּת כַּדָּת מֵחַלְּלוֹ,
Kol shomer Shabbat ka'dat me'ḥallelo,

His reward is great, according to his efforts.

שְׂכָרוֹ הַרְבֵּה מְאֹד עַל פִּי פָעֳלוֹ,
Skharo harbe meod 'al pi fo'olo,

Every man in his own camp, and every man by his standard.

אִישׁ עַל מַחֲנֵהוּ וְאִישׁ עַל דִּגְלוֹ.
Ish 'al maḥanehu ve'ish 'al diglo.

Lovers of God who await Jerusalem's rebuilding,

אוֹהֲבֵי יְיָ הַמְחַכִּים בְּבִנְיַן אֲרִיאֵל,
Ohavei Adonai ha'meḥakkim be'vinyan Ariel,

On the day of Shabbat, rejoice and exult, as when receiving [God's] gift.

בְּיוֹם הַשַּׁבָּת שִׂישׂוּ וְשִׂמְחוּ
כִּמְקַבְּלֵי מַתַּן נַחֲלִיאֵל.
Be'yom ha'Shabbat sisu ve'simḥu
ki'mekabbelei mattan naḥaliel.

Lift your hands in holiness, and say to God,

גַּם שְׂאוּ יְדֵיכֶם קֹדֶשׁ וְאִמְרוּ לָאֵל,
Gam seu yedeikhem kodesh ve'imru la'El,

"Blessed is God who has given repose to His people Israel."

בָּרוּךְ יְיָ אֲשֶׁר נָתַן מְנוּחָה
לְעַמּוֹ יִשְׂרָאֵל.
Barukh Adonai asher natan menuḥah
le'ammo Yisrael.

דּוֹרְשֵׁי יְיָ, זֶרַע אַבְרָהָם אוֹהֲבוֹ,

Dorshei Adonai, zera Avraham ohavo,

Pursuers of God, children of Abraham, His beloved,

הַמְאַחֲרִים לָצֵאת מִן הַשַּׁבָּת
וּמְמַהֲרִים לָבֹא,

Ha'meaḥarim latzet min ha'Shabbat
u'memaharim lavo,

Who tarry when parting from Shabbat, and hurry to its welcome,

וּשְׂמֵחִים לְשָׁמְרוֹ וּלְעָרֵב עֵרוּבוֹ,

U'smeḥim leshomro u'learev eruvo,

And rejoice in its observance, and its *eruv* arrangement,

זֶה הַיּוֹם עָשָׂה יְיָ, נָגִילָה וְנִשְׂמְחָה בוֹ.

Ze ha'yom asah Adonai, nagilah ve'nismeḥah vo.

This is the day God has made; let us celebrate and rejoice in it.

זִכְרוּ תּוֹרַת מֹשֶׁה, בְּמִצְוַת שַׁבָּת גְּרוּסָה,

Zikhru torat Moshe, be'mitzvat Shabbat grusah,

Remember the Torah of Moses, be well-versed in its Shabbat commandments—

חֲרוּתָה לְיוֹם הַשְּׁבִיעִי כְּכַלָּה
בֵּין רֵעוֹתֶיהָ מְשֻׁבָּצָה,

Ḥarutah le'yom ha'shvii ke'khallah
bein re'otehah meshubbatzah,

Engraved [on the Tablets] for the seventh day, a finely dressed bride among her companions.

טְהוֹרִים יִירָשׁוּהָ וִיקַדְּשׁוּהָ
בְּמַאֲמַר כָּל אֲשֶׁר עָשָׂה,

Tehorim yirashuhah vi'ykaddshuhah
be'maamar kol asher asah,

The pure ones inherit and sanctify her with the words "All [His work] which He had done."

וַיְכַל אֱלֹהִים בַּיּוֹם הַשְּׁבִיעִי
מְלַאכְתּוֹ אֲשֶׁר עָשָׂה.

Va'ykhal Elohim ba'yom ha'shvii
melakhto asher asah.

And God finished by the seventh day His work which He had done.

יוֹם קָדוֹשׁ הוּא מִבּוֹאוֹ וְעַד צֵאתוֹ,

Yom kadosh hu mi'bo-o ve'ad tzeto,

It is a day of holiness from its arrival to its departure;

כָּל זֶרַע יַעֲקֹב יְכַבְּדוּהוּ כִּדְבַר
הַמֶּלֶךְ וְדָתוֹ,

Kol zera Yaakov yekhabduhu ki'dvar ha'melekh ve'dato,

All of Jacob's descendants honor it—[for it is] the King's word and decree,

לָנוּחַ בּוֹ וְלִשְׂמֹחַ בְּתַעֲנוּג אָכוֹל וְשָׁתוֹ,

Lanuaḥ bo ve'lismoaḥ be'taanug akhol ve'shato,

To rest on it and to rejoice, and delight in eating and drinking.

כָּל עֲדַת יִשְׂרָאֵל יַעֲשׂוּ אוֹתוֹ.

Kol adat Yisrael yaasu oto.

All the congregation of Israel shall observe it.

מְשֹׁךְ חַסְדְּךָ לְיוֹדְעֶיךָ אֵל
קַנֹּא וְנוֹקֵם,

Meshokh ḥasdekha le'yodekha, El kanno ve'nokem,

Direct Your kindness toward those who know You, vengeful God,

נוֹטְרֵי לַיּוֹם הַשְּׁבִיעִי זָכוֹר
וְשָׁמוֹר לְהָקֵם,

Notrei la'yom ha'shvii zakhor ve'shamor lehakem,

Who wait for the seventh day to fulfill "Remember" and "Safe guard."

שַׂמְּחֵם בְּבִנְיַן שָׁלֵם, בְּאוֹר
פָּנֶיךָ תַּבְהִיקֵם,

Sammḥem be'vinyan shalem, be'or panekha tavhikem,

Gladden them with the complete rebuilding [of the Temple]; illumine them with the light of Your countenance.

They will be satiated with the delight of Your House; let them drink from the stream of Your bliss.

יִרְוְיֻן מִדֶּשֶׁן בֵּיתֶךָ, וְנַחַל
עֲדָנֶיךָ תַּשְׁקֵם.

Yirveyun mi'deshen beitekha, ve'naḥal adanekha tashkem.

Support those who forever avoid plowing and harvesting on the Seventh,

עֲזוֹר לַשּׁוֹבְתִים בַּשְּׁבִיעִי, בֶּחָרִישׁ
וּבַקָּצִיר עוֹלָמִים,

Azor la'shovtim ba'shvii, be'ḥarish uva'katzir olamim,

[Those who on Shabbat] walk modestly, and have festive meals to bless [You] three times.

פּוֹסְעִים בּוֹ פְּסִיעָה קְטַנָּה, סוֹעֲדִים בּוֹ
לְבָרֵךְ שָׁלֹשׁ פְּעָמִים.

Posim bo psiah ktanah, soadim bo levarekh shalosh peamim.

May their righteousness shine brilliantly like the light of the seven days.

צִדְקָתָם תַּצְהִיר כְּאוֹר שִׁבְעַת הַיָּמִים,

Tzidkatam tatzhir ke'or shivat ha'yamim,

Lord, God of Israel, grant us perfection!

יְיָ אֱלֹהֵי יִשְׂרָאֵל, הָבָה תָּמִים,

Adonai Elohei Yisrael, havah tamim,

Lord, God of Israel—a pure love; Lord, God of Israel—the eternal Redemption!

יְיָ אֱלֹהֵי יִשְׂרָאֵל, תְּשׁוּעַת עוֹלָמִים.

Adonai Elohei Yisrael tshuat olamim.

מנוחה ושמחה

Menuḥah ve'Simḥah

This *piyyut* likewise was composed by an author named Moshe, whose name appears as the first letters of the first three verses, and who lived about four hundred years ago.

Rest and joy and light for the Jews,	מְנוּחָה וְשִׂמְחָה, אוֹר לַיְּהוּדִים, *Menuḥah ve'simḥah, or la'yehudim,*
[Brings] the Sabbath day, day of delights;	יוֹם שַׁבָּתוֹן, יוֹם מַחֲמַדִּים, *Yom shabbaton, yom maḥamaddim,*
Those who keep and remember it testify,	שׁוֹמְרָיו וְזוֹכְרָיו הֵמָּה מְעִידִים, *Shomrav ve'zokhrav hemma meidim,*
That all things were created and rose in six days.	כִּי לְשִׁשָּׁה כֹּל בְּרוּאִים וְעוֹמְדִים. *Ki le'shisha kol bruim ve'omdim.*
The furthermost skies and the earth and the seas,	שְׁמֵי שָׁמַיִם אֶרֶץ וְיַמִּים, *Shmei shamayim, eretz ve'yamim,*
All the hosts of Heaven, exalted and high,	כָּל צְבָא מָרוֹם גְּבוֹהִים וְרָמִים, *Kol tzeva marom, gvohim ve'ramim,*
Serpents of the deep, and man, and the wild ox,	תַּנִּין וְאָדָם וְחַיַּת רְאֵמִים, *Tannin ve'adam ve'ḥayyat re'emim,*
Proclaim God Lord and Rock of the worlds.	כִּי בְּיָהּ יְיָ צוּר עוֹלָמִים. *Ki be'Yah Adonai tzur olamim.*
This is as He said to His chosen people:	הוּא אֲשֶׁר דִּבֶּר לְעַם סְגֻלָּתוֹ, *Hu asher dibber le'am segullato,*

"Keep it to make it holy from coming to closing";

The sacred Sabbath, day of God's delight,

For on it He rested from all of His work.

Through the Sabbath commandments God gives you strength;

Rise up and call on Him, He hurries to your help.

[Pray] "The soul of all life" and "We will adore You!"

[Then] eat in joy, for His favor is granted.

With two loaves of bread, with holy words over wine,

With many lovely foods and with a generous heart,

Those who delight in the Sabbath shall merit great good,

With the redeemer's arrival, for life in the world to come!

שָׁמוֹר לְקַדְּשׁוֹ מִבֹּאוֹ וְעַד צֵאתוֹ,
Shamor lekaddsho mi'boo ve'ad tzeto,
שַׁבַּת קֹדֶשׁ, יוֹם חֶמְדָּתוֹ,
Shabbat kodesh, yom ḥemdato,

כִּי בוֹ שָׁבַת אֵל מִכָּל מְלַאכְתּוֹ.
Ki vo shavat El mi'kol melakhto.

בְּמִצְוַת שַׁבָּת אֵל יַחֲלִיצָךְ,
Be'mitzvat Shabbat El yaḥalitzakh,

קוּם קְרָא אֵלָיו יָחִישׁ לְאַמְּצָךְ,
Kum kra elav yaḥish leamtzakh,

נִשְׁמַת כָּל חַי וְגַם נַעֲרִיצָךְ,
Nishmat kol ḥai ve'gam naaritzakh,

אֱכוֹל בְּשִׂמְחָה כִּי כְּבָר רָצָךְ.
Ekhol be'shimhah ki kvar ratzakh.

בְּמִשְׁנֶה לֶחֶם וְקִדּוּשׁ רַבָּה,
Be'mishneh leḥem ve'Kiddush rabbah,

בְּרוֹב מַטְעַמִּים וְרוּחַ נְדִיבָה,
Be'rov matamim ve'ruaḥ nedivah,

יִזְכּוּ לְרַב טוּב הַמִּתְעַנְּגִים בָּהּ,
Yizku le'rav tuv ha'mitanngim bah,

בְּבִיאַת גּוֹאֵל לְחַיֵּי הָעוֹלָם הַבָּא.
Be'viat goel le'ḥayey ha'olam ha'ba.

מה ידידות

Mah Yedidut

This *piyyut* is more than four hundred years old. Its author's name, Menaḥem, is alluded to in the first letters of the stanzas.

מַה יְּדִידוּת מְנוּחָתֵךְ, אַתְּ שַׁבָּת הַמַּלְכָּה,
Mah yedidut menuḥatekh, at Shabbat ha'malkah.

How lovely is your rest, you Sabbath queen!

בְּכֵן נָרוּץ לִקְרָאתֵךְ, בּוֹאִי כַלָּה נְסוּכָה.
Be'khen narutz likratekh, boi khallah nesukhah.

Therefore do we run to greet you: Come, anointed bride!

לְבוּשׁ בִּגְדֵי חֲמוּדוֹת, לְהַדְלִיק נֵר בִּבְרָכָה,
Levush bigdei ḥamudot, lehadlik ner bi'vrakhah,

Clothed in favorite garments, we light candles with a blessing;

וַתֵּכֶל כָּל הָעֲבוֹדוֹת, לֹא תַעֲשׂוּ מְלָאכָה.
Va'tekhel kol ha'avodot, lo taasu melakhah.

All labors must be finished, you shall do no work.

[פִּזְמוֹן]
לְהִתְעַנֵּג בְּתַעֲנוּגִים, בַּרְבּוּרִים
וּשְׂלָו וְדָגִים.

Lehitanneg be'taanugim, barburim
u'slav ve'dagim.

Chorus:
Let us rejoice in [a round of] delights, with swans and quails and fish!

מֵעֶרֶב מַזְמִינִים כָּל מִינֵי מַטְעַמִּים,
Me'erev mazminim kol minei matammim,

On the previous day one prepares all kinds of tasty foods:

מִבְּעוֹד יוֹם מוּכָנִים תַּרְנְגוֹלִים מְפֻטָּמִים.
Mi'beod yom mukhanim tarnegolim mefuttamim,

On the eve of the day fatted chickens are readied,

וְלַעֲרוֹךְ כַּמָּה מִינִים, שְׁתוֹת יֵינוֹת מְבֻשָּׂמִים,
Ve'laarokh kamma minim, shetot yeinot mevussamim,

With a spread of many dishes, with fragrant wines to drink,

וְתַפְנוּקֵי מַעֲדַנִּים, בְּכָל שָׁלֹשׁ פְּעָמִים.
Ve'tafnukei maadamin, be'khol shalosh pe'amim.

And dainties delightful for each of the three meals!

[פִּזְמוֹן]

[Chorus]

נַחֲלַת יַעֲקֹב יִירָשׁ, בְּלִי מְצָרִים נַחֲלָה,
Naḥalat Yaakov yirash, bli meitzarim naḥalah,

[You] shall inherit the portion of Jacob, heritage without bounds.

וִיכַבְּדוּהוּ עָשִׁיר וָרָשׁ, וְתִזְכּוּ לִגְאֻלָּה.
Vi'ykhabduhu ashir va'rash, ve'tizku li'geullah.

Rich and poor will honor [the Sabbath], you shall merit redemption;

יוֹם שַׁבָּת אִם תִּשְׁמֹרוּ, וִהְיִיתֶם לִי סְגֻלָּה,
Yom Shabbat im tishmoru, vi'hyitem li segullah,

You shall be my treasured people, if you honor the Sabbath day.

שֵׁשֶׁת יָמִים תַּעֲבֹדוּ, וּבַשְּׁבִיעִי נָגִילָה.
Sheshet yamim taavodu, uva'shvii nagilah.

Six days shall you labor, on the seventh let us rejoice!

[פִּזְמוֹן]

[Chorus]

חֲפָצֶיךָ אֲסוּרִים, וְגַם לַחֲשׁוֹב חֶשְׁבּוֹנוֹת,
Ḥafatzekha asurim, ve'gam laḥashov ḥeshbonot,

Your business interests are forbidden, considering money matters.

הִרְהוּרִים מֻתָּרִים, וּלְשַׁדֵּךְ הַבָּנוֹת.
Hirhurim muttarim, u'leshaddekh ha'banot.

But thinking is permitted, and making matches for one's daughters,

Instructing little children in books, such as Psalms and songs,	וְתִינוֹק לְלַמְּדוֹ סֵפֶר, לַמְנַצֵּחַ בִּנְגִינוֹת, *Ve'tinnok le'lammdo sefer, la'menatzeaḥ bi'nginot,*
And meditating on the goodly word in every camp and corner.	וְלַהֲגוֹת בְּאִמְרֵי שֶׁפֶר, בְּכָל פִּנּוֹת וּמַחֲנוֹת. *Ve'lahagot be'imrei shefer, be'khol pinnot u'maḥanot.*
[Chorus]	[פִּזְמוֹן]
Let your walk and manner be gentle, call the Sabbath a delight;	הִלּוּכָךְ תְּהֵא בְנַחַת, עֹנֶג קְרָא לַשַּׁבָּת, *Hillukhakh tehe be'naḥat, 'oneg kra la'Shabbat,*
Sleep is to be praised, when it serves to restore the soul.	וְהַשֵּׁנָה מְשֻׁבַּחַת, כְּדָת נֶפֶשׁ מְשִׁיבַת. *Veha'sheina meshubbaḥat, ke'dat nefesh meshivat.*
Therefore my soul longs for you, for resting lovingly;	בְּכֵן נַפְשִׁי לְךָ עָרְגָה, וְלָנוּחַ בְּחִבַּת, *Bkhen, nafshi lekha argah, ve'lanuaḥ be'ḥibbat,*
Fenced about as with lilies, son and daughter rest.	כַּשּׁוֹשַׁנִּים סוּגָה, בּוֹ יָנוּחוּ בֵּן וּבַת. *Ka'shoshanim sugah, bo yanuḥu ben u'vat.*
[Chorus]	[פִּזְמוֹן]
A taste of the world to come is the Sabbath day of rest;	מֵעֵין עוֹלָם הַבָּא, יוֹם שַׁבָּת מְנוּחָה, *Me'eyn olam ha'ba, yom Shabbat menuḥah,*
All those who rejoice in it shall merit exceeding joy,	כָּל הַמִּתְעַנְּגִים בָּהּ יִזְכּוּ לְרוֹב שִׂמְחָה. *Kol ha'mitangim bah yizku le'rov simḥah.*

Protected and delivered from the pains that precede the Messiah.

מֵחֶבְלֵי מָשִׁיחַ יֻצָּלוּ לִרְוָחָה,
Me'ḥevlei mashiaḥ yutzalu li'rvaḥah,

O, make our redemption flourish, and sorrow and anguish fly!

פְּדוּתֵנוּ תַּצְמִיחַ, וְנָס יָגוֹן וַאֲנָחָה.
Pdutenu tatzmiaḥ, ve'nas yagon va'anaḥah.

[Chorus]

[פִּזְמוֹן]

יום שבת קודש הוא
Yom Shabbat Kodesh Hu

The name of the author of this *piyyut,* concealed in an acrostic in the initial letters of the stanzas, is Yehonatan. This name is followed, also in acrostic form, by the word *ḥazak*, which is not a family name, but simply a word of blessing and encouragement—"may he be strong."

The day of Shabbat is holy; happy is he who guards it,

יוֹם שַׁבָּת קוֹדֶשׁ הוּא, אַשְׁרֵי הָאִישׁ שׁוֹמְרֵהוּ,
Yom Shabbat kodesh hu, ashrei ha'ish shomrehu,

And over wine remembers it, and does not take to heart.

וְעַל הַיַּיִן זָכְרֵהוּ, וְאַל יָשִׂים אֶל לִבּוֹ.
Ve'al ha'yayin zokhrehu, ve'al yasim el libbo.

The empty pocket, without a coin—rejoice, be content,

הַכִּיס רֵיק וְאֵין בּוֹ, יִשְׂמַח וְיִרְוֶה,
Ha'kis rek ve'ein bo, yismaḥ ve'yirveh,

And if you borrow, the Creator will repay your loan.

וְאִם לֹוֶה, הַצּוּר יִפְרַע אֶת חוֹבוֹ.
Ve'im loveh—ha'tzur yifra et ḥovo.

Meat, wine, and fish—and do not leave out pleasures.

הַבָּשָׂר יַיִן וְדָגִים, וְאַל יֶחְסַר בְּתַעֲנוּגִים,
Ha'basar, yayin ve'dagim, ve'al yeḥsar be'taanugim,

And if these three are present, his reward for wishing her honor will be:

וְאִם שְׁלֹשׁ אֵלֶּה לְפָנָיו צָגִים, זֶה
יִהְיֶה שְׂכָרוֹ.

Ve'im shlosh elle lefanav tzagim, zeh yihyeh sekharo.

[The treasure of] Yosef, who, opening a fish [he had acquired to honor Shabbat], found a priceless pearl inside.

אֲשֶׁר חָפֵץ בִּיקָרוֹ, יוֹסֵף חָצָה דָּג,
וּמָצָא מַרְגָּלִית בִּבְשָׂרוֹ.

Asher ḥafetz bi'ykaro, Yosef ḥatzah dag, u'matza margalit be'vsaro.

And if his table is arranged as befits, God's angel will say, "Blessed!

וְאִם שֻׁלְחָן כַּדָּת עָרוּךְ, וּמַלְאַךְ אֵל
יַעֲנֶה בָּרוּךְ,

Ve'im shulḥan ka'dat 'arukh, u'malakh El ya'aneh barukh,

May it be thus for many a year!" His enemies will be speechless.

זֶה יִהְיֶה זְמַן אָרוּךְ, וְאוֹיְבָיו יִהְיוּ כְּדוֹמֶן.

Zeh yihyeh zman arukh, ve'oyvav yihyu ke'domen.

And the evil angel will answer, "Amen," grudgingly reciting his acclaim;

וּמַלְאַךְ רַע יַעֲנֶה אָמֵן, בְּעַל כָּרְחוֹ
יְסַפֵּר שִׁבְחוֹ,

U'malakh ra' yaaneh amen, be'al korḥo yesapper shvaḥo,

His name will soar like goodly oil.

שְׁמוֹ יַעֲלֶה כְּטוֹב שָׁמֶן.

Shmo yaaleh ke'tov shemen.

Women light Shabbat candles, and hold fast to family purity laws,

נָשִׁים נֵרוֹת תַּדְלֵקְנָה, וְחֹק נִדּוֹת
תְּחַזֵּקְנָה,

Nashim nerot tadleknah, ve'ḥok niddot taḥazeknah,

And burn the challah dough's tithes. Their merit [from these three] will protect them,

וְהַחַלּוֹת תַּסֵּקְנָה, יָגֵן בַּעֲדָן זְכוּתָן,

Veha'ḥallot tasseknah, yagen ba'adan zkhutan,

When their birthing day arrives. And, having avoided transgression,

יוֹם בֹּא עֵת לֵדָתָן. וְאִם לֹא עָבְרוּ וְנִזְהָרוּ,

Yom bo et leidatan. Ve'im lo avru ve'nizharu,

Their children will come forth with ease.

אֲזַי קְרוֹבָה לֵדָתָן.

Azai krovah leidatan.

Give praise and song to God, who created Shabbat,

תְּנוּ שֶׁבַח וְשִׁירָה, לָאֵל אֲשֶׁר שַׁבָּת בָּרָא,

Tnu shevaḥ ve'shirah, la'El asher Shabbat bara,

And, on that day, gave us Torah, calling to Moses: "I have a gift,

וְלָנוּ בּוֹ נָתַן תּוֹרָה, קָרָא לְמֹשֶׁה
מַתָּנָה.

Ve'lanu bo natan Torah, kara le'Moshe mattanah.

Hidden in My treasure-house, She is fitting for you—take Her,

בְּבֵית גְּנָזַי הִיא טְמוּנָה, לְךָ יָאֲתָה
וְקַח אוֹתָהּ,

Be'veit genazai hi tmunah, lekha yaatah ve'kaḥ otah,

Give Her to the congregation without number."

תְּנָהּ לַעֲדַת מִי מָנָה.

Tnah la'adat mi manah.

For the soul that laments, Shabbat comes, and with it—rest,

נֶפֶשׁ כִּי נֶאֱנָחָה, בָּא שַׁבָּת בָּא מְנוּחָה,

Nefesh ki ne'enaḥah, ba Shabbat ba menuḥah,

גִּיל וְשָׂשׂוֹן וְשִׂמְחָה. בֵּרְכוֹ
וְקִדְּשׁוֹ בְּמָן,

Gil ve'sason ve'simḥah. Berkho
ve'kiddsho be'man,

Rapture, gladness, and joy. He blessed it and sanctified it with manna,

מִלְּרֶדֶת לְעַם לֹא אַלְמָן,
וְהַשַּׁבָּת נֶפֶשׁ מְשִׁיבַת,

Mile'redet le'am lo alman.
Veha'Shabbat nefesh meshivat,

Which [on Shabbat] ceased falling to a nation still bound to God. And Shabbat restores the soul

בְּפִסַּת בָּר אֲשֶׁר טָמָן.

Be'fissat bar asher taman.

With plentiful grain, hidden away.

חֻקּוֹתֶיהָ בְּמָרָה, נִצְטַוּוּ בְּאַזְהָרָה,

Ḥukkoteha be'marah, nitztavvu be'azharah,

Its laws and forewarnings were decreed at Marah;

כַּהֲרָרִים בִּשְׂעָרָה תְּלוּיִם הִלְכוֹתֶיהָ.

Ka'hararim bi'se'arah tluyim hilkhotehah.

Its rules are like mountains suspended on strands of hair.

שׁוֹמְרֵי מִצְוֹתֶיהָ יִנְחָלוּ לְיוֹם
שֶׁכֻּלּוֹ שַׁבָּת בְּצִבְאוֹתֶיהָ.

Shomrei mitzvoteha yinḥalu leyom
she'kullo Shabbat be'tzivotehah.

Those keeping its commandments will inherit a time—wholly Shabbat—with the whole nation together.

זֶה הָאוֹת אֲשֶׁר שָׂם אֵל, בֵּינוֹ וּבֵין בְּנֵי יִשְׂרָאֵל,

Zeh ha'ot asher sam El, beino u'vein bnei Yisrael,

[Shabbat] is the sign God gave between Himself and the children of Israel,

וּבַשְּׁבִיעִי אֲשֶׁר הוֹאֵל. סַמְבַּטְיוֹן הַנָּהָר,

Uva'shvii asher hoel. Sambatyon ha'nahar,

On the seventh day which He willed. That the river Sambatyon—

שֶׁבְּכָל יוֹם רָץ וְנִמְהָר, יוֹכִיחַ בּוֹ מָנוֹחַ,
Shebe'khol yom ratz ve'nimhar, yokhiaḥ bo manoaḥ,

Raging all week—will flow serenely, showing repose,

תָּשִׁיב לְמִין אֲשֶׁר שׁוֹאֵל.
Tashiv le'min asher shoel.

Thus answer the non-believer's question.

קוֹלֵי קוֹלוֹת יֶחְדָּלוּן, בְּעֵת שִׁירַי יִגְדָּלוּן,
Kolei kolot yeḥdalun, be'et shirai yigdalun,

All voices become still, when my songs soar in grace

כִּי כְּטַל הֵם יִזָּלוּן, וְאַל יַשִּׂיגוּ גְּבוּלִי.
Ki kha'tal hem yizzalun, ve'al yasigu gvuli.

Gently, drifting like dew. None approach my [melodic] craft;

בְּאוֹרַח שִׁיר נָפַל חֶבְלִי, הִתְקוֹשְׁשׁוּ
וְאַל תְּשַׁמְּשׁוּ,
Be'oraḥ shir nafal ḥevli, hitkosheshu ve'al teshammshu,

My destiny has become the art of song. Enhance yourselves [in other paths], but do not exploit

בְּנֵזֶר שִׁיר שֶׁפְּרָה לִי.
Be'nezer shir shafrah li.

[This] diadem of music which is mine alone.

יה ריבון
Yah Ribbon

This piyyut was written by Rabbi Israel Najara, whose name is alluded to in the initial letters of the stanzas. Rabbi Israel Najara, one of the greatest Jewish poets after the expulsion from Spain, lived 350 years ago in the city of Gaza, where he served as rabbi. His wonderful poetry is noted for its intense attachment to God, its description of the troubles of Israel, and its longing for redemption. He learned much from the great Spanish poets, but his poetry also contains original forms and content; it is outstanding for its linguistic richness and polished style, as well as for the depth and subtlety of feeling that it expresses. His poems are widespread primarily among Sephardic Jewry and are sung in synagogues.

Chorus:

O Lord and Master of worlds and times, Ruler, King of kings,

[פִּזְמוֹן]

יָהּ רִבּוֹן עָלַם וְעָלְמַיָּא,
אַנְתְּ הוּא מַלְכָּא מֶלֶךְ מַלְכַיָּא .

Yah ribbon alam ve'almaya,
ant hu malka melekh malkhaya,

The power and wonder of Your works, how fine and fitting to tell!

עוֹבַד גְּבוּרְתֵּךְ וְתִמְהַיָּא,

Ovad gvurtekh ve'timhaya,

שְׁפַר קֳדָמָךְ לְהַחֲוָיָא.

Shefar kodomakh lehaḥavaya.

[Chorus]

[פִּזְמוֹן]

I offer my praises at dawn and dusk

שְׁבָחִין אֲסַדֵּר צַפְרָא וְרַמְשָׁא,

Shvaḥin asadder tzafra ve'ramsha,

To You, holy God, who created all life,

לָךְ אֱלָהָא קַדִּישָׁא דִּי בְרָא כָּל נַפְשָׁא.

Lakh Elaha kaddisha di vra kol nafsha.

The holy angels, the children of men,

עִירִין קַדִּישִׁין וּבְנֵי אֱנָשָׁא,

Irin kaddishin u'vnei enasha,

Beasts of the field and birds of the sky.

חֵיוַת בָּרָא וְעוֹפֵי שְׁמַיָּא.

Ḥeivat bara ve'ofei shmaya.

[Chorus]

[פִּזְמוֹן]

How manifold and mighty are Your works!

רַבְרְבִין עוֹבְדֵךְ וְתַקִּיפִין,

Ravrevin ovdekh ve'takkifin,

מָכִיךְ רָמַיָּא וְזָקִיף כְּפִיפִין.
Makhikh remaya ve'zakkif kefifin.
You humble the haughty, You raise up the low.

לוּ יִחְיֶה גְּבַר שְׁנִין אַלְפִין,
Lu yiḥyeh gvar shnin alfin,
Were a man to live for thousands of years,

לָא יֵעוֹל גְּבוּרְתֵּךְ בְּחוּשְׁבְּנַיָּא.
La yeol gvurtekh be'ḥushbenayya.
His mind could not compass Your power.

[פִּזְמוֹן]
[Chorus]

אֱלָהָא דִּי לֵיהּ יְקַר וּרְבוּתָא,
Elaha di leh yekar u'revuta,
God, for Yours are majesty and glory;

פְּרוֹק יַת עָנָךְ מִפּוּם אַרְיְוָתָא.
Perok yat anakh mi'pum aryevata,
Save Your flock from the lion's jaws,

וְאַפֵּיק יַת עַמֵּךְ מִגּוֹ גָּלוּתָא,
Ve'appek yat ammekh mi'go galuta,
And bring Your people home from exile,

עַמֵּךְ דִּי בְחַרְתְּ מִכָּל אֻמַּיָּא.
Ammekh di vekhart mi'kol ummaya.
Your people whom You chose from all the nations.

[פִּזְמוֹן]
[Chorus]

לְמִקְדָּשֵׁךְ תּוּב וּלְקֹדֶשׁ קוּדְשִׁין,
Le'mikdashekh tuv ule'kodesh kudshin,
Return to Your temple, to the holy of holies,

אֲתַר דִּי בֵיהּ יֶחֱדוּן רוּחִין וְנַפְשִׁין,
Atar di veh yeḥdun ruḥin ve'nafshin,
There, where body and soul rejoice,

וִיזַמְּרוּן לָךְ שִׁירִין וְרַחֲשִׁין,
Vi'yzammrun lakh shirin ve'raḥashin,
And they shall sing You songs and praises

In Jerusalem, beautiful city.

בִּירוּשְׁלֵם קַרְתָּא דְשׁוּפְרַיָּא.

Bi'yrushlem karta de'shufraya.

[Chorus]

[פִּזְמוֹן]

יום זה לישראל
Yom Zeh le'Yisrael

The initials of the stanzas of this *piyyut* carry the name of The Holy Ari (Yitzḥak Luria Ḥazak), but, unlike most of his *piyyutim*, it is composed in the Hebrew language. There are many researchers who contend, for this and other reasons, that he did not write this *piyyut*.

Chorus:

[פִּזְמוֹן]

This day brings Israel light and joy, the Sabbath, day of rest.

יוֹם זֶה לְיִשְׂרָאֵל אוֹרָה וְשִׂמְחָה
שַׁבָּת מְנוּחָה.

Yom zeh le'Yisrael orah ve'simḥah,
Shabbat menuḥah.

You commanded us precepts [when we stood] at Sinai,

צִוִּיתָ פִּקּוּדִים בְּמַעֲמַד הַר סִינַי,

Tzivvita pikkudim be'maamad har Sinai,

Sabbath and festivals, for keeping year by year;

שַׁבָּת וּמוֹעֲדִים לִשְׁמֹר בְּכָל שָׁנַי,

Shabbat u'moadim lishmor be'khol shanai,

Setting before me presents and repasts, [on] the Sabbath, day of rest.

לַעֲרֹךְ לְפָנַי מַשְׂאֵת וַאֲרוּחָה,
שַׁבָּת מְנוּחָה.

Laarokh lefanai maset va'aruḥah,
Shabbat menuḥah.

[Chorus]

[פִּזְמוֹן]

Heart's delight to a nation broken,

An extra soul to spirits in pain,

For the troubled spirits, the removal of sorrow, [is] the Sabbath, day of rest.

חֶמְדַּת הַלְּבָבוֹת לְאֻמָּה שְׁבוּרָה,
Ḥemdat ha'levavot le'ummah shvurah,

לִנְפָשׁוֹת נִכְאָבוֹת נְשָׁמָה יְתֵרָה,
Li'nfashot nikhavot—neshamah yeterah,

לְנֶפֶשׁ מְצֵרָה תָּסִיר אֲנָחָה,
שַׁבָּת מְנוּחָה.
Le'nefesh metzerah tasir anaḥah,
Shabbat menuḥah.

[Chorus]

[פִּזְמוֹן]

You sanctified and blessed it above all other days,

When in six days You completed the making of the worlds.

On it, the sorrowful find safety and quiet, [on] the Sabbath, day of rest.

קִדַּשְׁתָּ, בֵּרַכְתָּ אוֹתוֹ מִכָּל יָמִים,
Kiddashta, berakhta oto mi'kol yamim,

בְּשֵׁשֶׁת כִּלִּיתָ מְלֶאכֶת עוֹלָמִים.
Be'sheshet killita melekhet olamim.

בּוֹ מָצְאוּ עֲגוּמִים הַשְׁקֵט וּבִטְחָה,
שַׁבָּת מְנוּחָה.
Bo matzu agumim hashket u'vitḥah,
Shabbat menuḥah.

[Chorus]

[פִּזְמוֹן]

You commanded, awesome God, that work be forbidden;

I shall merit splendid majesty if I keep the Sabbath.

לְאִסּוּר מְלָאכָה צִוִּיתָנוּ, נוֹרָא,
Le'issur melakhah tzivvitanu, nora,

אֶזְכֶּה הוֹד מְלוּכָה אִם שַׁבָּת אֶשְׁמֹרָה.
Ezkeh hod melukhah im Shabbat eshmora.

I bring, feared God, gifts and fragrant offerings, [on] the Sabbath, day of rest.

אַקְרִיב שַׁי לַמּוֹרָא מִנְחָה מֶרְקָחָה,
שַׁבָּת מְנוּחָה.

Akriv shai la'mora, minḥah merkaḥah,
Shabbat menuḥah.

[Chorus]

[פִּזְמוֹן]

Songs shall I set before You with melody and music;

וְשִׁיר אֶעֱרֹךְ לְךָ בְּנִגּוּן וּנְעִימָה,

Ve'shir e'erokh lakh be'niggun u'neimah,

Before the beauty of Your greatness my soul for You does yearn.

מוּל תִּפְאֶרֶת גָּדְלְךָ נַפְשִׁי לְךָ כָּמְהָה,

Mul tiferet godlekha nafshi lekha kamhah.

Keep the promise which You made Your perfect treasured people, [on] the Sabbath, day of rest.

לִסְגֻלָּה תְּמִימָה קַיֵּם הַבְטָחָה,
שַׁבָּת מְנוּחָה.

Li'sgullah tmimah kayyem havtaḥah,
Shabbat menuḥah.

[Chorus]

[פִּזְמוֹן]

Accept my prayer like Nahshon's sacrifice;

רְצֵה תְּפִלָּתִי כְּמוֹ קָרְבַּן נַחְשׁוֹן,

Retzeh tefillati kemo korban Naḥshon,

May my day of rest, with joyous song and happiness,

וְיוֹם מְנוּחָתִי בְּרִנָּה וּבְשָׂשׂוֹן,

Ve'yom menuḥati be'rinnah uve'sason,

Be precious as the apple of Your eye, and greatly prosperous, the Sabbath, day of rest.

חָבִיב כְּבַת אִישׁוֹן, בְּרֹב הַצְלָחָה,
שַׁבָּת מְנוּחָה.

Ḥaviv ke'vat ishon, be'rov hatzlaḥah,
Shabbat menuḥah.

[Chorus]

[פִּזְמוֹן]

יֶשְׁעֲךָ קִוִּינוּ, יָהּ אַדִּיר אַדִּירִים,
Yeshakha kivvinu, Yah addir addirim,

For Your salvation have we hoped, God, greatest of the great.

בֶּן־דָּוִד מַלְכֵּנוּ שְׁלַח נָא לָעִבְרִים,
Ben David malkenu shlaḥ na la'ivrim,

Send, please, David's son, our king, to the Israelite people.

וְיִקְרָא לִדְרוֹרִים, רֶוַח וַהֲנָחָה,
שַׁבָּת מְנוּחָה.
Ve'yikra li'drorim revaḥ ve'hanaḥah,
Shabbat menuḥah.

He shall proclaim freedom, respite, and relief, [on] the Sabbath, day of rest.

[פִּזְמוֹן]

[Chorus]

אָנָּא עֶלְיוֹן נוֹרָא, הַבִּיטָה, עֲנֵנוּ,
Anna elyon nora' habbita, 'anenu,

We beseech you, God awesome and exalted, behold and answer us!

פְּדֵנוּ בִּמְהֵרָה, חָנֵּנוּ חָנֵּנוּ,
Pdenu bi'mhera, ḥonnenu, ḥonnenu,

Speedily save us! Be gracious, O, be gracious unto us!

שַׂמַּח נַפְשֵׁנוּ בְּאוֹר וְשִׂמְחָה,
שַׁבָּת מְנוּחָה.
Sammaḥ nafshenu be'or ve'simḥah,
Shabbat menuḥah.

Cause our souls to rejoice amidst light and joy, [on] the Sabbath, day of rest.

[פִּזְמוֹן]

[Chorus]

חַדֵּשׁ מִקְדָּשֵׁנוּ, זָכְרָה נֶחֱרֶבֶת,
Ḥaddesh mikdashenu, zokhra neḥerevet,

Restore our holy temple; remember her who was destroyed!

טוּבְךָ מוֹשִׁיעֵנוּ תְּנָה לַנֶּעֱצֶבֶת,
Tuvkha, moshi'enu, tna la'ne'etzevet,

Redeemer, bestow Your goodness on her who is sad!

She sits down each Sabbath to sing and to praise [You], [on] the Sabbath, day of rest.

בְּשַׁבָּת יוֹשֶׁבֶת בְּזֶמֶר וּשְׁבָחָה,
שַׁבָּת מְנוּחָה.

Be'Shabbat yoshevet be'zemer u'shvaḥah,
Shabbat menuḥah.

[Chorus]

[פִּזְמוֹן]

Remember us, Holy One, and by the virtue of this precious day,

זְכוֹר קָדוֹשׁ לָנוּ, בִּזְכוּת יִקְרַת הַיּוֹם,

Zekhor, kadosh, lanu, bi'zkhut yikrat ha'yom,

Preserve us, please, on this day and every day,

שְׁמוֹר נָא אוֹתָנוּ, בְּיוֹם זֶה וּבְכָל יוֹם,

Shmor na otanu, beyom zeh uve'khol yom,

My beloved, radiant and awesome, bring respite, [on] the Sabbath, day of rest.

דּוֹדִי צַח וְאָיֹם, תָּבִיא רְוָחָה,
שַׁבָּת מְנוּחָה.

Dodi tzaḥ ve'ayom, tavi revaḥah,
Shabbat menuḥah.

[Chorus]

[פִּזְמוֹן]

Let Israel hear the voice of joy and of salvation,

קוֹל רִנָּה וִישׁוּעָה לְיִשְׂרָאֵל הַשְׁמִיעָה,

Kol rinnah vi'yshuah le'Yisrael hashmiah,

When the vision of salvation comes to be, Rock who makes salvation flourish;

בְּבֹא חֶזְיוֹן תְּשׁוּעָה, צוּר מַצְמִיחַ יְשׁוּעָה,

Be'vo ḥezyon teshuah, tzur matzmiaḥ yeshuah,

Cause the light of my sun to appear, and let it always shine, [on] the Sabbath, day of rest.

אוֹר שִׁמְשִׁי הוֹפִיעָה, תָּמִיד הַזְרִיחָה,
שַׁבָּת מְנוּחָה.

Or shimshi hofiah, tamid hazriḥah,
Shabbat menuḥah.

[פִּזְמוֹן]

[Chorus]

צמאה נפשי

Tzamah Nafshi

This *piyyut* was composed by Rabbi Abraham ibn Ezra, whose name appears as an acrostic at the start of the line of each chapter. The last line of each stanza quotes a verse, or fragment of a verse, containing the word *ḥai* ("lives" or "living"). As indicated by the final line, this *piyyut* was originally a *reshut* (introductory poem) to the prayer *Nishmat kol Ḥai*, recited on Shabbat and festivals.

צָמְאָה נַפְשִׁי לֵאלֹהִים לְאֵל חָי.
Tzamah nafshi l'Elohim, le'El ḥai ,

My soul thirsts for God, the living God.

[פִּזְמוֹן]
לִבִּי וּבְשָׂרִי יְרַנְּנוּ לְאֵל חָי.
Libbi u'vsari yerannenu le'El ḥai.

Chorus:
My heart and my flesh sing out to the living God.

אֵל אֶחָד בְּרָאָנִי, וְאָמַר חַי אָנִי,
El eḥad braani, ve'amar ḥai ani,

The one God created me and said to me, "I live,

כִּי לֹא יִרְאַנִי הָאָדָם וָחָי.
Ki lo yirani ha'adam va'ḥai.

For no man shall see me and yet live."

[פִּזְמוֹן]

[Chorus]

Rabbi Abraham ibn Ezra, born in Spain about eight hundred years ago, was a poet, grammarian, biblical exegete, philosopher, astronomer, and physician. Most of his life was spent wandering from place to place. His poems are, for the most part, reflective poetry in which he describes his observations of the world and its vagaries from a stance of emotional quiet, stemming from his extensive knowledge and rich life experience. Many of his poems have been incorporated within the prayer book.

He created all with wisdom, with counsel and with purpose;	בָּרָא כֹּל בְּחָכְמָה, בְּעֵצָה וּבִמְזִמָּה, *Bara kol be'ḥokhmah, be'etzah uvi'mzimah,*
Deeply are they hidden from the sight of all who live.	מְאֹד נֶעֱלָמָה מֵעֵינֵי כָּל חָי. *Meod neelamah me'einei kol ḥai.*
[Chorus]	[פִּזְמוֹן]
Exalted above all is His glory, every tongue declares His splendor;	רָם עַל כָּל כְּבוֹדוֹ, כָּל פֶּה יְחַוֶּה הוֹדוֹ, *Ram al kol kvodo, kol peh yeḥaveh hodo,*
Blessed He, in whose hands are the souls of all who live.	בָּרוּךְ אֲשֶׁר בְּיָדוֹ נֶפֶשׁ כָּל חָי. *Barukh asher be'yado nefesh kol ḥai.*
[Chorus]	[פִּזְמוֹן]
He set apart [Jacob's], the perfect man's, descendants	הִבְדִּיל נִינֵי תָם, חֻקִּים לְהוֹרוֹתָם, *Hivdil ninei tam ḥukkim lehorotam,*
To teach them the decrees that man should do, and thereby live.	אֲשֶׁר יַעֲשֶׂה אוֹתָם הָאָדָם וָחָי. *Asher yaaseh otam ha'adam va'ḥai.*
[Chorus]	[פִּזְמוֹן]
What [man]—[who is] compared to the fine dust—can claim to be righteous?	מִי זֶה יִצְטַדָּק, נִמְשַׁל לְאָבָק דָּק, *Mi zeh yitztadak, nimshal le'avak dak,*
Truly, righteous before You there are none who live.	אֱמֶת כִּי לֹא יִצְדַּק לְפָנֶיךָ כָּל חָי. *Emet ki lo yitzdak lefanekha kol ḥai.*
[Chorus]	[פִּזְמוֹן]
The inclination of the heart may be likened to the viper's venom;	בְּלֵב יֵצֶר חָשׁוּב, כִּדְמוּת חֲמַת עַכְשׁוּב, *Be'lev yetzer ḥashuv, ki'dmut ḥamat akhshuv,*

How then can [mere] flesh return to You and live?	וְאֵיכָכָה יָשׁוּב הַבָּשָׂר הֶחָי. *Ve'eikhakha yashuv ha'basar ha'ḥai.*
[Chorus]	[פִּזְמוֹן]
The wayward, if they have the will, can turn back from their paths,	נְסוֹגִים אִם אָבוּ, וּמִדַּרְכָּם שָׁבוּ, *Nesogim im avu, umi'darkam shavu,*
Before they go to lie where all must meet that live.	טֶרֶם יִשְׁכָּבוּ בֵּית מוֹעֵד לְכָל חָי. *Terem yishkavu beit mo'ed lekhol ḥai.*
[Chorus]	[פִּזְמוֹן]
For all things I thank You, let every tongue proclaim You one;	עַל כֹּל אֲהוֹדֶךָ, כָּל פֶּה תְּיַחֲדֶךָ, *Al kol ahodekha, kol peh teyaḥadekha,*
You [who] open out Your hand and satisfy all who live.	פּוֹתֵחַ אֶת יָדֶךָ, וּמַשְׂבִּיעַ לְכָל חָי. *Poteaḥ et yadekha, u'masbia lekhol ḥai.*
[Chorus]	[פִּזְמוֹן]
Remember [our] ancient love! Bring those who slumber back to life,	זְכוֹר אַהֲבַת קְדוּמִים, וְהַחֲיֵה נִרְדָּמִים, *Zkhor ahavat kdumim, ve'haḥayeh nirdamim,*
And draw near the days when Jesse's son shall live.	וְקָרֵב הַיָּמִים אֲשֶׁר בֶּן יִשַׁי חָי. *Ve'karev ha'yamim asher ben Yishai ḥai.*
[Chorus]	[פִּזְמוֹן]
Show that the truth is with the lady, when the maid is holding forth,	רְאֵה לִגְבֶרֶת אֱמֶת, שִׁפְחָה נוֹאֶמֶת, *Reeh li'geveret emet, shifḥah noemet,*
"Not so! Your son is the dead one; it is my son who does live!"	לֹא, כִּי בְּנֵךְ הַמֵּת וּבְנִי הֶחָי. *Lo, khi bnekh ha'met u'vni ha'ḥai.*
[Chorus]	[פִּזְמוֹן]

I prostrate myself before You, I spread out to You my hands,

אֶקֹּד עַל אַפִּי, וְאֶפְרוֹשׂ לְךָ כַּפִּי,
Ekkod al appi, ve'efros lekha kappi,

When I open my mouth in prayer with "The souls of all that live."

עֵת אֶפְתַּח פִּי בְּנִשְׁמַת כָּל חָי.
Et eftaḥ pi be'nishmat kol ḥai.

[Chorus] [פִּזְמוֹן]

יה אכסוף
Yah Ekhsof

This hymn was composed by Rabbi Aharon (the Great) of Karlin. The initial letters of its four stanzas combine into the Ineffable Name of God; the initial letters in the second word of each verse combine into the name Aharon, while the first letter of the third word of each of the stanzas form the word neshamah ("soul").

God, I yearn for the Sabbath's sweetness; it partners, it unites with Your treasured people.

יָא אֶכְסֹף נֹעַם שַׁבָּת,
Yah ekhsof noam Shabbat,

הַמַּתְאֶמֶת וּמִתְאַחֶדֶת בִּסְגֻלָּתֶךָ.
Ha'matemmet u'mitaḥedet bi'sgullatekha,

Draw the sweetness of Your awe over the people who seek Your favor.

מְשֹׁךְ נֹעַם יִרְאָתֶךָ לְעַם
מְבַקְשֵׁי רְצוֹנֶךָ,
Meshokh noam yiratekha le'am
mevakshei retzonekha,

Rabbi Aharon of Karlin was one of the disciples of the Maggid of Mezerich and founder of the Karlin-Stolin Hasidic dynasty. Even though he died young, he left behind a deeply felt influence, not only upon individuals, but also upon the many communities that he visited.

Make them holy with the holiness of the Sabbath that unites with Your Torah.

קַדְּשֵׁם בִּקְדֻשַּׁת הַשַּׁבָּת הַמִּתְאַחֶדֶת בְּתוֹרָתֶךָ,

Kaddshem bi'kdushat ha'Shabbat ha'mitahedet be'Toratekha,

Open unto them the sweetness and favor with which to open the gates of Your favor.

פְּתַח לָהֶם נֹעַם וְרָצוֹן לִפְתּוֹחַ שַׁעֲרֵי רְצוֹנֶךָ.

Ptah lahem noam ve'ratzon liftoah shaarei retzonekha.

God, who was and is, keep the keepers of Your holy Sabbath, awaiting it eagerly;

הָיָה הֹוֶה שְׁמוֹר שׁוֹמְרֵי וּמְצַפִּים שַׁבַּת קָדְשֶׁךָ,

Hayah, hoveh, shemor shomrei u'metzappim Shabbat kodshekha,

As the deer longs for streams of water, their souls long to receive (the sweetness) of the Sabbath that unites with Your holy Name.

כְּאַיָּל תַּעֲרֹג עַל אֲפִיקֵי מָיִם, כֵּן נַפְשָׁם תַּעֲרֹג לְקַבֵּל קְדוּשַׁת (נֹעַם) שַׁבָּת הַמִּתְאַחֶדֶת בְּשֵׁם קָדְשֶׁךָ.

Ke'ayal taarog al afikei mayim, ken nafsham taarog lekabbel noam Shabbat, ha'mitahedet be'shem kodshekha.

Save those who put off parting from the Sabbath, lest You hide Yourself from them on the six days, which receive holiness from Your holy Sabbath;

הַצֵּל מְאַחֲרֵי לִפְרשׁ מִן הַשַּׁבָּת, לְבִלְתִּי תִהְיֶה סָגוּר מֵהֶם, שִׁשָּׁה יָמִים הַמְקַבְּלִים קְדֻשָּׁה מִשַּׁבַּת קָדְשֶׁךָ.

Hatzel meaharei lifrosh min ha'Shabbat, le'vilti tihyeh sagur mehem, shisha yamim ha'mekabblim kdushah mi'Shabbat kodshekha,

And purify their hearts to serve You in truth and in faith.

וְטַהֵר לִבָּם בֶּאֱמֶת וּבֶאֱמוּנָה לְעָבְדֶךָ.

Ve'taher libbam be'emet uve'emunah le'ovdekha.

And may Your mercies prevail (over Your just measures! And may Your mercies prevail toward) Your people,

וְיִהְיוּ רַחֲמֶיךָ מִתְגּוֹלְלִים (עַל מִדּוֹתֶיךָ, וְיִהְיוּ רַחֲמֶיךָ מִתְגּוֹלְלִים) עַל עַם קָדְשֶׁךָ,

Ve'yihyu raḥamekha mitgolelim (al middotekha, veyihyu raḥamekha mitgolelim) al am kodshekha,

Giving drink to those who thirst for Your love, from the river that goes forth from Eden,

לְהַשְׁקוֹת צְמֵאֵי חַסְדֶּךָ מִנָּהָר הַיּוֹצֵא מֵעֵדֶן.

Lehashkot tzmeei ḥasdekha mi'nahar ha'yotze me'eden,

Crowning Israel with the glory, who glorify You (on the Sabbath) through Your holy Sabbath,

לְעַטֵּר אֶת יִשְׂרָאֵל בְּתִפְאֶרֶת, הַמְפָאֲרִים אוֹתְךָ (בְּיוֹם שַׁבָּת) עַל יְדֵי שַׁבַּת קָדְשֶׁךָ,

Le'atter et Yisrael be'tiferet, ha'mefaarim otkha (beyom Shabbat) al yedei Shabbat kodshekha,

Setting them through all the six days in the portion of Jacob, Your chosen.

כָּל שִׁשָּׁה יָמִים לְהַנְחִילָם נַחֲלַת יַעֲקֹב בְּחִירֶךָ.

Kol shisha yamim lehanḥilam naḥalat Ya'akov bḥirekha.

The Sabbath is the soul's sweetness, the seventh day is the spirit's joy, the soul's delight,

הַשַּׁבָּת נֹעַם הַנְּשָׁמוֹת, וְהַשְּׁבִיעִי
עֹנֶג הָרוּחוֹת וְעֵדֶן הַנְּפָשׁוֹת,

Ha'Shabbat noam ha'neshamot, veha'shvii oneg ha'ruḥot ve'eden ha'nefashot,

Where to delight in Your love and in Your awe.

לְהִתְעַדֵּן בְּאַהֲבָתְךָ וְיִרְאָתֶךָ.

Lehitaden be'ahavatkha ve'yiratekha.

Holy Sabbath, my soul is sick for love of You.

שַׁבָּת קֹדֶשׁ, נַפְשִׁי חוֹלַת אַהֲבָתֶךָ.

Shabbat kodesh, nafshi ḥolat ahavatekha.

Holy Sabbath, in the shade of Your wings the souls of Israel shelter, satisfied with the rich plenty in Your house.

שַׁבָּת קֹדֶשׁ, נַפְשׁוֹת יִשְׂרָאֵל בְּצֵל
כְּנָפֶיךָ יֶחֱסָיוּן, יִרְוְיֻן
מִדֶּשֶׁן בֵּיתֶךָ.

Shabbat kodesh, nafshot Yisrael be'tzel kenafekha yeḥesayun, yirveyun mi'deshen beitekha.

צור משלו אכלנו
Tzur mi'Shelo Akhalnu

This hymn, whose author is unknown, is very early, and is intended to be sung just before the Blessing after Meals. Its verses are parallel to the first three sections of this blessing (the last two stanzas corresponding to the blessing of Jerusalem).

Chorus:

The Creator, whose food we have eaten—bless Him, my friends. We have filled our needs and left something over, according to God's word.

[פִּזְמוֹן]

צוּר מִשֶּׁלּוֹ אָכַלְנוּ, בָּרְכוּ אֱמוּנַי,
שָׂבַעְנוּ וְהוֹתַרְנוּ כִּדְבַר יְיָ.

Tzur mi'shelo akhalnu, barkhu emunai, Savanu ve'hotarnu, ki'dvar Adonai.

Our Shepherd, our Father—He sustains His world.

הַזָּן אֶת עוֹלָמוֹ, רוֹעֵנוּ אָבִינוּ,

Ha'zan et olamo, ro'enu, avinu,

We have eaten His bread and drunk His wine.

אָכַלְנוּ אֶת לַחְמוֹ וְיֵינוֹ שָׁתִינוּ.

Akhalu et laḥmo ve'yeyno shatinu.

So let us give thanks and praise to His Name:

עַל כֵּן נוֹדֶה לִשְׁמוֹ, וּנְהַלְלוֹ בְּפִינוּ,

Al ken nodeh li'shmo, u'nehallelo be'finu,

There is none as holy as God.

אָמַרְנוּ וְעָנִינוּ: אֵין קָדוֹשׁ כַּיְיָ.

Amarnu ve'aninu, ein kadosh k'Adonai.

[Chorus]

[פִּזְמוֹן]

With appreciative songs let us bless our God

בְּשִׁיר וְקוֹל תּוֹדָה נְבָרֵךְ לֵאלֹהֵינוּ,

Be'shir ve'kol todah nevarekh l'Eloheinu,

For the good, precious land He bequeathed our fathers.

עַל אֶרֶץ חֶמְדָּה טוֹבָה שֶׁהִנְחִיל לַאֲבוֹתֵינוּ.

Al eretz ḥemdah tovah she'hinḥil l'avoteinu.

With plentiful sustenance he has nurtured our souls;

מָזוֹן וְצֵדָה הִשְׂבִּיעַ לְנַפְשֵׁנוּ,

Mazon ve'tzeidah hisbia le'nafshenu,

His kindness overcomes us, and God's truth.

חַסְדּוֹ גָּבַר עָלֵינוּ וֶאֱמֶת יְיָ.

Ḥasdo gavar aleinu ve'emet Adonai.

[Chorus]

[פִּזְמוֹן]

In Your compassion, have mercy for Your people,

רַחֵם בְּחַסְדֶּךָ עַל עַמְּךָ צוּרֵנוּ,

Raḥem be'ḥasdekha al ammkha, tzurenu,

For Zion, the abode of Your Glory,
the site of our Temple.

עַל צִיּוֹן מִשְׁכַּן כְּבוֹדֶךָ,
זְבוּל בֵּית תִּפְאַרְתֵּנוּ.

Al Tziyyon mishkan kvodekha,
zvul beit tifartenu.

May Your servant, David's son,
come redeem us,

בֶּן דָּוִד עַבְדֶּךָ יָבֹא וְיִגְאָלֵנוּ,

Ben David avdekha yavo ve'yigalenu,

The breath of our life: God's
Messiah.

רוּחַ אַפֵּינוּ, מְשִׁיחַ יְיָ.

Ruaḥ appenu, meshiaḥ Adonai.

[Chorus]

[פִּזְמוֹן]

Let the Temple be rebuilt, let Zion
be filled;

יִבָּנֶה הַמִּקְדָּשׁ, עִיר צִיּוֹן תְּמַלֵּא,

Yibbaneh ha'mikdash, ir Tziyyon temalle,

We will sing a new song there, and
soar in joy.

וְשָׁם נָשִׁיר שִׁיר חָדָשׁ,
וּבִרְנָנָה נַעֲלֶה.

Ve'sham nashir shir ḥadash,
uvi'rnanah naaleh.

Then the Merciful One will be
blessed and exalted,

הָרַחֲמָן הַנִּקְדָּשׁ. יִתְבָּרַךְ וְיִתְעַלֶּה,

Ha'raḥaman ha'nikdash yitbarakh ve'yitaleh,

With a cup of wine, filled with the
blessing of God.

עַל כּוֹס יַיִן מָלֵא, כְּבִרְכַּת יְיָ.

Al kos yayin male, ke'virkat Adonai.

[Chorus]

[פִּזְמוֹן]

Shabbat Day

If Friday evening represents the transition from the week days to the Shabbat, the daytime of Shabbat is, so to speak, Shabbat itself. Nighttime in general is the time of concealment. On this particular night, the weekdays are concealed, while the night also contains within itself the coming day, the Shabbat. It is a time of darkness, like one of the symbols of the Shekhinah, the moon, which has no light of its own. For that very reason, it can receive illumination from the Shabbat and be filled with it. Precisely because it only receives an illumination from the Shabbat, it ascends toward it with longing, like a bride going out to greet her groom. (For that reason—because the illumination is always more strongly felt than the thing itself, and because of the element of transition and newness involved—we often feel the sanctity of the Shabbat more strongly during Friday night.)

Shabbat day, by contrast, represents the light of Shabbat itself. From this point on, we not only see the Shabbat, but also are within it. That is, we are with the Almighty Himself, above and separated from all the worlds, on that level known in kabbalistic language as *Attika Kaddisha*. This level is experienced within the soul as a connection with the intrinsic pleasure of the Shabbat day itself. Thus, the meal of the Shabbat day is called the meal of *Attika Kaddisha,* because it partakes of the level of the most Supreme that is utterly separated from every thing—that is the source of all pleasures.

Order of Shabbat Day

Shabbat lunch, the second Shabbat meal, follows the end of synagogue services, which begin in the morning and conclude with the *Musaf* prayer. This meal is preceded by a short Kiddush. Even though this Kiddush is known as ***Kiddusha Rabbah*** ("the Great Kiddush"), it is in fact very short. Strictly speaking, it is enough to merely recite the blessing over wine. Some explain this name as being given out of respect, precisely because this Kiddush is so short. Others explain that since the blessing over wine appears in every ceremony of Kiddush, it is in fact "the great Kiddush." It is customary to recite various verses prior to the blessing itself, as well as the ***Atkinu Seudata*** hymn (see page 93).

אתקינו סעודתא
Atkinu Seudata

Prepare the meal of perfect faith,

אַתְקִינוּ סְעוּדָתָא דִּמְהֵימְנוּתָא שְׁלֵימָתָא,

Atkinu seudata di'mheimnuta shleimata,

Which is the delight of the holy King;

חֶדְוָתָא דְּמַלְכָּא קַדִּישָׁא,

Ḥedvata de'malka kaddisha,

Prepare the meal of the King.	אַתְקִינוּ סְעוּדָתָא דְמַלְכָּא. *Atkinu seudata de'malka.*
This is the meal of the holy Ancient One,	דָּא הִיא סְעוּדָתָא דְעַתִּיקָא קַדִּישָׁא, *Da hi seudata de'attika kaddisha,*
And *Zeir Anpin* and the holy *Ḥakal Tappuḥin*	וּזְעֵיר אַנְפִּין וַחֲקַל תַּפּוּחִין קַדִּישִׁין *U'zeir anpin va'ḥakal tappuḥin kaddishin*
Come to join Him in the meal [Zohar II: 88a–b].	אַתְיָן לְסַעֲדָא בַּהֲדֵיהּ. *Atyan le'saada ba'hadeh.*

אסדר לסעודתא
Asadder li'Seudata

Asadder li'Seudata, the hymn written by Rabbi Isaac Luria (see *Azammer bi'Shvaḥin,* page 30) for the Shabbat lunch, is then recited. Here, too, his name is found in the initial letters of the stanzas.

I shall offer praise at the Shabbat morning meal,	אֲסַדֵּר לִסְעוּדָתָא בְּצַפְרָא דְשַׁבַּתָּא, *Asadder li'seudata be'tzafra de'shabbata*
And shall now invite the holy Ancient One.	וְאַזְמִין בָּהּ הַשְׁתָּא עַתִּיקָא קַדִּישָׁא. *Ve'azmin bah hashta attika kaddisha.*
May the supernal light shine on through the great Kiddush,	נְהוֹרֵיהּ יִשְׁרֵי בָהּ בְּקִידּוּשָׁא רַבָּא, *Nehoreh yishrei vah be'Kiddusha rabba*
And good wine that gladdens the soul.	וּבְחַמְרָא טָבָא דְּבֵהּ תֶּחְדֵי נַפְשָׁא. *Uve'ḥamra tava de'veh teḥdei nafsha.*

May He send to us its resplendence,
and we shall behold its glory

יְשַׁדֵּר לָן שׁוּפְרֵיהּ וְנֶחֱזֵי בִּיקָרֵיהּ,
Yeshadder lan shufreh, ve'neḥezei vi'ykareh

May He reveal to us His hidden
things which are said in secret.

וְיַחֲזֵי לָן סִתְרֵהּ דְּאִתְאֲמַר בִּלְחִישָׁא.
Ve'yaḥazei lan sitreh de'itammar bi'lḥisha.

May He disclose to us the reason
for the twelve breads

יְגַלֵּה לָן טַעֲמֵי דִּבְתְרֵיסַר נַהֲמֵי,
Yegalleh lan taamei devi'treisar nahamei,

Which symbolize a letter of His
Name—both in the combined and
the single form.

דְּאִינּוּן אָת בִּשְׁמֵיהּ כְּפִילָא וּקְלִישָׁא.
De'innun at bi'shmeh, kfila u'klisha.

May we be united with the
Supreme One in whom is the life
of all things;

צְרוֹרָא דִלְעֵילָא דְּבֵיהּ חַיֵּי כֹלָּא,
Tzrora dil'eyla, de'veh ḥayey kholla,

May our strength be increased, and
may [our prayer] ascend and
become [a diadem] upon His head.

וְיִתְרַבֵּי חֵילָא וְתִיסַּק עַד רֵישָׁא.
Ve'yitrabbei ḥeila ve'tisak ad reisha.

Field laborers [Torah scholars],
rejoice with speech and voice,

חֲדוּ חַצְדֵי חַקְלָא בְּדִבּוּר וּבְקָלָא,
Ḥadu ḥatzdei ḥakla, be'dibbur uve'kala,

And speak the words [of Torah]
which are sweet as honey.

וּמַלְּלוּ מִלָּה מְתִיקָא כְּדוּבְשָׁא.
U'mallelu millah metika ke'duvsha.

Before the Master of the worlds
you will reveal words in the
secrets [of the Torah],

קֳדָם רִבּוֹן עָלְמִין בְּמִלִּין סְתִימִין,
Kodam Ribbon Almin, be'millin stimin,

And deliver new insights [in it];

תְּגַלּוּן פִּתְגָּמִין וְתֵימְרוּן חִדּוּשָׁא.
Tegallun pitgamin ve'teimrun ḥiddusha.

To adorn the table with the precious secrets [of the Torah],

לְעַטֵּר פְּתוֹרָא בְּרָזָא יַקִּירָא,
Leatter petora be'raza yakkira,

Profound and hidden, which are ordinarily not to be revealed.

עֲמִיקָא וּטְמִירָא, וְלָאו מִלְּתָא אַוְשָׁא.
Amika u'tmira, ve'lav milta avsha.

And these words will become firmaments.

וְאִלֵּין מִלַּיָּא יְהוֹן לִרְקִיעַיָּא,
Ve'ileyn millaya yehon li'rkiaya,

Who will abide therein? None other than the [Shekhinah, which is allegorically called the] sun.

וְתַמָּן מָאן שַׁרְיָא, הֲלָא הַהוּא שִׁמְשָׁא.
Ve'tamman man sharya, hala ha'hu shimsha.

He will ascend to a more lofty level;

רְבוּ יַתִּיר יַסְגֵּי לְעֵילָּא מִן דַּרְגֵּהּ,
Revu yattir yasgei, le'eyla min dargeh,

And He will take to Himself His mate [Israel], from whom He was separated [during the week].

וְיִסַּב בַּת זוּגֵהּ דַּהֲוַת פְּרִישָׁא.
Ve'yissav bat zugeh da'havat prisha.

Many do not recite these last two verses altogether; others recite them at the very end of the meal, immediately before washing the fingers for the Blessing after Meals.

I cleanse my hands into one vessel,

יָדַי אַסְחֶה אֲנָא לְגַבֵּי חַד מָנָא,
Yaday asḥeh ana le'gabbei ḥad mana,

Toward the Other Side, which has no substance.

לְסִטְרָא חוֹרִינָא, דְּלֵית בָּהּ מַמָּשָׁא.
Le'sitra ḥorina, de'leit ba mammasha.

I shall make *Zimmun* with three, over a cup of blessing,

אֲזַמֵּן בִּתְלָתָא, בְּכַסָּא דְבִרְכָתָא,
Azammen bi'tlata, be'khasa de'virkhata,

To the Cause of Causes, the holy Ancient One.

לְעִלַּת עִלָּתָא, עַתִּיקָא קַדִּישָׁא.
Le'illat illata, attika kaddisha.

חי יי וברוך צורי

Ḥai Adonai u'Varukh Tzuri

The author of this *piyyut,* evidently written some three hundred years ago, left his name, *Ḥayyim Yitzḥak,* in the initial letters of the stanzas. The song speaks of, among other things, the five things that a person needs to prepare on the eve of the Shabbat: candles, double loaves of bread, a laid table, a made bed, and a cup of wine for Kiddush.

The living God! Blessed is my Rock. My soul praises itself in God.

חַי יְיָ וּבָרוּךְ צוּרִי,
בַּיְיָ תִּתְהַלֵּל נַפְשִׁי,

Ḥai Adonai u'varukh tzuri,
b'Adonai tithallel nafshi,

For He illumines my soul's light,
His fire brilliant over my head.

כִּי יְיָ יָאִיר נֵרִי, בְּהִלּוֹ נֵרוֹ עֲלֵי רֹאשִׁי.

Ki Adonai yair neri, be'hillo nero aley roshi.

God is my shepherd, I shall not feel want; He leads me beside still waters.

יְיָ רֹעִי לֹא אֶחְסָר,
עַל מֵי מְנוּחוֹת יְנַהֲלֵנִי,

Adonai ro'i, lo eḥsar,
al mei menuḥot yenahaleni,

He who gives food to all flesh,
provide me my daily portion.

נוֹתֵן לֶחֶם לְכָל בָּשָׂר,
לֶחֶם חֻקִּי הַטְרִיפֵנִי.

Noten leḥem le'khol basar,
leḥem ḥukki hatrifeni.

Let it be Your will—my God, my Holy One—

יְהִי רָצוֹן מִלְּפָנֶיךָ, אַתָּה אֱלֹהַי קְדוֹשִׁי,

Yehi ratzon mi'lfanekha, attah Elohai kdoshi,

Prepare Your table before me;
anoint my head with oil.

תַּעֲרֹךְ לְפָנַי שֻׁלְחָנֶךָ,
תְּדַשֵּׁן בַּשֶּׁמֶן רֹאשִׁי.

Taarokh lefanai shulḥanekha,
tedashen ba'shemen roshi.

Who will grant me rest before the Master of peace?

מִי יִתֵּן מְנוּחָתִי לִפְנֵי אֲדוֹן הַשָּׁלוֹם,

Mi yitten menuḥati lifnei adon ha'shalom,

—That my children be pure,
[blessed with] life and peace.

וְהָיְתָה שְׁלֵמָה מִטָּתִי,
הַחַיִּים וְהַשָּׁלוֹם.

Ve'haytah shlemah mittati,
ha'ḥayyim veha'shalom.

Let Him send His angel ahead to accompany me.

יִשְׁלַח מַלְאָכוֹ לְפָנַי לְלַוּוֹתִי לְוָיָה,

Yishlaḥ malakho lefanai lelavvoti levayah,

I lift my gaze to the cup of salvation; my share is abundant.

בְּכוֹס יְשׁוּעוֹת אֶשָּׂא פָנַי,
מְנָת כּוֹסִי רְוָיָה.

Be'khos yeshuot essa fanai,
menat kosi revayah.

My soul thirsts for God; may He fill my storehouses abundantly.

צָמְאָה נַפְשִׁי אֶל יְיָ,
יְמַלֵּא שֹׂבַע אֲסָמַי,

Tzamah nafshi el Adonai,
yemalle sova asamay,

I lift my eyes to the mountains [teachers], to Hillel's rather than Shammai's [path].

אֶל הֶהָרִים אֶשָּׂא עֵינַי,
כְּהִלֵּל וְלֹא כְּשַׁמַּאי.

El he'harim essa einay,
ke'Hillel ve'lo ke'Shammai.

Joyous days and boundless years—
Awake, my soul, awake!

חֶדְוַת יָמִים וּשְׁנוֹת עוֹלָמִים,
עוּרָה כְבוֹדִי עוּרָה,

Ḥedvat yamim u'shnot olamim,
urah khvodi urah,

And over my head let the lamp of the commandments and the light of Torah shine.

וְעַל רֹאשִׁי יִהְיוּ תַמִּים,
נֵר מִצְוָה וְאוֹר תּוֹרָה.

Ve'al roshi yihyu tammim,
ner mitzvah ve'or Torah.

Rise up, O God, to my rest, You and the Ark of Your Might.

קוּמָה יְיָ לִמְנוּחָתִי,
אַתָּה וַאֲרוֹן עֻזֶּךָ,

Kumah Adonai li'mnuḥati,
attah va'aron uzzekha,

Accept now, God, my blessing; strengthen the power of Your prophet.

קַח נָא אֵל אֶת בִּרְכָתִי,
וְהַחֲזֵק מָגֵן חוֹזֶךָ.

Kaḥ na El et birkhati,
ve'haḥazek magen ḥozekha.

מזמור לדוד
Mizmor le'David

This psalm, Psalm 23, accompanies all of the Shabbat meals and some of the Shabbat prayers. Although it does not refer directly to Shabbat, it portrays the inner feeling of Shabbat, of Shabbat rest and Shabbat delight. After the busy weekdays, Jews come to the Shabbat table, where they find pleasure, calm, and contentment. They merely need to pray that this situation of peacefulness will continue. (For a more detailed commentary on this psalm, see page 125).

A Psalm by David. The Lord is my shepherd, I shall lack nothing.

מִזְמוֹר לְדָוִד, יְיָ רֹעִי לֹא אֶחְסָר.

Mizmor le'David. Adonai roi lo eḥsar.

He makes me lie down in green pastures; He leads me beside still waters.

בִּנְאוֹת דֶּשֶׁא יַרְבִּיצֵנִי,
עַל מֵי מְנוּחוֹת יְנַהֲלֵנִי.

Bi'neot deshe yarbitzeni,
al mei menuḥot yenahaleni.

He revives my soul; He directs me in paths of righteousness for the sake of His Name.

נַפְשִׁי יְשׁוֹבֵב, יַנְחֵנִי בְמַעְגְּלֵי
צֶדֶק לְמַעַן שְׁמוֹ.

Nafshi yeshovev, yanḥeni be'maaglei
tzedek lemaan shmo.

Even if I will walk in the valley of the shadow of death, I will fear no evil, for You are with me;

גַּם כִּי אֵלֵךְ בְּגֵיא צַלְמָוֶת,
לֹא אִירָא רָע, כִּי אַתָּה עִמָּדִי,

Gam ki elekh be'gey tzalmavet,
lo ira ra, ki attah immadi,

Your rod and Your staff—they will comfort me.

שִׁבְטְךָ וּמִשְׁעַנְתֶּךָ הֵמָּה יְנַחֲמֻנִי.

Shivtekha u'mishantekha hemmah yenaḥ.amuni.

You will prepare a table for me before my enemies;

תַּעֲרֹךְ לְפָנַי שֻׁלְחָן נֶגֶד צֹרְרָי,

Taarokh lefanai shulḥan neged tzorerai,

You have anointed my head with oil; my cup is full.

דִּשַּׁנְתָּ בַשֶּׁמֶן רֹאשִׁי, כּוֹסִי רְוָיָה.

Dishanta va'shemen roshi, kosi revayah.

Only goodness and kindness shall follow me all the days of my life,

אַךְ טוֹב וָחֶסֶד יִרְדְּפוּנִי כָּל יְמֵי חַיָּי,

Akh tov va'ḥesed yirdefuni kol yemey ḥayyay,

And I shall dwell in the House of the Lord for many long years.

וְשַׁבְתִּי בְּבֵית יְיָ לְאֹרֶךְ יָמִים.

Ve'shavti be'veit Adonai le'orekh yamim.

Kiddush for Shabbat Day

קידוש ליום השבת

Kiddush for Shabbat Day

אִם תָּשִׁיב מִשַּׁבָּת רַגְלֶךָ, עֲשׂוֹת חֲפָצֶךָ בְּיוֹם קָדְשִׁי, וְקָרָאתָ

Im tashiv mi'Shabbat raglekha, asot ḥafatzekha be'yom kodshi, ve'karata

לַשַּׁבָּת עֹנֶג, לִקְדוֹשׁ יְיָ מְכֻבָּד וְכִבַּדְתּוֹ מֵעֲשׂוֹת דְּרָכֶיךָ,

la'Shabbat oneg, li'kdosh Adonai mekhubbad, ve'khibadto me'asot drakhekha,

מִמְּצוֹא חֶפְצְךָ וְדַבֵּר דָּבָר. אָז תִּתְעַנַּג עַל יְיָ, וְהִרְכַּבְתִּיךָ עַל

mi'metzo ḥeftzekha ve'dabber davar. Az titannag al Adonai ve'hirkavtikha al

בָּמֳתֵי אָרֶץ, וְהַאֲכַלְתִּיךָ נַחֲלַת יַעֲקֹב אָבִיךָ, כִּי פִּי יְיָ דִּבֵּר.

bamotei aretz, ve'haakhaltikha naḥalat Yaakov avikha, ki pi Adonai dibber.

וְשָׁמְרוּ בְנֵי יִשְׂרָאֵל אֶת הַשַּׁבָּת, לַעֲשׂוֹת אֶת הַשַּׁבָּת לְדֹרֹתָם בְּרִית עוֹלָם.

Ve'sahmru vnei Yisrael et ha'Shabbat, laasot et ha'Shabbat le'dorotam brit olam.

בֵּינִי וּבֵין בְּנֵי יִשְׂרָאֵל אוֹת הִיא לְעוֹלָם, כִּי שֵׁשֶׁת יָמִים עָשָׂה יְיָ אֶת

Beini u'vein bnei Yisrael ot hi le'olam, ki sheshet yamim asah Adonai et

הַשָּׁמַיִם וְאֶת הָאָרֶץ, וּבַיּוֹם הַשְּׁבִיעִי שָׁבַת וַיִּנָּפַשׁ.

ha'shamayim ve'et ha'aretz, uva'yom ha'shvii shavat va'yinnafash.

זָכוֹר אֶת יוֹם הַשַּׁבָּת לְקַדְּשׁוֹ. שֵׁשֶׁת יָמִים תַּעֲבֹד וְעָשִׂיתָ כָּל

Zakhor et yom ha'Shabbat lekaddsho. Sheshet yamim taavod ve'asita kol

מְלַאכְתֶּךָ. וְיוֹם הַשְּׁבִיעִי שַׁבָּת לַיְיָ אֱלֹהֶיךָ, לֹא תַעֲשֶׂה כָל

melakhtekha. Ve'yom ha'shvii Shabbat l'Adonai Elohekha, lo taaseh khol

מְלָאכָה אַתָּה וּבִנְךָ וּבִתֶּךָ, עַבְדְּךָ וַאֲמָתְךָ וּבְהֶמְתֶּךָ וְגֵרְךָ

melakhah, attah u'vinkha u'vitekha, avdekha va'amatkha u'vhemtekha, ve'gerkha

אֲשֶׁר בִּשְׁעָרֶיךָ. כִּי שֵׁשֶׁת יָמִים עָשָׂה יְיָ אֶת הַשָּׁמַיִם וְאֶת הָאָרֶץ,

asher bi'she'arekha. Ki sheshet yamim asah Adonai et ha'shamayim ve'et ha'aretz,

אֶת הַיָּם וְאֶת כָּל אֲשֶׁר בָּם, וַיָּנַח בַּיּוֹם הַשְּׁבִיעִי,

et ha'yam ve'et kol asher bam, va'yanaḥ ba'yom ha'shvii,

עַל כֵּן בֵּרַךְ יְיָ אֶת יוֹם הַשַּׁבָּת וַיְקַדְּשֵׁהוּ.

Al ken berakh Adonai et yom ha'Shabbat va'yekaddshehu.

סַבְרִי מָרָנָן וְרַבָּנָן וְרַבּוֹתַי:

Savri maranan ve'rabbanan ve'rabbotai

בָּרוּךְ אַתָּה יְיָ, אֱלֹהֵינוּ מֶלֶךְ הָעוֹלָם, בּוֹרֵא פְּרִי הַגָּפֶן.

Barukh attah Adonai, Eloheinu melekh ha'olam, bore' pri ha'gafen.

Translation of the Kiddush Text

If you restrain your feet, because of the Shabbat, from attending to your affairs on My holy day and you call the Shabbat "delight," the day made holy by the Lord "honored," and you honor it by not following your customary ways, refraining from pursuing your affairs and from speaking profane things—then you shall delight in the Lord, and I will make you ride on the high places of the earth, and I will nourish you with the heritage of Jacob your father; thus the mouth of the Lord has spoken [Isaiah 58:13–14].

And the children of Israel shall observe the Shabbat, establishing the Shabbat throughout their generations as an everlasting covenant. It is a sign between Me and the children of Israel for all time, for in six days the Lord made the heavens and the earth, and on the seventh day He ceased from work and rested [Exodus 31:16–17].

Remember the Shabbat day, to sanctify it. Six days you shall labor and do all your work, but the seventh day is Shabbat for the Lord your God; you shall not do any work—you, your son or your daughter, your manservant or your womanservant, or your cattle, or the stranger within your gates. For [in] six days the Lord made the heavens, the earth, the sea, and all that is in them, and rested on the seventh day.

Therefore the Lord blessed the Shabbat day and made it holy [Exodus 20:8-11].

Attention, friends!

Blessed are You, Lord our God, King of the universe, who creates the fruit of the vine.

נטילת ידיים

Washing of Hands

After the Kiddush and before the second Shabbat meal, the ritual washing of hands is done, and the following blessing is recited:

בָּרוּךְ אַתָּה יְיָ, אֱלֹהֵינוּ מֶלֶךְ הָעוֹלָם, אֲשֶׁר קִדְּשָׁנוּ
בְּמִצְוֹתָיו וְצִוָּנוּ עַל נְטִילַת יָדָיִם.

Barukh attah Adonai, Eloheinu melekh ha'olam, asher kiddshanu be'mitzvotav ve'tzivvanu al netilat yadayim.

Blessed are You, Lord our God, King of the universe, who has sanctified us with His commandments, and commanded us concerning the washing of the hands.

ברכת המוציא

Blessing over Bread

The bread is dipped in salt. At mealtimes, the table should always have a salt container on it, just as salt had to be on the holy altar of the Temple. Before breaking bread, the following blessing is recited:

בָּרוּךְ אַתָּה יְיָ, אֱלֹהֵינוּ מֶלֶךְ הָעוֹלָם, הַמּוֹצִיא לֶחֶם מִן הָאָרֶץ.

Barukh attah Adonai, Eloheinu melekh ha'olam, ha'motzi leḥem min ha'aretz.

Blessed are You, Lord our God, King of the universe, who brings forth bread from the earth.

Then, the second Shabbat meal is held.

זמירות ליום השבת
Zemirot *for Shabbat Day*

ברוך יי יום יום
Barukh Adonai Yom Yom

The author of this *piyyut* is Rabbi Shimon bar Yitzḥak, who lived in the city of Magence (Mainz) some one thousand years ago.

בָּרוּךְ אֲדֹנָי יוֹם יוֹם,
יַעֲמָס לָנוּ יֶשַׁע וּפִדְיוֹם,

Barukh Adonai yom yom,
yaamos lanu yesha u'fidyom,

Bless God each day; His salvation
and deliverance overwhelm us.

וּבִשְׁמוֹ נָגִיל כָּל הַיּוֹם,
וּבִישׁוּעָתוֹ נָרִים רֹאשׁ עֶלְיוֹן,

Uvi'shmo nagil kol ha'yom,
uvi'yeshuato narim rosh elyon,

We will rejoice in His Name forever,
and through His redemption, lift
our heads Above,

כִּי הוּא מָעוֹז לַדָּל וּמַחֲסֶה לָאֶבְיוֹן.

Ki hu maoz la'dal u'maḥaseh la'evyon.

For He is a fortress to the
wretched, a haven to the miserable.

שִׁבְטֵי יָהּ לְיִשְׂרָאֵל עֵדוּת, בְּצָרָתָם לוֹ צָר,

Shivtei Yah le'Yisrael edut, be'tzaratam lo tzar,

God's tribes of Israel bear [Him]
testimony. He suffers with them,

Through servitude and slavery; in sapphire stonework He showed His love's strength,

בְּסִבְלוּת וּבְעַבְדוּת,
בְּלִבְנַת הַסַּפִּיר הֶרְאָם עֹז יְדִידוּת,

Be'sivlut uve'avdut,
be'livnat ha'sappir heram oz yedidut,

And—revealed—lifted them from chasm and dungeon,

וְנִגְלָה לְהַעֲלוֹתָם מֵעֹמֶק בּוֹר וָדוּת,

Ve'niglah lehaalotam me'omek bor va'dut,

For lovingkindness is with Him; His deliverance abounds.

כִּי עִם יְיָ הַחֶסֶד וְהַרְבֵּה עִמּוֹ פְדוּת.

Ki im Adonai ha'ḥesed, ve'harbeh immo fedut.

How precious is His love; in its shadow [He] protects them;

מַה יָּקָר חַסְדּוֹ בְּצִלּוֹ לְגוֹנְנֵמוֹ,

Mah yakar ḥasdo be'tzillo legoneneimo,

In exile in Babylon [the Shekhinah] was sent [to accompany] us,

בְּגָלוּת בָּבֶלָה שֻׁלַּח לְמַעֲנֵמוֹ,

Be'galut Bavelah shullaḥ lemaaneimo,

[His Presence] was with us [when we were] chained in ships' holds,

לְהוֹרִיד בָּרִיחִים נִמְנָה בֵינֵימוֹ,

Lehorid bariḥim nimnah veineimo,

Begging our captors to regard us with mercy,

וַיִּתְּנֵם לְרַחֲמִים לִפְנֵי שׁוֹבֵימוֹ,

Va'yittnem le'raḥamim lifnei shoveimo,

For God will not forsake His people—for the sake of His Great Name.

כִּי לֹא יִטֹּשׁ יְיָ אֶת עַמּוֹ,
בַּעֲבוּר הַגָּדוֹל שְׁמוֹ.

Ki lo yittosh Adonai et ammo,
baavur ha'gadol shmo.

He set His Throne in Eilam [Persia] to rescue His beloved,

עֵילָם שָׂת כִּסְאוֹ לְהַצִּיל יְדִידָיו,

Eylam shat kiso le'hatzil yedidav,

Vanquishing from there the strongholds of the defiant,

לְהַעֲבִיר מִשָּׁם מָעֻזְנֵי מוֹרְדָיו,

Lehaavir mi'sham ma'uznei mordav,

Saving His servants from the sword, He redeemed them [from destruction].

מֵעֲבוֹר בַּשֶּׁלַח פָּדָה אֶת עֲבָדָיו,
Me'avor ba'shellaḥ padah et avadav,

He exalts His people's renown, [apportioning] praise to all His pious ones.

קֶרֶן לְעַמּוֹ יָרִים תְּהִלָּה לְכָל חֲסִידָיו,
Keren le'ammo yarim, tehillah le'khol ḥasidav,

For though He brings suffering, [in the end] His mercy shines through boundless love.

כִּי אִם הוֹגָה
וְרִחַם כְּרַחֲמָיו וּכְרֹב חֲסָדָיו.

Ki im hogah
ve'riḥam ke'raḥamav ukhe'rov ḥasadav.

The young goat [Alexander the Great] reigned supreme,

וּצְפִיר הָעִזִּים הִגְדִּיל עֲצוּמָיו,
U'tzfir ha'izzim higdil atzumav,

And the four kingdoms [of Daniel's prophetic vision] rose to the heavens,

וְגַם חָזוּת אַרְבַּע עָלוּ לִמְרוֹמָיו,
Ve'gam ḥazut arba alu li'mromav,

Conspiring in their hearts to destroy His cherished ones,

וּבְלִבָּם דִּמּוּ לְהַשְׁחִית אֶת רְחוּמָיו,
Uve'libbam dimmu lehashḥit et reḥumav,

But through His priests [the Hasmoneans], He overthrew their foes.

עַל יְדֵי כֹהֲנָיו מִגֵּר מִתְקוֹמְמָיו,
Al yedey khohanav migger mitkomemav,

God's love is endless; His compassion is never exhausted.

חַסְדֵי יְיָ כִּי לֹא תָמְנוּ,
כִּי לֹא כָלוּ רַחֲמָיו.

Ḥasdei Adonai ki lo tamnu,
ki lo khalu raḥamav.

My quarrelsome brethren gave me over to Edom [Rome],

נִסְגַּרְתִּי לֶאֱדוֹם בְּיַד רֵעַי מְדָנַי,
Nisgarti le'Edom be'yad reai medanai,

Who—taking my wealth—gorged themselves daily.

שֶׁבְּכָל יוֹם וָיוֹם מְמַלְאִים
כְּרֵסָם מֵעֲדָנַי,

Shebe'khol yom va'yom memalim
kresam me'adanai,

[Yet] His support was with me, strengthening my foundations,

עֶזְרָתוֹ עִמִּי לִסְמֹךְ אֶת אֲדָנַי,

Ezrato immi lismokh et adanai,

Never deserting me throughout my exile,

וְלֹא נְטַשְׁתַּנִי כָּל יְמֵי עִדָּנַי,

Ve'lo netashtani kol yemei iddanai,

For my God will never cast aside forever.

כִּי לֹא יִזְנַח לְעוֹלָם אֲדֹנָי.

Ki lo yiznaḥ le'olam Adonai.

When He returns from Edom with bloodstained garments,

בְּבֹאוֹ מֵאֱדוֹם חֲמוּץ בְּגָדִים,

Be'vo'o me'Edom ḥamutz bgadim,

[From] slaughtering [Edom's angel] in Bozrah and [avenging His people],

זֶבַח לוֹ בְּבָצְרָה וְטֶבַח לוֹ בְּבוֹגְדִים,

Zevaḥ lo be'votzrah ve'tevaḥ lo be'vogdim,

Their blood will drip with crimson stains.

וְיֵז נִצְחָם מַלְבּוּשָׁיו לְהַאְדִּים,

Ve'yez nitzḥam malbushav lehaadim,

His great power will annul their high-born conceit,

בְּכֹחוֹ הַגָּדוֹל יִבְצֹר רוּחַ נְגִידִים,

Be'khoḥo ha'gadol yivtzor ruaḥ negidim,

On the day of His harsh east wind.

הָגָה בְּרוּחוֹ הַקָּשָׁה בְּיוֹם קָדִים.

Hagah be'ruḥo ha'kasha be'yom kadim.

When Edom's oppressing angel foresees [his downfall],

רְאוֹתוֹ כִּי כֵן אֲדוֹמִי הָעוֹצֵר,

Reoto ki khen adomi ha'otzer,

He will misjudge—seeking shelter in Bozrah [as he would in the refuge city of] Betzer—

יַחְשׁוֹב לוֹ בְּבָצְרָה תִּקְלֹט כְּבֶצֶר,
Yaḥshov lo be'votzrah tiklot ke'vetzer,

Thinking that angels, like men, will be protected there,

וּמַלְאָךְ כְּאָדָם בְּתוֹכָהּ יִנָּצֵר,
U'malakh ke'adam be'tokhah yinnatzer,

And that deliberate murderers, like inadvertent ones, find refuge and asylum.

וּמֵזִיד כַּשּׁוֹגֵג בְּמִקְלָט יֵעָצֵר,
U'mezid ka'shogeg be'miklat ye'atzer,

Love God, all His pious ones—waiting for the Redemption—for He protects the faithful.

אֶהֱבוּ אֶת יְיָ כָּל חֲסִידָיו אֱמוּנִים נוֹצֵר.
Ehevu et Adonai kol ḥasidav, emunim notzer.

The Creator will command to bring His communities together

יְצַוֶּה צוּר חַסְדּוֹ קְהִלּוֹתָיו לְקַבֵּץ,
Yetzaveh Tzur ḥasdo kehillotav lekabbetz,

From the four corners of the earth, to assemble

מֵאַרְבַּע רוּחוֹת עָדָיו לְהִקָּבֵץ,
Me'arba ruḥot adav lehikkavetz,

On lofty Mount [Moriah in His Holy Temple], and settle us [there].

וּבְהַר מְרוֹם הָרִים אוֹתָנוּ לְהַרְבֵּץ,
Uve'har merom harim otanu leharbetz,

And the Gatherer of exiles will return with us,

וְאִתָּנוּ יָשׁוּב נִדָּחִים קוֹבֵץ,
Ve'ittanu yashuv niddaḥim kovetz,

For "He will bring back" is not written, rather: "He will return"—and bring together.

יָשִׁיב לֹא נֶאֱמַר, כִּי אִם וְשָׁב וְקִבֵּץ.
Yashiv lo ne'emar, ki im ve'shav ve'kibbetz.

Blessed is our God who has granted us goodness,

בָּרוּךְ הוּא אֱלֹהֵינוּ אֲשֶׁר טוֹב גְּמָלָנוּ,
Barukh hu Eloheinu asher tov gmalanu,

And in His loving compassion has brought us wondrous salvations.

כְּרַחֲמָיו וּכְרֹב חֲסָדָיו הִגְדִּיל לָנוּ,

Ke'rahamav ukhe'rov hasadav higdil lanu,

So, too, may He increase the like,

אֵלֶּה וְכָאֵלֶּה יוֹסֵף עִמָּנוּ,

Elleh vekha'elleh yosef immanu

To make manifest His mighty and awesome Name that was called upon us.

לְהַגְדִּיל שְׁמוֹ הַגָּדוֹל הַגִּבּוֹר וְהַנּוֹרָא
שֶׁנִּקְרָא עָלֵינוּ.

Lehagdil shmo ha'gadol ha'gibbor veha'nora she'nikra aleinu.

Blessed is our God who has created us for His Glory,

בָּרוּךְ הוּא אֱלֹהֵינוּ שֶׁבְּרָאָנוּ לִכְבוֹדוֹ,

Barukh hu Eloheinu she'braanu likhvodo,

To praise and acclaim Him, to relate His splendor.

לְהַלְלוֹ וּלְשַׁבְּחוֹ וּלְסַפֵּר הוֹדוֹ.

Lehallelo u'leshabbho u'lesapper hodo.

He has done more mercies for us than for all other nations;

מִכָּל אוֹם גָּבַר עָלֵינוּ חַסְדּוֹ,

Mi'kol om gavar aleinu hasdo,

Therefore, with all our heart and soul, with everything we have, we proclaim Him our King and unite His Name.

לָכֵן בְּכָל לֵב וּבְכָל נֶפֶשׁ
וּבְכָל מְאוֹד נַמְלִיכוֹ וּנְיַחֲדוֹ.

Lakhen be'khol lev uve'khol nefesh uve'khol meod namlikho u'neyahado.

May He, to whom peace belongs, grant us blessing and peace;

שֶׁהַשָּׁלוֹם שֶׁלּוֹ יָשִׂים עָלֵינוּ בְּרָכָה
וְשָׁלוֹם,

Sheha'shalom shelo yasim aleinu brakha ve'shalom,

Peace, resting on Israel from right and left [north and south],

מִשְּׂמֹאל וּמִיָּמִין עַל יִשְׂרָאֵל שָׁלוֹם,

Mi'smol umi'yamin al Yisrael shalom,

May the Merciful One bless His people with peace,

הָרַחֲמָן הוּא יְבָרֵךְ אֶת עַמּוֹ בַשָּׁלוֹם,
Ha'raḥaman hu yevarekh et ammo va'shalom,

And may they merit seeing children and grandchildren

וְיִזְכּוּ לִרְאוֹת בָּנִים וּבְנֵי בָנִים
Ve'yizku lirot banim u'vnei vanim

Pursuing Torah and good deeds.

עוֹסְקִים בַּתּוֹרָה וּבְמִצְוֹת,
Oskim ba'Torah uva'mitzvot,

Peace for Israel—

עַל יִשְׂרָאֵל שָׁלוֹם,
Al Yisrael shalom,

[From] the Wonderful Counselor, Almighty God, Eternal Father, the Master of Peace.

פֶּלֶא יוֹעֵץ, אֵל גִּבּוֹר, אֲבִי עַד, שַׂר שָׁלוֹם.
Pele yoetz, El gibbor, avi ad, sar shalom.

ברוך אל עליון
Barukh El Elyon

This *piyyut* (whose initial letters form the name Barukh Ḥazak) was composed by Barukh ben Shmuel of Magence.

Blessed is exalted God who gave our souls calm; release from suffering and lament.

בָּרוּךְ אֵל עֶלְיוֹן אֲשֶׁר נָתַן מְנוּחָה,
לְנַפְשֵׁנוּ פִּדְיוֹן מִשֵּׁאת וַאֲנָחָה,
Barukh El elyon asher natan menuḥah,
le'nafshenu fidyon mi'shet va'anaḥah,

May He look after Zion, the forsaken city. How much longer must our souls grieve?

וְהוּא יִדְרֹשׁ לְצִיּוֹן, עִיר הַנִּדָּחָה,
עַד אָנָה תּוּגְיוֹן נֶפֶשׁ נֶאֱנָחָה.
Ve'hu yidrosh le'Tziyyon, ir ha'niddaḥah,
ad ana tugyon nefesh ne'enaḥah?

Chorus:

All who sanctify the Sabbath—sons and daughters together—may they give the Divine pleasure, like the Temple offerings.

[פִּזְמוֹן]

הַשּׁוֹמֵר שַׁבָּת, הַבֵּן עִם הַבַּת,
לָאֵל יֵרָצוּ כְּמִנְחָה עַל מַחֲבַת.

Ha'shomer Shabbat, ha'ben im ha'bat,
la'El yeratzu ke'minḥah al maḥavat.

The King of the universe, spanning the firmaments, in gentle words inspired His people's rest;

רוֹכֵב בָּעֲרָבוֹת, מֶלֶךְ עוֹלָמִים,
אֶת עַמּוֹ לִשְׁבּוֹת אִזֵּן בַּנְּעִימִים,

Rokhev ba'aravot, melekh olamim,
et ammo lishbot izzen ba'neimim,

With rich delicacies and sweet, tasty foods, splendid finery, and family celebration.

בְּמַאֲכָלֵי עֲרֵבוֹת בְּמִינֵי מַטְעַמִּים,
בְּמַלְבּוּשֵׁי כָבוֹד, זֶבַח מִשְׁפָּחָה.

Be'maakhalei arevot, be'minei matamim,
be'malbushei kavod, zevaḥ mishpaḥah.

[Chorus]

[פִּזְמוֹן]

Happy are all who await their double reward from Him who dwells in the mist, who sees all.

וְאַשְׁרֵי כָּל חוֹכֶה לְתַשְׁלוּמֵי כֵפֶל,
מֵאֵת כָּל סוֹכֶה שׁוֹכֵן בָּעֲרָפֶל,

Ve'ashrei kol ḥokheh le'tashlumei khefel,
me'et kol sokheh shokhen ba'arafel,

Hills and valleys shall they inherit; the inheritance of him [Jacob] for whom the sun shone.

נַחֲלָה לוֹ יִזְכֶּה בָּהָר וּבַשָּׁפֶל,
נַחֲלָה וּמְנוּחָה כַּשֶּׁמֶשׁ לוֹ זָרְחָה.

Naḥalah lo yizkeh ba'har uva'shafel,
naḥalah u'mnuḥah, ka'shemesh lo zarḥah.

[Chorus]

[פִּזְמוֹן]

All who guard Shabbat from profaning it, their destiny is holy; worthy of His love.

כָּל שׁוֹמֵר שַׁבָּת כַּדָּת מֵחַלְּלוֹ,
הֵן הֶכְשֵׁר חִבַּת קֹדֶשׁ גּוֹרָלוֹ,

Kol shomer Shabbat ka'dat me'ḥallelo,
hen hekhsher ḥibbat kodesh goralo,

Meeting the holy day's obligations: how fortunate he is, a gift to his Creator.

וְאִם יָצָא חוֹבַת הַיּוֹם אַשְׁרֵי לוֹ,
אֶל אֵל אָדוֹן מְחוֹלְלוֹ מִנְחָה הִיא שְׁלוּחָה.

Ve'im yatza ḥovat ha'yom—ashrei lo,
el El adon meḥolelo minḥah hi shluḥah.

[Chorus]

[פִּזְמוֹן]

The choicest of days, my God, my Rock, called it, and happy are the earnest, protecting its sanctity.

חֶמְדַּת הַיָּמִים קְרָאוֹ אֵלִי צוּר,
וְאַשְׁרֵי לִתְמִימִים אִם יִהְיֶה נָצוּר,

Ḥemdat ha'yamim krao Eli tzur,
ve'ashrei li'tmimim im yihyeh natzur.

The Creator of all worlds fashions a golden crown for those who bring Him delight.

כֶּתֶר הִלּוּמִים עַל רֹאשָׁם יָצוּר,
צוּר הָעוֹלָמִים רוּחוֹ בָּם נָחָה.

Keter hillumim al rosham yatzur,
tzur ha'olamim, ruḥo vam naḥah.

[Chorus]

[פִּזְמוֹן]

Remember the Sabbath day, to sanctify it. It will be like a diadem on the heads of those who honor it.

זָכוֹר אֶת יוֹם הַשַּׁבָּת לְקַדְּשׁוֹ,
קַרְנוֹ כִּי גָבְהָה, נֵזֶר עַל רֹאשׁוֹ,

Zakhor et yom ha'Shabbat lekaddsho,
karno ki gavhah, nezer al rosho,

Therefore, man will give his soul pleasure and joy [on Shabbat], which will be [for him] as anointing oils.

עַל כֵּן יִתֵּן הָאָדָם לְנַפְשׁוֹ,
עֹנֶג וְגַם שִׂמְחָה בָּהֶם לְמָשְׁחָה.

Al ken yitten ha'adam le'nafsho,
oneg ve'gam simḥah bahem lemoshḥah.

[Chorus]

[פִּזְמוֹן]

The Sabbath Queen is holy for you,
bringing blessings into your homes.

קֹדֶשׁ הִיא לָכֶם שַׁבָּת הַמַּלְכָּה,
אֶל תּוֹךְ בָּתֵּיכֶם לְהָנִיחַ בְּרָכָה,

Kodesh hi lakhem Shabbat ha'malkah,
el tokh bateikhem lehaniaḥ brakhah,

In all your dwellings no work must be
done: not your sons or daughters,
servants or maids.

בְּכָל מוֹשְׁבוֹתֵיכֶם לֹא תַעֲשׂוּ מְלָאכָה,
בְּנֵיכֶם וּבְנוֹתֵיכֶם, עֶבֶד וְגַם שִׁפְחָה.

Be'khol moshvoteikhem lo taasu melakhah,
bneikhem u'vnoteikhem, eved ve'gam shifḥah.

[Chorus]

[פִּזְמוֹן]

יום זה מכובד
Yom Zeh Mekhubbad

The name of the author of this hymn, Yisrael (or perhaps Yisrael ha'Ger [Israel the Proselyte]), is alluded to in the initial letters of the verses, but we do not know who he was or when he lived.

Chorus:
This day is honored more than
every other, for on it, the Creator
of the worlds rested.

[פִּזְמוֹן]

יוֹם זֶה מְכֻבָּד מִכָּל יָמִים,
כִּי בוֹ שָׁבַת צוּר עוֹלָמִים.

Yom zeh mekhubbad mi'kol yamim,
ki vo shavat tzur olamim.

Six days shall you do your work;
the seventh is for your God.

שֵׁשֶׁת יָמִים תַּעֲשֶׂה מְלַאכְתֶּךָ,

Sheshet yamim taaseh mlakhtekha,

וְיוֹם הַשְּׁבִיעִי לֵאלֹהֶיךָ,

Ve'yom ha'shevii le'Eloheikha,

On Shabbat you must not work,
for He created all in six days.

שַׁבָּת לֹא תַעֲשֶׂה בוֹ מְלָאכָה,
Shabbat lo taaseh vo melakhah,
כִּי כֹל עָשָׂה שֵׁשֶׁת יָמִים.
Ki khol asah sheshet yamim.

[Chorus]

[פִּזְמוֹן]

The first of all the holy days: a time of rest, a time of Sabbath. Let every man sanctify it with wine, and the pure-hearted bless the bounteous loaves.

רִאשׁוֹן הוּא לְמִקְרָאֵי קֹדֶשׁ,
Rishon hu le'mikraei kodesh,

יוֹם שַׁבָּתוֹן יוֹם שַׁבַּת קֹדֶשׁ,
Yom shabbaton yom Shabbat kodesh,
עַל כֵּן כָּל אִישׁ בְּיֵינוֹ יְקַדֵּשׁ,
Al ken kol ish be'yeyno yekaddesh,
עַל שְׁתֵּי לֶחֶם יִבְצְעוּ תְמִימִים.
Al shtei leḥem yivtzeu tmimim.

[Chorus]

[פִּזְמוֹן]

Eat rich foods and savor sweet drinks, for God rewards all who cleave to Him: clothes to wear and ample bread; fish and meat, and every delicacy.

אֱכוֹל מַשְׁמַנִּים, שְׁתֵה מַמְתַּקִּים,
Ekhol mashmanim, shteh mamtakim,
כִּי אֵל יִתֵּן לְכָל בּוֹ דְבֵקִים,
Ki El yitten le'khol bo dvekim,
בֶּגֶד לִלְבּשׁ, לֶחֶם חֻקִּים,
Beged lilbosh, leḥem ḥukkim,
בָּשָׂר וְדָגִים וְכָל מַטְעַמִּים.
Basar ve'dagim ve'khol matamim.

[Chorus]

[פִּזְמוֹן]

You will lack nothing [on the Sabbath], so eat to your content, and bless God—whom you love—for He has blessed you above all nations.

לֹא תֶחְסַר כֹּל בּוֹ, וְאָכַלְתָּ וְשָׂבָעְתָּ
Lo teḥsar kol bo ve'akhalta, ve'savata
וּבֵרַכְתָּ אֶת יְיָ אֱלֹהֶיךָ אֲשֶׁר אָהַבְתָּ,
U'verakhta et Adonai Elohekha asher ahavta,
כִּי בֵרַכְךָ מִכָּל הָעַמִּים.
Ki verakhakha mi'kol ha'ammim.

[Chorus]

[פִּזְמוֹן]

The heavens declare His Glory; His Love fills the earth. Look, His Hand has made it all—the Master Craftsman's perfect work.

הַשָּׁמַיִם מְסַפְּרִים כְּבוֹדוֹ,
Ha'shamayim mesapprim kvodo,
וְגַם הָאָרֶץ מָלְאָה חַסְדּוֹ,
Ve'gam haaretz malah ḥasdo,
רְאוּ כִּי כָל אֵלֶּה עָשְׂתָה יָדוֹ,
Reu ki khol elleh asta yado,
כִּי הוּא הַצּוּר פָּעֳלוֹ תָמִים.
Ki hu ha'tzur po'olo tamim.

[Chorus]

[פִּזְמוֹן]

כי אשמרה שבת
Ki Eshmerah Shabbat

This *piyyut* was written by Rabbi Abraham ibn Ezra (see his description, on the *piyyut* for Friday night, *Tzamah Nafshi*, page 73).

When I keep the Sabbath, surely God keeps me;

כִּי אֶשְׁמְרָה שַׁבָּת אֵל יִשְׁמְרֵנִי,
Ki eshmerah Shabbat, El yishmereni,

[פִּזְמוֹן]

אוֹת הִיא לְעוֹלְמֵי עַד בֵּינוֹ וּבֵינִי.

Ot hi le'olmey ad beino u'veini.

Chorus:
It is a sign eternal, binding Him and me.

אָסוּר מְצֹא חֵפֶץ, עֲשׂוֹת דְּרָכִים,

Asur metzo ḥefetz, asot drakhim,

It is forbidden to do business or engage in such affairs,

גַּם מִלְּדַבֵּר בּוֹ דִּבְרֵי צְרָכִים,

Gam mi'ledabber bo divrei tzerakhim,

Even to talk of them at all,

דִּבְרֵי סְחוֹרָה אַף דִּבְרֵי מְלָכִים,

Divrei sḥorah af divrei melakhim,

Nor of deals or politics;

אֶהְגֶּה בְּתוֹרַת אֵל וּתְחַכְּמֵנִי.

Ehegeh be'Torat El u'teḥakmeni.

Let me ponder God's Torah, and it shall make me wise.

[פִּזְמוֹן]

[Chorus]

בּוֹ אֶמְצָא תָמִיד נֹפֶשׁ לְנַפְשִׁי,

Bo emtza tamid nofesh le'nafshi,

On the Sabbath I shall always find restoration for my soul,

הִנֵּה לְדוֹר רִאשׁוֹן נָתַן קְדוֹשִׁי

Hinneh le'dor rishon natan kdoshi

For my holy God gave to the first generation

מוֹפֵת, בְּתֵת לֶחֶם מִשְׁנֶה בַּשִּׁשִּׁי,

Mofet, be'tet leḥem mishneh ba'shishi,

Double manna, as a sign,

כָּכָה בְּכָל שִׁשִּׁי יַכְפִּיל מְזוֹנִי.

Kakha be'khol shishi yakhpil mezoni.

And each sixth day thereafter He gives me double food.

[פִּזְמוֹן]

[Chorus]

רָשַׁם בְּדַת הָאֵל חֹק אֶל סְגָנָיו,

Rasham be'dat ha'El ḥok el sganav,

God made a statute in His law, that on this day His holy priests

בּוֹ לַעֲרוֹךְ לֶחֶם פָּנִים בְּפָנָיו,

Bo laarokh leḥem panim be'fanav,

Set sacred bread before Him,

That fasting be, by His sages' word, utterly forbidden,

Except on the day my sins are atoned.

[Chorus]

The Sabbath is a noble day, a day of delights,

Of bread, fine wines, and meat and fish;

A day when it is wrong to mourn,

A day whose joys are manifold, when You make me rejoice!

[Chorus]

Who starts to work, profaning the Sabbath, will surely be cut off;

I therefore scour with lye my heart,

And evening and morning pray,

And noon and afternoon, to God who answers me.

[Chorus]

עַל כֵּן לְהִתְעַנּוֹת בּוֹ, עַל פִּי נְבוֹנָיו,
Al ken lehitanot bo, al pi nevonav,

אָסוּר, לְבַד מִיּוֹם כִּפּוּר עֲוֹנִי.
Asur, levad mi'yom kippur avoni.

[פִּזְמוֹן]

הוּא יוֹם מְכֻבָּד, הוּא יוֹם תַּעֲנוּגִים,
Hu yom mekhubbad, hu yom taanugim,

לֶחֶם וְיַיִן טוֹב, בָּשָׂר וְדָגִים.
Leḥem ve'yayin tov, basar ve'dagim.

הַמִּתְאַבְּלִים בּוֹ אָחוֹר נְסוֹגִים,
Ha'mitablim bo aḥor nesogim,

כִּי יוֹם שְׂמָחוֹת הוּא וּתְשַׂמְּחֵנִי.
Ki yom smaḥot hu u'tesamḥeni.

[פִּזְמוֹן]

מֵחֵל מְלָאכָה בּוֹ סוֹפוֹ לְהַכְרִית,
Meḥel melakha bo, sofo lehakhrit,

עַל כֵּן אֲכַבֵּס בּוֹ לִבִּי כְּבוֹרִית,
Al ken akhabbes bo libbi ke'vorit,

וְאֶתְפַּלְּלָה אֶל אֵל עַרְבִית וְשַׁחֲרִית,
Ve'etpallelah el El arvit ve'shaḥarit,

מוּסָף וְגַם מִנְחָה, הוּא יַעֲנֵנִי.
Musaf ve'gam minḥah, hu yaaneni.

[פִּזְמוֹן]

שמרו שבתותי

Shimru Shabbtotai

The initial letters of the stanzas of this *piyyut* are Shlomo Ḥazak, and it is ascribed by some to Rabbi Solomon ibn Gabirol.

שִׁמְרוּ שַׁבְּתוֹתַי, לְמַעַן תִּינְקוּ וּשְׂבַעְתֶּם
Shimru shabbtotai lemaan tinku u'svaatem
מִזִּיו בִּרְכוֹתַי, אֶל הַמְּנוּחָה כִּי בָאתֶם,
Mi'ziv birkhotai, el ha'menuḥah ki vatem.

Observe my Sabbaths, so that the light of My blessings nurture and fill you when you reach your rest.

[פִּזְמוֹן]
וּלְווּ עָלַי, בָּנַי, וְעִדְנוּ מַעֲדָנַי,
U'lvu alay, banay, ve'idnu maadanai,
שַׁבָּת הַיּוֹם לַיְיָ.
Shabbat ha'yom l'Adonai.

Chorus:
And [if needed], My children, borrow money on My account; take delight in My pleasures—for today is God's Shabbat.

לֶעָמֵל קִרְאוּ דְּרוֹר, וְנָתַתִּי אֶת בִּרְכָתִי,
Le'amel kiru dror, venatati et birkhati,
אִשָּׁה אֶל אֲחוֹתָהּ לִצְרוֹר, לְגַלּוֹת עַל יוֹם שִׂמְחָתִי,
Ishah el aḥotah litzror, legallot al yom simḥati.

Proclaim freedom from workday effort, and I will call forth My blessings, each tied to the next; to rejoice in My day of bliss.

Rabbi Solomon ibn Gabirol (Spain, some nine hundred years ago) was an outstanding Spanish Jewish philosopher and poet. His poetry includes secular poetry, philosophical poems, nature poems, ethical and rebuke poetry, national poetry, mystical poetry (reaching its height in *Keter Malkhut,* which also entered the Siddur), and, primarily, religious poetry, expressing deep longing for God together with submissive humility.

בִּגְדֵי שֵׁשׁ עִם שָׁנִי, וְהִתְבּוֹנְנוּ מִזְּקֵנַי,

Bigdei shesh im shani, ve'hitbonenu mi'zkenai,

שַׁבָּת הַיּוֹם לַיְיָ.

Shabbat hayom l'Adonai.

Array yourself in fine linen and silk; contemplate [the words] of My sages—for today is God's Shabbat.

[פִּזְמוֹן]

[Chorus]

מַהֲרוּ אֶת הַמָּנֶה, לַעֲשׂוֹת אֶת דְּבַר אֶסְתֵּר,

Maharu et ha'maneh, laasot et dvar Ester,

וְחִשְׁבוּ עִם הַקּוֹנֶה, לְשַׁלֵּם אָכוֹל וְהוֹתֵר,

Ve'ḥishvu im ha'koneh, leshallem akhol ve'hoter.

Hurry, prepare the festive meal, [as when they rushed] to obey Queen Esther's decree. Apprise the universe's Proprietor [of all your expenses]; He will repay for food and beyond.

בִּטְחוּ בִי אֱמוּנַי, וּשְׁתוּ יֵין מַשְׁמַנַּי,

Bitḥu vi emunai, u'shtu yeyn mashmannai,

שַׁבָּת הַיּוֹם לַיְיָ.

Shabbat ha'yom l'Adonai.

Trust Me, My faithful ones, and drink choice wine—for today is God's Shabbat.

[פִּזְמוֹן]

[Chorus]

הִנֵּה יוֹם גְּאֻלָּה, יוֹם שַׁבָּת אִם תִּשְׁמֹרוּ,

Hinneh yom geullah, yom Shabbat im tishmoru,

וִהְיִיתֶם לִי סְגֻלָּה, לִינוּ וְאַחַר תַּעֲבֹרוּ,

Vi'hyitem li sgullah, linu ve'aḥar taavoru,

The day of Redemption is here, if you keep My Sabbath; and you will be My treasure. Rest, and then move forward [to Redemption].

וְאָז תִּחְיוּ לְפָנַי, וְתִמָּלְאוּ צְפוּנַי,

Ve'az tiḥyu lefanay ve'timmallu tzfunay,

שַׁבָּת הַיּוֹם לַיְיָ.

Shabbat ha'yom l'Adonai.

And then, live before Me, filled with My hidden riches—for today is God's Shabbat.

[פִּזְמוֹן]

[Chorus]

Almighty God, strengthen my city; restore my Temple with jubilant song.

חַזֵּק קִרְיָתִי, אֵל אֱלֹהִים עֶלְיוֹן,
Ḥazzek kiryati, El Elohim elyon,
וְהָשֵׁב אֶת נְוָתִי, בְּשִׂמְחָה וּבְהִגָּיוֹן,
Ve'hashev et nevati be'simḥah uve'higgayon.

Let my choirs burst forth, my Levites, my priests,

יְשׁוֹרְרוּ שָׁם רְנָנַי, לְוִיַּי וְכֹהֲנַי,
Yeshoreru sham renanai, leviyai ve'khohanai,

And then [we] will delight in God—for today is God's Shabbat.

וְאָז תִּתְעַנַּג עַל יְיָ, שַׁבָּת הַיּוֹם לַייָ.
Ve'az titannag al Adonai, Shabbat ha'yom l'Adonai.

[Chorus]

[פִּזְמוֹן]

יום שבתון
Yom Shabbaton

This *piyyut* was written by Rabbi Judah Halevi, whose name is alluded to in the headings of the stanza.

Unforgettable is the Sabbath day! Its memory is like a soothing incense.

יוֹם שַׁבָּתוֹן אֵין לִשְׁכֹּחַ,
זִכְרוֹ כְּרֵיחַ הַנִּיחֹחַ,

Yom shabbaton ein lishkoaḥ,
zikhro ke'reaḥ ha'nihoaḥ,

Rabbi Judah Halevi (Spain, some nine hundred years ago) was among the greatest Jewish poets of all generations, and an important philosopher, author of *The Kuzari*. At the end of his life he decided to go to the Land of Israel. According to legend, he was trampled by an Arab horseman while mourning or weeping over the Destruction of Jerusalem at the Western Wall. Others claim that he never reached the Land of Israel, but died in Egypt. About 750 of his poems are extant; many of them are elevated religious poems that have entered the Siddur.

Chorus:

The dove found resting on this day; there the weary rediscover strength.

[פִּזְמוֹן]

יוֹנָה מָצְאָה בוֹ מָנוֹחַ,
וְשָׁם יָנוּחוּ יְגִיעֵי כֹחַ.

Yonah matzah vo manoaḥ,
ve'sham yanuḥu yegiey khoaḥ.

The day is honored in the families of the faithful, with loving care they keep it, parent and child.

הַיּוֹם נִכְבָּד לִבְנֵי אֱמוּנִים,
זְהִירִים לְשָׁמְרוֹ אָבוֹת וּבָנִים,

Ha'yom nikhbad li'vnei emunim,
zehirim leshomro avot u'vanim,

For in the two stone tablets it was set, by God, great in power and mighty in strength.

חָקוּק בִּשְׁנֵי לוּחוֹת אֲבָנִים,
מֵרוֹב אוֹנִים וְאַמִּיץ כֹּחַ.

Ḥakuk bi'shnei luḥot avanim,
merov onim ve'amitz koaḥ.

[Chorus]

[פִּזְמוֹן]

At that time all the people came to one accord: "We will do and we will listen," they declared as one.

וּבָאוּ כֻלָּם בִּבְרִית יַחַד,
נַעֲשֶׂה וְנִשְׁמַע אָמְרוּ כְּאֶחָד,

U'vau khullam bi'vrit yaḥad,
naaseh ve'nishma amru ke'eḥad,

They spoke up, they answered: "The Lord, He is One," blessed He, who gives the weary strength.

וּפָתְחוּ וְעָנוּ יְיָ אֶחָד,
בָּרוּךְ הַנּוֹתֵן לַיָּעֵף כֹּחַ.

U'fatḥu ve'anu—Adonai eḥad,
barukh ha'noten la'yaef koaḥ.

[Chorus]

[פִּזְמוֹן]

From the fragrant mountain in holiness God spoke: Remember and preserve the Sabbath day;

דִּבֵּר בְּקָדְשׁוֹ בְּהַר הַמּוֹר,
יוֹם הַשְּׁבִיעִי זָכוֹר וְשָׁמוֹר,

Dibber be'kodsho be'har ha'mor,
yom ha'shvii zakhor ve'shamor,

Fulfill its precepts all together, so may God impart us vigor, and energy and strength.

וְכָל פִּקּוּדָיו יַחַד לִגְמֹר,
חַזֵּק מָתְנַיִם וְאַמֵּץ כֹּחַ.

Ve'khol pikkudav yahad ligmor,
ḥazzek motnayim ve'ammetz koaḥ.

[Chorus]

[פִּזְמוֹן]

The people that wanders, like a straying flock, remembers its master's covenant and oath:

הָעָם אֲשֶׁר נָע, כַּצֹּאן טָעָה,
יִזְכּוֹר לְפָקְדוֹ בִּבְרִית וּשְׁבוּעָה,

Ha'am asher na, ka'tzon taah,
yizkor lefokdo bi'vrit u'shvuah,

That no misfortune should befall them, as God swore upon the swell of Noah's flood.

לְבַל יַעֲבוֹר בָּם מִקְרֶה רָעָה,
כַּאֲשֶׁר נִשְׁבַּעְתָּ עַל מֵי נֹחַ.

Le'val yaavor bam mikreh raah,
kaasher nishbata al mei noaḥ.

[Chorus]

[פִּזְמוֹן]

דרור יקרא

Dror Yikra

This *piyyut* was written by Dunash ibn Labrat, whose name appears at the beginning of four of its six stanzas.

דְּרוֹר יִקְרָא לְבֵן עִם בַּת,
וְיִנְצָרְכֶם כְּמוֹ בָבַת,

Dror yikra le'ven im bat,
ve'yintzorkhem kemo vavat,

He will set son and daughter free, and guard you as the apple of His eye.

נְעִים שִׁמְכֶם וְלֹא יוּשְׁבַּת,
שְׁבוּ וְנוּחוּ בְּיוֹם שַׁבָּת.

Neim shimkhem ve'lo yushbat,
shevu ve'nuḥu be'yom Shabbat.

Your name is sweet, it will not be lost; come and rest on the Sabbath day.

דְּרֹשׁ נָוִי וְאוּלָמִי, וְאוֹת יֶשַׁע עֲשֵׂה עִמִּי,

Drosh navi ve'ulami, ve'ot yesha ase immi,

Show Your care for house and home, make me salvation's sign.

נְטַע שׂוֹרֵק בְּתוֹךְ כַּרְמִי,
שְׁעֵה שַׁוְעַת בְּנֵי עַמִּי.

Neta sorek be'tokh karmi,
sheeh shavat bnei ammi.

Plant the best vine in my vineyard, heed my people's cry for help.

Dunash ibn Labrat, a Hebrew philologist and poet, lived in Spain nearly one thousand years ago. A student of Rabbi Saadya Gaon in Baghdad, he was a rabbi and religious judge. He laid the foundations for medieval Hebrew poetry, adapting the meter of Arabic poetry to Hebrew poetry. Only a few of his poems have been discovered to date.

Tread the vine-press down in Botzrah, and in Babylon grown mighty,

דְּרֹךְ פּוּרָה בְּתוֹךְ בָּצְרָה,
וְגַם בָּבֶל אֲשֶׁר גָּבְרָה,

Drokh purah be'tokh Botzrah,
ve'gam Bavel asher gavrah,

Throw my enemies down in fury, hear my voice the day I call.

נְתֹץ צָרַי בְּאַף וְעֶבְרָה, שְׁמַע קוֹלִי בְּיוֹם אֶקְרָא.

Netotz tzarai be'af ve'evrah, shma koli be'yom ekra.

God, plant a mountain in the desert—myrtle, acacia, cypress, elm;

אֱלֹהִים תֵּן בַּמִּדְבָּר הַר,
הֲדַס שִׁטָּה בְּרוֹשׁ תִּדְהָר,

Elohim, ten ba'midbar har,
hadas shittah brosh tidhar,

To those who teach and those who learn, send Your peace like flowing streams.

וְלַמַּזְהִיר וְלַנִּזְהָר, שְׁלוֹמִים תֵּן כְּמֵי נָהָר.

Ve'lamazhir ve'lanizhar, shlomim ten ke'mei nahar.

Throw off my foes, God of zeal, crush the crust about their hearts.

הֲדוֹךְ קָמַי אֵל קַנָּא,
בְּמוֹג לֵבָב וּבַמְּגִינָּה,

Hadokh kamai, El kanna,
be'mog levav uva'mginah,

Then wide our mouths we will open; fill our throats with songs to You.

וְנַרְחִיב פֶּה וּנְמַלְאֶנָּה,
לְשׁוֹנֵנוּ לְךָ רִנָּה.

Ve'narḥiv peh u'nemalenah,
leshonenu lekha rinnah.

Lay this counsel to your soul, set it a crown upon your head;

דְּעֵה חָכְמָה לְנַפְשֶׁךָ,
וְהִיא כֶתֶר לְרֹאשֶׁךָ,

De'eh ḥokhmah le'nafshekha,
ve'hi kheter le'roshekha,

Keep your holy God's commandments, keep the Sabbath, your sacred day.

נְצוֹר מִצְוַת קְדוֹשֶׁךָ,
שְׁמוֹר שַׁבָּת קָדְשֶׁךָ.

Netzor mitzvat kdoshekha,
shmor Shabbat kodshekha.

שבת היום ליי

Shabbat ha'Yom l'Adonai

All that we know about the author of this *piyyut* is his name, Shmuel, which appears in the initial letters of the poem.

Chorus:

It is Shabbat today, given over to God.

[פִּזְמוֹן]

שַׁבָּת הַיּוֹם לַיְיָ.

Shabbat ha'yom l'Adonai,

Rejoice mightily with My songs, and generously be stow My treats; observing with care the command of God.

מְאֹד צַהֲלוּ בְּרִנּוּנַי, וְגַם הַרְבּוּ מַעֲדָנַי,
Meod tzahalu be'rinnunay, ve'gam harbu maadanai,
אוֹתוֹ לִשְׁמוֹר כְּמִצְוַת יְיָ.
Oto lishmor ke'mtizvat Adonai.

[Chorus]

[פִּזְמוֹן]

Traverse not distant borders, nor take on worldly labors; eat and drink, sing praises; this is the day which the Lord has made.

מֵעֲבוֹר דֶּרֶךְ וּגְבוּלִים, מֵעֲשׂוֹת הַיּוֹם פְּעָלִים,
Me'avor derekh u'gvulim, me'asot ha'yom pealim,
לֶאֱכֹל וְלִשְׁתּוֹת בְּהִלּוּלִים,
Le'ekhol ve'lishtot be'hillulim,
זֶה הַיּוֹם עָשָׂה יְיָ.
Zeh ha'yom asah Adonai.

[Chorus]

[פִּזְמוֹן]

And if you keep it, God will preserve you, the apple of His eye, also your son, as well as your daughter; and call Shabbat: Delight—then you will soar in His rapture.

וְאִם תִּשְׁמְרֶנּוּ, יָהּ יִנְצָרְךָ כְּבָבַת,
Ve'im tishmerenu, Yah yintzorkha ke'vavat,
אַתָּה וּבִנְךָ וְגַם הַבַּת,
Attah u'vinkha ve'gam ha'bat,
וְקָרָאתָ עֹנֶג לַשַּׁבָּת, אָז תִּתְעַנַּג עַל יְיָ.
Ve'karata oneg la'Shabbat, az titannag al Adonai.

[Chorus]

[פִּזְמוֹן]

Eat rich foods and delicacies, tasty morsels of all descriptions, soft-shelled nuts and pomegranates; and when you have eaten and are satisfied, bless the Lord.

אֱכֹל מַשְׁמַנִּים וּמַעֲדַנִּים,
Ekhol mashmannim u'maadanim,
וּמַטְעַמִּים הַרְבֵּה מִינִים,
U'matamim harbeh minnim,
אֱגוֹזֵי פֶרֶךְ וְרִמּוֹנִים,
Egozei ferekh ve'rimmonim,
וְאָכַלְתָּ וְשָׂבָעְתָּ וּבֵרַכְתָּ אֶת יְיָ.
Ve'akhalta ve'savata u'verakhta et Adonai.

[Chorus]

[פִּזְמוֹן]

Arrange the table with choice loaves of bread, serve today three festive meals; bless [God's] Honored Name and give thanks. Observe it diligently, my sons; do all [I have said].

לַעֲרֹךְ בְּשֻׁלְחָן לֶחֶם חֲמוּדוֹת,
Laarokh be'shulḥan leḥem ḥamudot,
לַעֲשׂוֹת הַיּוֹם שָׁלֹשׁ סְעוּדוֹת,
Laasot ha'yom shalosh seudot,
אֶת הַשֵּׁם הַנִּכְבָּד לְבָרֵךְ וּלְהוֹדוֹת,
Et ha'Shem ha'nikhbad levarekh u'lehodot,
שִׁקְדוּ וְשִׁמְרוּ וַעֲשׂוּ, בָּנַי.
Shikkdu ve'shimmru va'asu, banai.

[Chorus]

[פִּזְמוֹן]

The Third Shabbat Meal

The third meal is eaten following the ***Minḥah*** prayer, during the third time period of Shabbat. At this meal, too, the formula ***Atkinu Seudata*** (see page 85) is recited, this time saying, "This is the meal of ***Zeir Anpin***" (a kabbalistic term).

This meal, like that of Shabbat midday, is conducted during the daytime of Shabbat, before sunset. At this time, the glories of the whole Shabbat focus and concentrate. It is said of this meal, "I will nourish you with the heritage of Jacob your father" (Isaiah 58:14)—that is, an utterly unlimited inheritance (as said about Jacob the patriarch himself: "You shall spread out to the west and east and north and south" (Genesis 28:14). From this level of boundless inheritance, of pressing reality, the boundaries of our limitations, Shabbat illuminates also the work days that will follow.

The light and revelation of Shabbat reach their culmination at twilight. On weekdays, the afternoon hours are a time of descent and of waning vitality, a time of judgment, and the weekday ***Minḥah*** prayer is associated with "the fear of [our patriarch] Isaac." But on Shabbat it is just the opposite: the afternoon hours are considered the time of the "will of all wills" and of the supreme illumination. The atmosphere at that time is one of conciliation, "a rest of peace, tranquillity, serenity, and security," combined with a spiritual thirst and longing for the ultimate goal of Shabbat. In the Talmudic and Mishnaic periods, the Shabbat afternoon hours were devoted to Torah study. People gathered in the synagogue to hear the homilies of the local sage, which usually were addressed to the general public. It is the custom among Hasidim, who follow the Sepharad rite, to join in a communal third meal, and to devote it to issues of Torah and faith.

A few have the custom of drinking wine with this meal, and a kind of Kiddush was even instituted, to be recited in the course of the meal, after eating some bread.

אתקינו סעודתא
Atkinu Seudata

Prepare the meal of perfect faith,	אַתְקִינוּ סְעוּדָתָא דִּמְהֵימְנוּתָא שְׁלֵמָתָא, ***Atkinu seudata di'meheimenuta shlemata,***
Which is the delight of the holy King;	חֶדְוָתָא דְּמַלְכָּא קַדִּישָׁא. ***Ḥedvata de'malka kaddisha.***
Prepare the meal of the King.	אַתְקִינוּ סְעוּדָתָא דְּמַלְכָּא. ***Atkinu seudata de'malka.***
This is the meal of *Zeir Anpin*,	דָּא הִיא סְעוּדָתָא דִּזְעֵיר אַנְפִּין, ***Da hi seudata di'zeir anpin,***
And the holy Ancient One and the holy *Ḥakal Tappuḥin*	וְעַתִּיקָא קַדִּישָׁא וַחֲקַל תַּפּוּחִין קַדִּישִׁין ***Ve'attika kaddisha va'ḥakal tappuḥin kaddishin***
Come to join him in the meal [Zohar II:88a–b]	אַתְיָן לְסַעֲדָא בַּהֲדָא. ***Atyan le'saada ba'hada.***

נטילת ידיים

Washing of Hands

The ritual washing of hands is done, and the following blessing recited:

בָּרוּךְ אַתָּה יְיָ, אֱלֹהֵינוּ מֶלֶךְ הָעוֹלָם, אֲשֶׁר קִדְּשָׁנוּ
בְּמִצְוֹתָיו וְצִוָּנוּ עַל נְטִילַת יָדָיִם.

Barukh attah Adonai, Eloheinu melekh ha'olam, asher kiddshanu be'mitzvotav ve'tzivvanu al netilat yadayim.

Blessed are You, Lord our God, King of the universe, who has sanctified us with His commandments, and commanded us concerning the washing of the hands.

ברכת המוציא

Blessing over Bread

The bread is dipped in salt. At mealtimes, the table should always have a salt container on it, just as salt had to be on the holy altar of the Temple.
Before bread is broken, the following blessing is recited:

בָּרוּךְ אַתָּה יְיָ, אֱלֹהֵינוּ מֶלֶךְ הָעוֹלָם, הַמּוֹצִיא לֶחֶם מִן הָאָרֶץ.

Barukh attah Adonai, Eloheinu melekh ha'olam, ha'motzi leḥem min ha'aretz.

Blessed are You, Lord our God, King of the universe, who brings forth bread from the earth.

Then, the third Shabbat meal is held.

זמירות לסעודה השלישית
Zemirot *for the Third Meal*

בני היכלא
Bnei Heikhala

Rabbi Isaac Luria's *piyyut*, *Bnei Heikhala*, the third of his special *piyyutim* for the Shabbat meals, is also recited.

בְּנֵי הֵיכָלָא דִּכְסִיפִין לְמֶחֱזֵי זִיו דִּזְעֵיר אַנְפִּין,

Bnei heikhala di'khsifin lemeḥzei ziv di'zeir anpin,

You princes of the palace, who yearn to behold the splendor of *Zeir Anpin:*

יְהוֹן הָכָא, בְּהַאי תַּכָּא,
דְּבֵיהּ מַלְכָּא בְּגִלּוּפִין:

Yehon hakha, be'hai takka,
de'veih malka be'gillufin.

Be present at this meal, at which the King leaves His imprint.

צְבוּ לַחֲדָא בְּהַאי וַעֲדָא,
בְּגוֹ עִירִין וְכָל גַּדְפִּין,

Tzvu la'ḥada be'hai vaada,
be'go irin ve'khol gaddfin,

Exult, rejoice in this gathering together, with the angels and all supernal beings;

חֲדוּ הַשְׁתָּא, בְּהַאי שַׁעְתָּא,
דְּבֵיהּ רַעֲוָא וְלֵית זַעְפִין,

Ḥadu hashta, be'hai shaata,
de'veh raava ve'leit zaafin.

Rejoice now, at this most propitious time, when there is joy, and no sadness.

Draw near to Me, behold My strength, for there are no harsh judgments.

קְרִיבוּ לִי, חֲזוּ חֵילִי, דְּלֵית דִּינִין דִּתְקִיפִין.

Krivu li, ḥazu ḥeili, de'leit dinnin di'tkifin.

They are cast out, they may not enter, those [forces of evil which are likened to] insolent dogs.

לְבַר נַטְלִין, וְלָא עָאלִין,
הָנֵי כַּלְבִּין דַּחֲצִיפִין:

Le'var natlin, ve'la alin,
hanei kalbin da'ḥatzifin.

I herewith invite the "Ancient of Days" at this auspicious time, and [the powers of impurity] will be utterly removed.

וְהָא אַזְמִין עַתִּיק יוֹמִין (לְמִנְחָה)
לְמִצְחָא עֲדֵי יְהוֹן חַלְפִין.

Ve'ha azmin attik yomin (le'minḥah)
le'mitzḥa adei yehon ḥalfin.

It is His revealed will to annul all the powers of impurity;

רְעוּ דִילֵהּ, דְּגַלֵּי לֵיהּ לְבַטָּלָא בְּכָל קְלִיפִין:

Reu di'leh de'gallei leh le'vattala be'khol klifin.

He will hurl them into their abysses, and they will hide in the clefts of the rocks.

יְשַׁוֵּי לוֹן בְּנֻקְבֵיהוֹן,
וִיטַמְרוּן בְּגוֹ כֵּפִין,

Yeshavvei lon be'nukveihon,
vi'ytamrun be'go kheifin.

For this time of *Minḥah* is a time of joy for *Zeir Anpin*.

אֲרֵי הַשְׁתָּא, בְּמִנְחָתָא,
בְּחֶדְוָתָא דִּזְעֵיר אַנְפִּין.

Arei hashta, be'minḥata,
be'ḥedvata di'zeir anpin.

מזמור לדוד
Mizmor le'David

A Psalm by David. The Lord is my shepherd, I shall lack nothing.

מִזְמוֹר לְדָוִד, יְיָ רֹעִי לֹא אֶחְסָר.

Mizmor le'David. Adonai roi lo eḥsar.

He makes me lie down in green pastures; He leads me beside still waters.

בִּנְאוֹת דֶּשֶׁא יַרְבִּיצֵנִי,
עַל מֵי מְנוּחוֹת יְנַהֲלֵנִי.

Bi'neot deshe yarbitzeni,
al mei menuḥot yenahaleni.

He revives my soul; He directs me in paths of righteousness for the sake of His Name.

נַפְשִׁי יְשׁוֹבֵב, יַנְחֵנִי בְמַעְגְּלֵי צֶדֶק
לְמַעַן שְׁמוֹ.

Nafshi yeshovev, yanḥeni ve'maaglei tzedek
lemaan shmo.

Even if I will walk in the valley of the shadow of death, I will fear no evil, for You are with me;

גַּם כִּי אֵלֵךְ בְּגֵיא צַלְמָוֶת,
לֹא אִירָא רָע, כִּי אַתָּה עִמָּדִי,

Gam ki elekh be'gey tzalmavet,
lo ira ra, ki attah immadi,

Your rod and Your staff— they will comfort me.

שִׁבְטְךָ וּמִשְׁעַנְתֶּךָ הֵמָּה יְנַחֲמֻנִי.

Shivtekha u'mishantekha hemmah yenaḥamuni.

You will prepare a table for me before my enemies;

תַּעֲרֹךְ לְפָנַי שֻׁלְחָן נֶגֶד צֹרְרָי,

Taarokh lefanai shulḥan neged tzorerai,

You have anointed my head with oil; my cup is full.

דִּשַּׁנְתָּ בַשֶּׁמֶן רֹאשִׁי, כּוֹסִי רְוָיָה.

Dishanta va'shemen roshi, kosi revayah.

Only goodness and kindness shall follow me all the days of my life,

אַךְ טוֹב וָחֶסֶד יִרְדְּפוּנִי כָּל יְמֵי חַיָּי,

Akh tov va'ḥesed yirdefuni kol yemey ḥayyay,

And I shall dwell in the House of the Lord for many long years.

וְשַׁבְתִּי בְּבֵית יְיָ לְאֹרֶךְ יָמִים.

Ve'shavti be'veit Adonai le'orekh yamim.

Commentary to Mizmor le'David

The 23rd Psalm's central image is taken from the world of shepherds; indeed, King David was a shepherd in his youth, and his rise to kingship is depicted as being taken "from the sheepcote" (2 Samuel 7:8). But the uniqueness of this psalm is that it depicts the pasture not from the viewpoint of the shepherd, but from the other side, that of the flock. It is, so to speak, the song of a lamb, pouring out its heart with words of gratitude to the devoted shepherd.

The psalm begins with an explanation of the essence: **The Lord is my shepherd**—God is depicted not as Creator or Ruler of the world, but as the Good Shepherd.

Part of the unique charm of this psalm lies in its constant back-and-forth switching from the image of the lamb to the human analogy. The opening words depict the lamb's trust in the shepherd and its cuddling against him: **I shall lack nothing**—because the shepherd is near me, I fear no want. Then comes a series of pastoral images: **He makes me lie down in green pastures**—in a place where the flock can rest and graze peacefully; **He leads me beside still waters**—beside a spring that is not threatening, but flows gently, without endangering those who drink from it; **He revives my soul**—with grass and water.

With the phrase **He directs me in paths of righteousness for the sake of His Name** we return to the human aspect, to the fact that God leads us in ways of justice. However, this is also a continuation of the primary image: the lamb being led by the shepherd along paths and routes among the hills.

This confidence in the shepherd is expressed in the continuation as well. **Even if I will walk in the valley of the shadow of death**—even when the cycle of life and the routes of pasture lead to frightening, threatening places overshadowed by death, even then **I will fear no evil**, because I know that **You are with me. Your rod and Your staff**—"rod" is the stick with which the shepherd beats the wayward lambs, while "staff" is the shepherd's crooked stave with which he rescues lambs that fall into pits and nooks. Although the rod seems to be an instrument of punishment, while the staff, on the contrary, is used for help and rescue. Your rod and your staff, both, **they will comfort me**: even when the shepherd beats me, it is in order to return me to the right path.

Then comes another human statement: **You will prepare a table for me before my enemies**, an allusion both to a pasture in green fields and to the valley of the shadow of death. Even though there are enemies present there, I can sit down with a feeling of calm and security. **You have anointed my head with oil**, as I sit down at the festive table, my head bathed in oil. **My cup is full**—overflowing and satisfying.

Only goodness and kindness shall follow me—usually, it is only troubles and disasters that pursue us; here, this image is reversed, with an additional meaning. Sometimes, one does not know where the good is. One may go from one place to another, from one situation to another, because the place and the situation may not be good. Therefore, **goodness and kindness shall follow me**—even though I am not myself pursuing them. And this will happen not only on one occasion, but **all the days of my life.**

Finally, we reach the epitome of happiness: **and I shall dwell in the House of the Lord**: which, in other words, is the merit of the happiness of being with Him. The very feeling of nesting in His shadow is the greatest satisfaction—as King David says elsewhere: "It is good for me to draw near to God" (Psalms 73:28)—without any further request whatsoever, but merely to feel the full cup of contentment and happiness, not just as a momentary experience, but **for many long years**.

Kiddush-like Formulation for the Third Meal

Some people recite the following verses, which are a Kiddush-like formulation for the third meal:

וַיֹּאמֶר מֹשֶׁה: אִכְלֻהוּ הַיּוֹם, כִּי שַׁבָּת הַיּוֹם לַיְיָ, הַיּוֹם לֹא

Va'yomer Moshe: ikhluhu ha'yom, ki Shabbat ha'yom l'Adonai, ha'yom lo

תִמְצָאֻהוּ בַּשָּׂדֶה. רְאוּ כִּי יְיָ נָתַן לָכֶם הַשַּׁבָּת, עַל כֵּן הוּא נֹתֵן

timtza'uhu ba'sadeh. Reu ki Adonai natan lakhem ha'Shabbat, al ken hu noten

לָכֶם בַּיּוֹם הַשִּׁשִּׁי לֶחֶם יוֹמָיִם. שְׁבוּ אִישׁ תַּחְתָּיו, אַל יֵצֵא אִישׁ

lakhem ba'yom ha'shishi leḥem yomayim. Shevu ish taḥtav, al yetze ish

מִמְּקֹמוֹ בַּיּוֹם הַשְּׁבִיעִי. וַיִּשְׁבְּתוּ הָעָם בַּיּוֹם הַשְּׁבִעִי.

mi'mkomo bayom ha'shvii. Va'yishbbetu ha'am ba'yom ha'shvii.

עַל כֵּן בֵּרַךְ יְיָ אֶת יוֹם הַשַּׁבָּת וַיְקַדְּשֵׁהוּ.

Al ken berakh Adonai et yom ha'Shabbat va'yekaddshehu.

סַבְרִי מָרָנָן וְרַבָּנָן וְרַבּוֹתַי:

Savri maranan ve'rabbanan rabbotai

בָּרוּךְ אַתָּה יְיָ, אֱלֹהֵינוּ מֶלֶךְ הָעוֹלָם, בּוֹרֵא פְּרִי הַגָּפֶן.

Barukh attah Adonai, Eloheinu melekh ha'olam, bore' pri ha'gafen

Translation of the Kiddush-like Formulation

And Moses said, "Eat [the manna] today, for today is God's Sabbath; today you will not find it in the field. See: God has given you the Sabbath—therefore He gives you bread for two days on the sixth day. Let each man remain in his place; let no one go out on the seventh day." And the people rested on the seventh day [Exodus 16:25, 29–30].

Therefore the Lord blessed the Shabbat day and made it holy [Exodus 20:8–11].

Attention, Friends!

Blessed are You, Lord our God, King of the universe, who creates the fruit of the vine.

ידיד נפש
Yedid Nefesh

This is a poem of religious devotion, the initial letters of whose stanzas allude to the Divine Name. Composed by Rabbi Eliezer Azikri, this *piyyut* is deep and filled with feelings of *dvekut*—clinging to God. In some prayer rites, this poem appears in, or just before, *Kabbalat Shabbat*, and is also included among the *piyyutim* for *Tikkun Ḥatzot* (midnight supplications) and among the *zemirot* sung on Shabbat. In recent years, the original manuscript of the poem has been discovered, differing in a number of details from the text found in standard prayer books. The following text is according to the original manuscript.

יְדִיד נֶפֶשׁ, אָב הָרַחֲמָן,
מְשׁוֹךְ עַבְדָּךְ אֶל רְצוֹנָךְ,

Yedid nefesh, av ha'raḥaman,
meshokh avdakh el retzonakh,

Merciful Father, love of my life, draw Your servant whither You will.

יָרוּץ עַבְדָּךְ כְּמוֹ אַיָּל,
יִשְׁתַּחֲוֶה מוּל הֲדָרָךְ,

Yarutz avdakh kmo ayyal,
yishtaḥaveh mul hadarakh,

Your servant runs, fleet as the deer, he bows down before Your glory;

כִּי יֶעֱרַב לוֹ יְדִידוּתָךְ, מִנּוֹפֶת צוּף וְכָל טָעַם.

Ki yeerav lo yedidutakh mi'nofet tzuf ve'khol taam.

To him, Your fellowship is sweeter than wild honey or any other savor.

הָדוּר, נָאֶה, זִיו הָעוֹלָם, נַפְשִׁי חוֹלַת אַהֲבָתָךְ,

Hadur, naeh, ziv ha'olam, nafshi ḥolat ahavatakh,

You, with whose glory the whole world is radiant, my soul is lovesick for You.

אָנָּא, אֵל נָא, רְפָא נָא לָהּ, בְּהַרְאוֹת לָהּ נוֹעַם זִיוָךְ,

Anna, El na, refa na lah, be'harot lah noam zivakh,

Lord, I beseech You, I beg You, heal her; show her the beauty of Your light;

Rabbi Eliezer Azikri of Safed (d. 1600), kabbalist and preacher, was the author of *Sefer Ḥaredim*, a mystical-ethical work in which the commandments are presented according to the organs of the body to which they correspond.

אָז תִּתְחַזֵּק וְתִתְרַפֵּא, וְהָיְתָה לָךְ שִׁפְחַת עוֹלָם:

Az titḥazzek ve'titrappe, ve'haytah lakh shifḥat olam.

Then she will be strong again, then she will be healed, and be Your servant forevermore.

וָתִיק, יֶהֱמוּ נָא רַחֲמֶיךָ,
וְחוּס נָא עַל בֵּן אוֹהֲבָךְ.

Vatik, yehemu na raḥamekha,
ve'ḥus na al ben ohavakh.

Faithful friend, let Your mercies move You to pity the child whom You love.

כִּי זֶה כַּמָּה נִכְסוֹף נִכְסַף, לִרְאוֹת בְּתִפְאֶרֶת עֻזָּךְ.

Ki zeh kammah nikhsof nikhsaf, lirot be'tiferet uzzakh.

For all this long time I have longed, longed, to set eyes on Your glorious might;

אָנָּא, אֵלִי, מַחְמַד לִבִּי, חוּשָׁה נָּא, וְאַל תִּתְעַלָּם:

Anna, Eli, maḥmad libbi, ḥushah na, ve'al titallam.

Please, O God, the treasure of my heart, I beseech You, hurry, do not hide Yourself.

הִגָּלֶה נָא וּפְרוֹס, חֲבִיב, עָלַי אֶת סֻכַּת שְׁלוֹמָךְ.

Higgaleh na u'fros, ḥaviv, alai, et sukkat shlomakh.

Show Yourself, I beg you; spread over me, Beloved, the canopy of Your peace.

תָּאִיר אֶרֶץ מִכְּבוֹדָךְ, נָגִילָה וְנִשְׂמְחָה בָּךְ.

Tair eretz mi'kvodakh, nagilah ve'nismeḥah bakh.

Set the whole world alight with Your glory, let us rejoice and delight in You.

מַהֵר, אָהוּב, כִּי בָא מוֹעֵד, וְחָנֵּנִי כִּימֵי עוֹלָם:

Maher, ahuv, ki va moed, ve'ḥonneni ki'ymei olam.

Hurry, Beloved, for the due time has come; show me favor, as once in former days.

אל מסתתר
El Mistatter

This is a kabbalistic *piyyut* describing the ten *sefirot*. It was composed by a disciple of Rabbi Moshe Cordovero (Safed, about four hundred years ago), the initials of whose name (Avraham mi'Yamin Ḥazak) appear at the beginning of its stanzas.

O God, You who hide Yourself behind the veil of Your pavilion,	אֵל מִסְתַּתֵּר בְּשַׁפְרִיר חֶבְיוֹן, *El mistatter be'shafrir ḥevyon,*
Intellect concealed beyond access of all thought,	הַשֵּׂכֶל הַנֶּעְלָם מִכָּל רַעְיוֹן, *Ha'sekhel ha'ne'elam mi'kol raayon,*
Cause of causes, crowned with the Crown most high,	עִלַּת הָעִלּוֹת, מוּכְתָּר בְּכֶתֶר עֶלְיוֹן, *Illat ha'illot, mukhtar be'kheter elyon,*
A Crown do they give You, O Lord.	כֶּתֶר יִתְּנוּ לְךָ, יְיָ. *Keter yittenu lekha, Adonai.*
In the beginning of Your primeval Torah	בְּרֵאשִׁית תּוֹרָתְךָ הַקְּדוּמָה, *Be'reshit toratekha ha'kdumah,*
Your secret Wisdom is recorded.	רְשׁוּמָה חָכְמָתְךָ הַסְּתוּמָה. *Reshumah ḥokhmatkha ha'stumah.*
From nought is it brought forth and it is concealed;	מֵאַיִן תִּמָּצֵא וְהִיא נֶעֱלָמָה, *Me'ayin timmatze, ve'hi neelamah,*
The beginning of Wisdom is the fear of the Lord.	רֵאשִׁית חָכְמָה יִרְאַת יְיָ. *Reshit ḥokhmah yirat Adonai.*
The breadths of the river are the currents of faith;	רְחוֹבוֹת הַנָּהָר נַחֲלֵי אֱמוּנָה, *Reḥovot ha'nahar naḥalei emunah,*

The man of understanding draws up the deep waters.

They flow out into the fifty gates of understanding.

The faithful are preserved by the Lord.

Great God, the eyes of all look to You.

Abundant in Grace, Your Grace is great above the heavens;

God of Abraham, remember [this] unto Your servant.

The Grace of the Lord I tell, the praises of the Lord.

Most High God, sublime in strength and power,

Who brings forth light, nothing transformed.

Fear of Isaac, enlighten our judgment;

Powerful are You forever, O Lord.

Who is a god like You, performing great deeds?—

מַיִם עֲמֻקִּים יִדְלֶם אִישׁ תְּבוּנָה.
Mayim amukim yidlem ish tvunah.

תּוֹצְאוֹתֶיהָ חֲמִשִּׁים שַׁעֲרֵי בִינָה,
Totzotehah ḥamishim shaarei vinah,

אֱמוּנִים נוֹצֵר יְיָ.
Emunim notzer Adonai.

הָאֵל הַגָּדוֹל, עֵינֵי כֹל נֶגְדֶּךָ,
Ha'El ha'gadol, einei khol negdekha,

רַב חֶסֶד גָּדוֹל, עַל הַשָּׁמַיִם חַסְדֶּךָ,
Rav ḥesed gadol, al ha'shamayim ḥasdekha,

אֱלֹהֵי אַבְרָהָם, זְכוֹר לְעַבְדֶּךָ,
Elohei Avraham, zkhor le'avdekha,

חַסְדֵי יְיָ אַזְכִּיר תְּהִלּוֹת יְיָ.
Ḥasdei Adonai azkir, tehillot Adonai.

מָרוֹם נֶאְדָּר בְּכֹחַ וּגְבוּרָה,
Marom ne'edar be'khoaḥ u'gvurah,

מוֹצִיא אוֹרָה מֵאֵין תְּמוּרָה.
Motzi orah me'eyn tmurah.

פַּחַד יִצְחָק, מִשְׁפָּטֵינוּ הָאִירָה,
Paḥad Yitzḥak, mishpateinu ha'irah,

אַתָּה גִבּוֹר לְעוֹלָם יְיָ:
Attah gibbor le'olam, Adonai.

מִי אֵל כָּמוֹךָ, עוֹשֶׂה גְדוֹלוֹת,
Mi el kamokha, oseh gdolot,

Mighty God of Jacob, awesome in praises,

אֲבִיר יַעֲקֹב, נוֹרָא תְהִלּוֹת,

Avir Yaakov, nora tehillot,

Beauty of Israel, who listens to prayers;

תִּפְאֶרֶת יִשְׂרָאֵל, שׁוֹמֵעַ תְּפִלּוֹת,

Tiferet Yisrael, shomea tfillot,

For He who hearkens to the needy is the Lord.

כִּי שׁוֹמֵעַ אֶל אֶבְיוֹנִים יְיָ.

Ki shomea el evyonim Adonai.

O God, may the merit of the fathers protect us!

יָהּ, זְכוּת אָבוֹת יָגֵן עָלֵינוּ,

Yah, zkhut avot yagen aleinu,

Eternity of Israel, redeem us from our troubles.

נֶצַח יִשְׂרָאֵל, מִצָּרוֹתֵינוּ גְּאָלֵנוּ,

Netzaḥ Yisrael, mi'tzaroteinu ge'alenu,

Draw down and raise us from the pit of exile,

וּמִבּוֹר גָּלוּת דְּלֵנוּ וְהַעֲלֵנוּ,

Umi'bor galut delenu ve'haalenu,

To oversee the work of the House of the Lord.

לְנַצֵּחַ עַל מְלֶאכֶת בֵּית יְיָ.

Lenatzeaḥ al melekhet beit Adonai.

From the right and the left flows the nourishment of the prophets,

מִיָּמִין וּמִשְּׂמֹאל יְנִיקַת הַנְּבִיאִים,

Mi'yamin umi'smol yenikat ha'nviim,

Eternity and Splendor derive their being from them:

נֶצַח וָהוֹד מֵהֶם נִמְצָאִים,

Netzaḥ va'hod mehem nimtzaim,

Jachin and Boaz are they called by name.

יָכִין וּבוֹעַז בְּשֵׁם נִקְרָאִים,

Yakhin u'Voaz beshem nikraim,

And all your children shall be learned in the Lord.

וְכָל בָּנַיִךְ לִמּוּדֵי יְיָ.

Ve'khol banayikh limmudei Adonai.

The Foundation is the righteous one, hidden in the seven;

He is a sign of the covenant forever.

The source of blessing, the righteous is the foundation of the world;

Righteous are You, O Lord.

Do You establish the Kingdom of David and Solomon,

With the crown with which his mother crowned him;

The Community of Israel is sweetly called "bride,"

Crown of Beauty in the hand of the Lord.

The Mighty God unites as one the ten *sefirot.*

He who separates Oneness will not see the lights;

Brilliant as a sapphire, they shine together.

May our song come before You, O Lord.

יְסוֹד צַדִּיק בְּשִׁבְעָה נֶעְלָם,
Yesod tzaddik be'shivah ne'elam,

אוֹת בְּרִית הוּא לְעוֹלָם,
Ot brit hu le'olam,

מַעְיַן הַבְּרָכָה, צַדִּיק יְסוֹד עוֹלָם,
Me'eyn ha'brakha, tzaddik yesod olam,

צַדִּיק אַתָּה יְיָ.
Tzaddik attah Adonai.

נָא הָקֵם מַלְכוּת דָּוִד וּשְׁלֹמֹה,
Na hakem malkhut David u'Shlomo,

בָּעֲטָרָה שֶׁעִטְּרָה לוֹ אִמּוֹ,
Ba'atarah she'ittrah lo immo,

כְּנֶסֶת יִשְׂרָאֵל כַּלָּה קְרוּאָה בִּנְעִימָה,
Kneset Yisrael kallah keruah bi'neimah,

עֲטֶרֶת תִּפְאֶרֶת בְּיַד יְיָ.
Ateret tiferet be'yad Adonai.

חָזָק מְיַחֵד כְּאֶחָד עֶשֶׂר סְפִירוֹת,
Ḥazak meyaḥed ke'eḥad eser sfirot,

וּמַפְרִיד אַלּוּף לֹא יִרְאֶה מְאוֹרוֹת.
U'mafrid alluf lo yireh meorot.

סַפִּיר גִּזְרָתָם, יַחַד מְאִירוֹת,
Sappir gizratam yaḥad meirot,

תִּקְרַב רִנָּתֵנוּ לְפָנֶיךָ יְיָ.
Tikrav rinnatenu lefanekha Adonai.

The Departure of Shabbat

גאט פון אברהם

Gott fun Avrohom

This prayer for the conclusion of Shabbat was originally meant mainly for women and children, and was therefore composed in Yiddish. However, Rabbi Levi Yitzḥak of Berditchev said that it should be recited three times by all—men, women, and children—at the conclusion of every Shabbat.

God of Abraham, of Isaac, and of Jacob, protect Your people, Israel, from all evil—in Your praise—as the beloved Holy Shabbat departs. May the coming week arrive to bring perfect faith, faith in Torah sages, love of and cleaving to good friends, attachment to the Creator, blessed be He, steadfast faith in Your Thirteen Principles, and in the complete and immediate redemption, soon in our days, in the resurrection of the dead, and in the prophecy of Moses our Teacher, may he rest in peace. Master of the universe, it is You who gives strength to the weary; give Your beloved Jewish children, too, the vitality to praise You, and to serve You alone, and no other. And let this coming week [be filled with] good deeds, good fortune, blessing, success, good health, wealth and honor, and children, life, and sustenance for ourselves and all [the people of] Israel. Amen.

גָאט פוּן אַבְרָהָם אוּן פוּן יִצְחָק אוּן פוּן יַעֲקֹב, בַּאהִיט דֵיין פָאלְק יִשְׂרָאֵל פוּן אַלֶע בֵּייזִין אִין דֵיינֶעם לוֹיבּ, אַז דֶער לִיבֶּער שַׁבָּת קוֹדֶשׁ גֵייט אַוֶועק, אַז דִיא וָואךְ זָאל אוּנְז קוּמֶען צוּ אֱמוּנָה שְׁלֵימָה, צוּ אֱמוּנַת חֲכָמִים, צוּ אַהֲבַת וְדִבּוּק חֲבֵרִים טוֹבִים, צוּ דְבֵיקוּת הַבּוֹרֵא בָּרוּךְ הוּא, מַאֲמִין צוּ זַיין בִּשְׁלֹשָׁה עָשָׂר עִיקָּרִים שֶׁלְּךָ וּבִגְאוּלָה שְׁלֵמָה וּקְרוֹבָה בִּמְהֵרָה בְּיָמֵינוּ, וּבִתְחִיַּת הַמֵּתִים, וּבִנְבוּאַת מֹשֶׁה רַבֵּנוּ עָלָיו הַשָּׁלוֹם. רִבּוֹנוֹ שֶׁל עוֹלָם, דוּא בִּיסְט הַנּוֹתֵן לַיָּעֵף כֹּחַ, גִיבּ דֵיינֶע לִיבֶּע אִידִישֶׁע קִינְדֶערְלָעךְ אוֹיךְ כֹּחַ דִיךְ צוּ לוֹיבִּין, אוּן דִיךְ צוּ דִינֶען אוּן וַוייטֶער קֵיינֶעם נִישְׁט, אוּן דִיא וָואךְ זָאל אוּנְז קוּמֶען צוּ חֶסֶד, אוּן צוּ מַזָּל, אוּן צוּ בְּרָכָה, אוּן צוּ הַצְלָחָה, אוּן צוּ גֶעזוּנְט, אוּן צוּ עֹשֶׁר וְכָבוֹד, אוּן צוּ בָּנֵי, חַיֵּי וּמְזוֹנֵי, לָנוּ וּלְכָל יִשְׂרָאֵל, אָמֵן.

The Havdalah Ceremony

At the end of Shabbat we make Havdalah, which is, in a sense, parallel to the Kiddush that ushered in the Shabbat.

In Havdalah, as in all the other customs we follow upon the conclusion of Shabbat, we honor Shabbat by escorting her out, just as we went out to greet her upon her arrival.

This parallelism is expressed in the detailed customs and in the very structure of the Havdalah. Apart from the various halakhic reasons for this practice, we both greet the Shabbat and bid it farewell with light—the Shabbat candles and the Havdalah torch—thereby fulfilling the verse "Glorify the Lord with light" (Isaiah 24:15). The various recitations, prayers, and *zemirot* for the departure of Shabbat are also connected with this idea, as is the *Melaveh Malkah* meal.

The ceremonies at the conclusion of Shabbat, which help us make the transition from Shabbat to weekdays, are also intended to draw the light of Shabbat into the profane, so that the weekdays will not be entirely gray and colorless, but rather illuminated by some of the Shabbat light. Therefore, Havdalah often is followed with prayers and petitions to begin the new week in a suitable and appropriate manner.

Although the formulation of Havdalah included in the evening *Ma'ariv* prayer (*Attah Ḥonantanu*) already allows us to work, the sages instituted the Havdalah rite expressly over a glass of wine, and forbade us to eat or drink anything prior to the ceremony.

In many congregations outside the Land of Israel, and in a few congregations in Israel as well, Havdalah is made in the synagogue right after the *Ma'ariv* prayer, for the sake of those who do not have wine at home; and then everybody goes home to make Havdalah for the family members. The ceremony is mandatory for both men and women. Women may perform their own ceremony, without the blessing of firelight.

The essential components of the Havdalah ceremony itself are quite ancient. Discussions regarding the details of the Havdalah ceremony appear in our sources (*Berakhot* 51b) among sages who lived at the end of the Second Temple era.

Havdalah is composed of several sections. There is a ceremonial opening, consisting of selected biblical verses (which are, in a sense, parallel to the verses of *Vayekhulu* in the Kiddush benediction) mentioning salvation, blessing, and light. These are followed by a series of blessings: on wine, aromatic spices, firelight, and the blessing of Havdalah itself.

The blessing on wine is intended to underscore the importance to Havdalah. Wine is a part of every blessing of special importance, such as Kiddush, the wedding blessings, and those of circumcision. The Havdalah cup should be filled to the brim, until it overflows and a little of its contents spills out, as a sign of blessing for a good week ahead.

After the ceremonial opening, one says, "Savri Maranan (ve'Rabbanan)" ("Attention, Friends [and Masters]!") and then makes the blessing on wine, "who creates the fruit of the vine." In case another drink is used, one makes the appropriate blessing for that drink. It is customary for the one pronouncing the blessing to pass the cup from his right hand to his left, so that he holds the container of spices in his right hand, and then also gazes at his hand in the light.

Following that, the blessing on spices is recited. On Shabbat—a day of spiritual exaltation devoted entirely to lofty and sanctified matters—one feels the presence of a *neshamah yeteirah* ("additional soul"). However, once Shabbat departs, we find ourselves as we had been before. This may lead to a measure of dejection and diminished vitality (described as "the departure of the additional soul"), apprehension and worry about weekday concerns and problems, along with a desire to hold on to some of the Shabbat and its sanctity. By smelling the spices, then, one is revived—just like any person who feels weak and needs to be strengthened. All those present smell the Havdalah spices; many people use a special, ornamented spice container.

This is followed by the blessing on firelight, "who creates the lights of fire." Since it is forbidden to create fire on Shabbat, we make a blessing here, upon its renewed use, at the conclusion of Shabbat. The sages of the Talmud say that the first fire made by humans was lit at the conclusion of the first Shabbat of creation, when the darkness of the first night began to fall (*Pesaḥim* 52b). This blessing over fire and light also expresses the distinctions between holy and profane, between Shabbat and weekdays, which are comparable to the distinction between light and darkness. The light of Havdalah also symbolizes the light of knowledge given to humankind, which enables people to distinguish between holy and profane, between Shabbat and the days of the week. In the words of our sages, "If there is no knowledge, how can there be differentiation?"

In order to recite the blessing on firelight, one is required to derive some benefit from it. It is customary to gaze at one's fingernails and to distinguish, by means of the candle-light, between the nail and the flesh on the finger. The candle used for Havdalah should be a taper with more than one wick. In most places, a special candle is used for this purpose, but one who does not have such a candle may use two regular candles, or even two matches, whose flames are put together so that they burn as one.

After reciting these blessings, one returns the cup to the right hand and pronounces the Havdalah blessing itself. At the end of this blessing, either the person who recited it, or one who had intended to do so from the outset, drinks the wine. It is the custom not to give any wine remaining in the Havdalah cup to others; it is also customary for women not to drink from it, unless a woman is making Havdalah for herself.

When the conclusion of the Shabbat falls on the eve of a Festival day, the Havdalah service is combined with the Kiddush service for the festival. If the Ninth of Av begins at the conclusion of Shabbat, the Havdalah service is not conducted, because no drinking can take place on the fast day. Only the blessing on firelight is recited, and the service is postponed to the following evening when the fast is over, and no blessing on aromatic spices or on firelight is made then.

A wide variety of customs connected with the Havdalah service reflect a special affection for this commandment. In most communities, the Havdalah candle is extinguished with the remaining wine, while some dip a finger into the spilled wine and touch it to their eyes or pockets.

In most communities, there are also special *piyyutim* and *zemirot* for the conclusion of Shabbat. These, like the *zemirot* of Shabbat itself, do not have a fully established order, and each family has its own customs. But with all the differences among the various customs, certain common elements appear, in varying forms, in all rites. Thus, for instance, Elijah the Prophet is universally mentioned at the conclusion of Shabbat. According to the sages (Jerusalem Talmud, *Pesaḥim* 3:6), Elijah will not come on Shabbat; hence, immediately upon the conclusion of Shabbat, we announce our expectation of Elijah's immediate arrival and of the Redemption. There are those who, on the basis of the Kabbalah, recite Elijah's name a total of 130 times in all the *zemirot* and *piyyutim* for the end of Shabbat. In addition, in all communities, additional prayers for the coming week are recited.

הבדלה
Havdalah

Taking the cup in one's hand, one says:

הִנֵּה אֵל יְשׁוּעָתִי, אֶבְטַח וְלֹא אֶפְחָד, כִּי עָזִּי וְזִמְרָת יָהּ יְיָ, וַיְהִי לִי לִישׁוּעָה.

Hinneh El yeshuati, evtaḥ ve'lo efḥad, ki ozzi ve'zimrat Yah Adonai, va'yhi li li'yshuah.

וּשְׁאַבְתֶּם מַיִם בְּשָׂשׂוֹן מִמַּעַיְנֵי הַיְשׁוּעָה. לַייָ הַיְשׁוּעָה, עַל עַמְּךָ

U'shavtem mayim be'sason mi'maayney ha'yshuah. L'Adonai ha'yshuah, al ammkha

בִּרְכָתֶךָ סֶּלָה. יְיָ צְבָאוֹת עִמָּנוּ, מִשְׂגָּב לָנוּ אֱלֹהֵי יַעֲקֹב סֶלָה. יְיָ
virkhatekha selah. Adonai tzevaot immanu, misgav lanu Elohei Yaakov selah. Adonai
צְבָאוֹת, אַשְׁרֵי אָדָם בֹּטֵחַ בָּךְ. יְיָ הוֹשִׁיעָה, הַמֶּלֶךְ יַעֲנֵנוּ בְיוֹם קָרְאֵנוּ.
tzevaot, ashrei adam bote'aḥ bakh. Adonai hoshiah, ha'melekh yaanenu ve'yom korenu.
לַיְּהוּדִים הָיְתָה אוֹרָה וְשִׂמְחָה וְשָׂשֹׂן וִיקָר, כֵּן תִּהְיֶה לָּנוּ. כּוֹס יְשׁוּעוֹת
La'yhudim hayta orah ve'simḥah ve'sason vi'ykar, ken tihyeh lanu. Kos yeshuot
אֶשָּׂא, וּבְשֵׁם יְיָ אֶקְרָא.
essa, uv'shem Adonai ekra.

Over the wine:

סַבְרִי מָרָנָן וְרַבָּנָן וְרַבּוֹתַי:

Savri maranan ve'rabbanan rabbotai

בָּרוּךְ אַתָּה יְיָ, אֱלֹהֵינוּ מֶלֶךְ הָעוֹלָם, בּוֹרֵא פְּרִי הַגָּפֶן.

Barukh attah Adonai, Eloheinu melekh ha'olam, bore' pri ha'gafen.

Over the fragrant spices:

בָּרוּךְ אַתָּה יְיָ, אֱלֹהֵינוּ מֶלֶךְ הָעוֹלָם, בּוֹרֵא מִינֵי בְשָׂמִים.

Barukh attah Adonai, Eloheinu melekh ha'olam, bore' minei vsamim.

On the candle:

(After the following blessing, one should fold the fingers over the thumb—the thumb is not to be seen—and look at the four fingernails.)

בָּרוּךְ אַתָּה יְיָ, אֱלֹהֵינוּ מֶלֶךְ הָעוֹלָם, בּוֹרֵא מְאוֹרֵי הָאֵשׁ.

Barukh attah Adonai, Eloheinu melekh ha'olam, bore' meorei ha'esh.

Then one continues:

בָּרוּךְ אַתָּה יְיָ, אֱלֹהֵינוּ מֶלֶךְ הָעוֹלָם, הַמַּבְדִּיל בֵּין קֹדֶשׁ לְחֹל,

Barukh attah Adonai, Eloheinu melekh ha'olam, ha'mavdil bein kodesh le'ḥol,

בֵּין אוֹר לְחֹשֶׁךְ, בֵּין יִשְׂרָאֵל לָעַמִּים, בֵּין יוֹם הַשְּׁבִיעִי לְשֵׁשֶׁת יְמֵי

bein or le'ḥoshekh, bein Yisrael la'ammim, bein yom ha'shvii le'sheshet yemei

הַמַּעֲשֶׂה .בָּרוּךְ אַתָּה יְיָ, אֱלֹהֵינוּ מֶלֶךְ הָעוֹלָם, הַמַּבְדִּיל בֵּין קֹדֶשׁ לְחֹל.

ha'maaseh. Barukh attah Adonai, ha'mavdil bein kodesh le'ḥol.

Translation of the Havdalah Text

Indeed, God is my deliverance; I am confident and shall not fear. For God the Lord is my strength and song, and He has been a help to me. You shall draw water with joy from the wellsprings of deliverance [Isaiah 12:2-3]. Deliverance is the Lord's; may Your blessing be upon Your people forever [Psalms 3:9]. The Lord of hosts is with us, the God of Jacob is our everlasting stronghold [Psalms 46:8]. Lord of hosts, happy is the person who trusts in You [Psalms 84:13]. Lord help us; may the King answer us on the day we call [Psalms 20:10]. For the Jews there was light and joy, gladness and honor [Esther 8:16]—so let it be with us. I raise the cup of deliverance and invoke the Name of the Lord [Psalms 116:13].

Over the wine:

Attention, friends!

Blessed are You, Lord our God, King of the universe, who creates the fruit of the vine.

Over the fragrant spices:

Blessed are You, Lord our God, King of the universe, who creates various kinds of spices.

On the candle:

(After the following blessing, one should fold the fingers over the thumb—the thumb is not to be seen—and look at the four fingernails.)

Blessed are You, Lord our God, King of the universe, who creates the lights of fire.

Then one continues:

Blessed are You, Lord our God, King of the universe, who makes a distinction between sacred and profane, between light and darkness, between Israel and the nations, between the Seventh Day and the six work days. Blessed are You, Lord, who makes a distinction between sacred and profane.

המבדיל
Ha'Mavdil

This *piyyut* is already mentioned in the *Maḥzor Vitry,* and was written by a man known as Yitzḥak, whose name (with the addition of the descriptive *ha'katan*, "the little one") appears in the initials of its verses.

He, who distinguishes between holy and profane, will pardon our sins, and make our seed and wealth as many as the sand, as the stars in the night.

הַמַּבְדִּיל בֵּין קֹדֶשׁ לְחוֹל, חַטֹּאתֵינוּ הוּא יִמְחֹל.
Ha'mavdil bein kodesh le'ḥol, ḥatoteinu hu yimḥol,
זַרְעֵנוּ וְכַסְפֵּנוּ יַרְבֶּה כַּחוֹל,
וְכַכּוֹכָבִים בַּלָּיְלָה.
Zarenu ve'khaspenu yarbeh ka'ḥol,
vekha'kokhavim ba'laylah.

The day has turned like the date palm's shadow, I call upon God to act for me; the watchman calls out, "Morning has come," also, "Night."

יוֹם פָּנָה כְּצֵל תֹּומֶר, אֶקְרָא לָאֵל עָלַי גּוֹמֵר,
Yom panah ke'tzel tomer, ekra la'El alay gomer,
אָמַר שׁוֹמֵר: אָתָא בֹקֶר וְגַם לַיְלָה.
Amar shomer—ata voker ve'gam laylah.

You, whose righteousness is like Mount Tabor, will surely pass over my sins, like yesterdays that pass quickly, like a watch in the night.

צִדְקָתְךָ כְּהַר תָּבוֹר, עַל חֲטָאַי עָבוֹר תַּעֲבֹר,
Tzidkatkha ke'har Tavor, al ḥataay avor taavor,
כְּיוֹם אֶתְמוֹל כִּי יַעֲבֹר, וְאַשְׁמוּרָה בַלָּיְלָה.
Ke'yom etmol ki yaavor, ve'ashmurah ba'laylah.

The time for the afternoon offering has passed; would that I might find rest! I am wearied by my sorrows and my tears flow every night.

My voice shall not be silenced; open for me the exalted gate! My hair is covered with dew, and my locks with the drops of night.

Hearken, awful, awesome God: I cry to You for ransom at twilight, when the day has sunk, in the very depth of night.

God, I call upon You, save me! Let me know the path of life; preserve me from poverty and sudden death, from break of day until night.

Cleanse the impurity of my deeds, lest my enemies taunt me, saying, "Where is the God who made him?" Who gives song in the night.

חָלְפָה עוֹנַת מִנְחָתִי, מִי יִתֵּן מְנוּחָתִי,

Ḥalfah onat minḥati, mi yitten menuḥati,

יָגַעְתִּי בְאַנְחָתִי, אַשְׂחֶה בְּכָל לַיְלָה.

Yagati be'anḥati, asḥeh be'khol laylah.

קוֹלִי בַּל יֻנְטַל, פְּתַח לִי שַׁעַר הַמְּנֻטָּל,

Koli bal yuntal, ptaḥ li shaar ha'menuttal,

שֶׁרֹּאשִׁי נִמְלָא טָל, קְוֻצּוֹתַי רְסִיסֵי לַיְלָה.

She'roshi nimla tal, kvutzotai resisei laylah.

הֵעָתֵר נוֹרָא וְאָיוֹם, אֲשַׁוֵּעַ תְּנָה פִדְיוֹם,

He'ater, nora ve'ayom, ashavvea tnah fidyom,

בְּנֶשֶׁף בְּעֶרֶב יוֹם, בְּאִישׁוֹן לַיְלָה.

Be'neshef be'erev yom, be'ishon laylah.

קְרָאתִיךָ, יָהּ, הוֹשִׁיעֵנִי, אֹרַח חַיִּים תּוֹדִיעֵנִי,

Kratikha, Yah, hoshieni, oraḥ ḥayyim todieni,

מִדַּלָּה תְּבַצְּעֵנִי, מִיּוֹם וְעַד לַיְלָה.

Mi'dallah tevatzeni, mi'yom ve'ad laylah.

טַהֵר טִנּוּף מַעֲשַׂי, פֶּן יֹאמְרוּ מַכְעִיסַי,

Taher tinnuf maasai, pen yomru makhisai:

אַיֵּה נָא אֱלוֹהַּ עֹשָׂי, הַנּוֹתֵן זְמִירוֹת בַּלַּיְלָה.

Ayeh na Eloha osai, ha'noten zmirot ba'laylah.

We are like clay in Your hands; forgive us, therefore, all the more, while day speaks to day, and night to night.

נַחְנוּ בְּיָדְךָ כַּחוֹמֶר, סְלַח נָא עַל קַל וָחוֹמֶר,

Naḥnu be'yadkha ka'ḥomer, slaḥ na al kal va'ḥomer,

יוֹם לְיוֹם יַבִּיעַ אֹמֶר, וְלַיְלָה לְלַיְלָה.

Yom le'yom yabia omer, ve'laylah le'laylah.

He, who distinguishes between holy and profane, will pardon our sins, and make our seed and wealth as many as the sand, as the stars in the night.

הַמַּבְדִּיל בֵּין קֹדֶשׁ לְחוֹל, חַטֹּאתֵינוּ הוּא יִמְחֹל.

Ha'mavdil bein kodesh le'ḥol, ḥatoteinu hu yimḥol,

זַרְעֵנוּ וְכַסְפֵּנוּ יַרְבֶּה כַּחוֹל,

וְכַכּוֹכָבִים בַּלָּיְלָה.

zarenu ve'khaspenu yarbeh ka'ḥol,

vekha'kokhavim ba'laylah.

ריבון העולמים

Ribbon ha'Olamim

This is an ancient prayer, mentioned in the Jerusalem Talmud (*Berakhot* 5:1).

Master of the universe, Father of compassion and forgiveness: in a good and auspicious time, start the six approaching days of activity for us in peace, free of any sin or transgression, and cleansed of all iniquity, wrongdoing, and evil; and cleaving to Torah study and good deeds. Grant us Your knowledge, understanding, and wisdom; and let us hear in them [the sound of]

רִבּוֹן הָעוֹלָמִים, אַב הָרַחֲמִים וְהַסְּלִיחוֹת, בְּסִמָּן
טוֹב וּבְמַזָּל טוֹב הָחֵל עָלֵינוּ אֶת שֵׁשֶׁת יְמֵי
הַמַּעֲשֶׂה הַבָּאִים לִקְרָאתֵנוּ לְשָׁלוֹם, חֲשׂוּכִים
מִכָּל חֵטְא, וּמְנֻקִּים מִכָּל עָוֹן וְאַשְׁמָה וָרֶשַׁע,
וּמְדֻבָּקִים בְּתַלְמוּד תּוֹרָה וּבְמַעֲשִׂים טוֹבִים, וְחָנֵּנוּ
דֵּעָה, בִּינָה וְהַשְׂכֵּל מֵאִתְּךָ, וְתַשְׁמִיעֵנוּ בָּהֶם שָׂשׂוֹן
וְשִׂמְחָה, וְלֹא תַעֲלֶה קִנְאָתֵנוּ עַל לֵב אָדָם וְלֹא
קִנְאַת אָדָם תַּעֲלֶה עַל לִבֵּנוּ. מַלְכֵּנוּ, אֱלֹהֵינוּ,
הָאָב הָרַחֲמָן, שִׂים בְּרָכָה וּרְוָחָה וְהַצְלָחָה בְּכָל
מַעֲשֵׂה יָדֵינוּ, וְכָל הַיּוֹעֵץ עַל עַמְּךָ בֵּית יִשְׂרָאֵל

gladness and rejoicing. Protect us from jealousy toward anyone, and let no one feel envy toward us. Our King, our God, Merciful Father: bestow blessing, relief, and success on all the efforts of our hands. And all those who make good counsel and [bear] good thoughts for your people, the house of Israel, strengthen them, bless them, make them great and enduring. Fulfill their counsel, as it is stated: "May He grant you your heart's desire, and fulfill your every counsel" [Psalms 20:5]. And it is stated: "And you will decree a ruling, and it will be securely established; and light will illuminate your path" [Job 22:28]. And anyone taking evil counsel toward us, and your people, the house of Israel, advice that is not worthy, or [harbors] improper thoughts [about them], let their scheme be undone, as it is stated: "God annuls the counsel of nations; he repeals people's schemes"

עֵצָה טוֹבָה וּמַחֲשָׁבָה טוֹבָה, אַמְּצוֹ, בָּרְכוֹ, גַּדְּלוֹ וְקַיְּמוֹ, קַיֵּם עֲצָתוֹ, כַּדָּבָר שֶׁנֶּאֱמַר: יִתֶּן לְךָ כִלְבָבֶךָ וְכָל עֲצָתְךָ יְמַלֵּא. וְנֶאֱמַר: וְתִגְזַר אֹמֶר וְיָקָם לָךְ, וְעַל דְּרָכֶיךָ נָגַהּ אוֹר. וְכָל הַיּוֹעֵץ עָלֵינוּ וְעַל עַמְּךָ בֵּית יִשְׂרָאֵל עֵצָה שֶׁאֵינָהּ טוֹבָה וּמַחֲשָׁבָה שֶׁאֵינָהּ טוֹבָה, תּוּפַר עֲצָתוֹ, כַּדָּבָר שֶׁנֶּאֱמַר: יְיָ הֵפִיר עֲצַת גּוֹיִם, הֵנִיא מַחְשְׁבוֹת עַמִּים. וְנֶאֱמַר: עֻצוּ עֵצָה וְתֻפָר, דַּבְּרוּ דָבָר וְלֹא יָקוּם, כִּי עִמָּנוּ אֵל. וּפְתַח לָנוּ, יְיָ אֱלֹהֵינוּ, אָב הָרַחֲמִים, אֲדוֹן הַסְּלִיחוֹת, בָּזֶה הַשָּׁבוּעַ וּבְכָל שָׁבוּעַ: שַׁעֲרֵי אוֹרָה, שַׁעֲרֵי אֹרֶךְ יָמִים וְשָׁנִים, שַׁעֲרֵי אֲרִיכַת אַפַּיִם, שַׁעֲרֵי בְרָכָה, שַׁעֲרֵי בִינָה, שַׁעֲרֵי גִילָה, שַׁעֲרֵי גְדֻלָּה, שַׁעֲרֵי גְאֻלָּה, שַׁעֲרֵי גְבוּרָה, שַׁעֲרֵי דִיצָה, שַׁעֲרֵי דֵעָה, שַׁעֲרֵי הוֹד, שַׁעֲרֵי הָדָר, שַׁעֲרֵי הַצְלָחָה, שַׁעֲרֵי הַרְוָחָה, שַׁעֲרֵי וַעַד טוֹב, שַׁעֲרֵי וָתִיקוּת, שַׁעֲרֵי זְרִיזוּת, שַׁעֲרֵי זִמְרָה, שַׁעֲרֵי זְכֻיּוֹת, שַׁעֲרֵי זִיו, שַׁעֲרֵי זֹהַר תּוֹרָה, שַׁעֲרֵי זֹהַר חָכְמָה, שַׁעֲרֵי זֹהַר בִּינָה, שַׁעֲרֵי זֹהַר דַּעַת, שַׁעֲרֵי חֶדְוָה, שַׁעֲרֵי חֶמְלָה, שַׁעֲרֵי חֵן וָחֶסֶד, שַׁעֲרֵי חַיִּים טוֹבִים, שַׁעֲרֵי חָכְמָה, שַׁעֲרֵי טוֹבָה, שַׁעֲרֵי טֹהַר, שַׁעֲרֵי יְשׁוּעָה, שַׁעֲרֵי יֹשֶׁר, שַׁעֲרֵי כַפָּרָה, שַׁעֲרֵי כַלְכָּלָה, שַׁעֲרֵי כָבוֹד, שַׁעֲרֵי לִמּוּד, שַׁעֲרֵי מָזוֹן, שַׁעֲרֵי מְנוּחוֹת, שַׁעֲרֵי מְחִילוֹת, שַׁעֲרֵי מַדָּע, שַׁעֲרֵי נֶחָמָה, שַׁעֲרֵי נְקִיּוּת, שַׁעֲרֵי סְלִיחָה, שַׁעֲרֵי סִיַּעְתָּא דִשְׁמַיָּא, שַׁעֲרֵי עֶזְרָה, שַׁעֲרֵי פְדוּת, שַׁעֲרֵי פַרְנָסָה טוֹבָה, שַׁעֲרֵי צְדָקָה, שַׁעֲרֵי צָהֳלָה, שַׁעֲרֵי קְדֻשָּׁה, שַׁעֲרֵי קוֹמְמִיּוּת, שַׁעֲרֵי רַחֲמִים, שַׁעֲרֵי רָצוֹן, שַׁעֲרֵי רְפוּאָה שְׁלֵמָה, שַׁעֲרֵי שָׁלוֹם, שַׁעֲרֵי שִׂמְחָה, שַׁעֲרֵי שְׁמוּעוֹת טוֹבוֹת,

146

שַׁעֲרֵי שַׁלְוָה, שַׁעֲרֵי תוֹרָה, שַׁעֲרֵי תְפִלָּה, שַׁעֲרֵי תְשׁוּבָה, שַׁעֲרֵי תְשׁוּעָה. כִּדְכְתִיב: וּתְשׁוּעַת צַדִּיקִים מֵיְיָ מָעוּזָּם בְּעֵת צָרָה. וַיַּעְזְרֵם יְיָ וַיְפַלְּטֵם, יְפַלְּטֵם מֵרְשָׁעִים וְיוֹשִׁיעֵם, כִּי חָסוּ בוֹ. וְנֶאֱמַר, חָשַׂף יְיָ אֶת זְרוֹעַ קָדְשׁוֹ לְעֵינֵי כָּל הַגּוֹיִם, וְרָאוּ כָּל אַפְסֵי אָרֶץ אֵת יְשׁוּעַת אֱלֹהֵינוּ. וְנֶאֱמַר: קוֹל צֹפַיִךְ נָשְׂאוּ קוֹל, יַחְדָּו יְרַנֵּנוּ, כִּי עַיִן בְּעַיִן יִרְאוּ בְּשׁוּב יְיָ צִיּוֹן. וְקַיֵּם לָנוּ יְיָ אֱלֹהֵינוּ מִקְרָא שֶׁכָּתוּב: מַה נָּאווּ עַל הֶהָרִים רַגְלֵי מְבַשֵּׂר, מַשְׁמִיעַ שָׁלוֹם, מְבַשֵּׂר טוֹב, מַשְׁמִיעַ יְשׁוּעָה, אֹמֵר לְצִיּוֹן מָלַךְ אֱלֹהָיִךְ. רִאשׁוֹן לְצִיּוֹן הִנֵּה הִנָּם, וְלִירוּשָׁלַיִם מְבַשֵּׂר אֶתֵּן, אָמֵן סֶלָה.

[Psalms 33:10]. And it is stated: "Contrive a scheme, but it will be foiled; conspire a plot, but it will not materialize, for God is with us" [Isaiah 8:10]. And open for us, Lord our God, Father of compassion, Lord of forgiveness, in this coming week and in every week: gates of light, gates of longevity, gates of patience, gates of blessing, gates of understanding, gates of glee, gates of greatness, gates of redemption, gates of might, gates of delight, gates of knowledge, gates of splendor, gates of beauty, gates of success, gates of relief, gates of good assemblies, gates of agility, gates of song, gates of merits, gates of illumination, gates of the Torah's radiance, gates of wisdom's radiance, gates of the radiance of perception, gates of the radiance of knowledge, gates of enjoyment, gates of empathy, gates of grace and loving-kindness, gates of good life, gates of wisdom, gates of goodness, gates of purity, gates of salvation, gates of integrity, gates of atonement, gates of livelihood, gates of honor, gates of learning, gates of sustenance, gates of calm, gates of forgiveness, gates of sagacity, gates of consolation, gates of cleanliness, gates of pardon, gates of Heavenly assistance, gates of help, gates of rescue, gates of ample sustenance, gates of righteous charity, gates of enthusiasm, gates of holiness, gates of uprightness, gates of mercy, gates of Divine Will, gates of complete healing, gates of peace, gates of happiness, gates of good news, gates of content, gates of Torah, gates of prayer, gates of repentance, gates of deliverance—as it is written: "And the deliverance of the righteous is from God—their strength in times of distress. And God will help and rescue them; He will save them from the evildoers, and redeem them, for they seek refuge in Him" [Psalms 37:39-40].

And it is stated: "God has uncovered His holy arm before the nations' eyes, and all the ends of the earth will see our God's deliverance" [Isaiah 52:10]; and it is stated: "The voice of Your watchmen [who have] lifted their voice—they will sing out in unison; for they will see vividly God's return to Zion" [Isaiah 52:8]. And fulfill for us, Lord our God, the verse "How beautiful, gracing the mountains, are the messenger's steps; [he] proclaims Peace; [he] proclaims Good; [he] proclaims Salvation—saying to Zion: 'Your God is King'" [Isaiah 52:7]. "The first to reach Zion [from Exile, calls out]: 'Here they are, here are your sons.' And I will bring a messenger [of good news] to Jerusalem" [Isaiah 41:27]. Amen, Selah.

The Melaveh Malkah Meal

As early as Talmudic times, it was customary to hold a special meal after the conclusion of Shabbat (*Shabbat* 119b), considered "the fourth Shabbat meal," and referred to in many sources as *Seudat Melaveh Malkah* (literally, "the meal for escorting the Queen"), or "the meal of King David," complementary to the three Shabbat meals, each one of which is parallel to one of the patriarchs. This meal, too—parallel to the first meal, on Shabbat eve—is held in honor of the Shabbat, so as to escort her out with great ceremony and joy, just as we welcomed her upon her arrival.

It is stated in the *halakhah* that one needs to prepare for this meal just as one does for all other Shabbat meals—by setting the table, spreading a tablecloth, etc.—even if one eats only an olive-sized morsel. It is customary among some to have two loaves of bread at this meal as well. Another custom is to eat both foods prepared for Shabbat itself and a special dish prepared specifically for this meal. It is also customary to stay in one's Shabbat clothes until after this meal, and to sing some of the *zemirot* for the end of Shabbat.

Many sages have commented upon the importance of this meal and the spiritual benefits bestowed on those who observe it meticulously. The food eaten at the *Melaveh Malkah* is said to sustain a certain bone in the body known as *luz*. Its exact location in the body is not known precisely, and indeed it may be seen as apocryphal. The *luz* has the unique quality of remaining even when the rest of the body decomposes after death. At the resurrection of the dead, following the coming of the Messiah, God will use the *luz* to rebuild the human body. When one rebuilds a Jew, one needs to restore not only the eyes and ears and other organs, but also the Jewish essence. This can be done even if there remains only one shred—the *luz* bone, which is sustained by the food eaten at *Melaveh Malkah*.

אתקינו סעודתא
Atkinu Seudata

Prepare the meal of perfect faith,	אַתְקִינוּ סְעוּדָתָא דִּמְהֵימְנוּתָא שְׁלֵמָתָא, *Atkinu seudata di'meheimnuta shleimata,*
Which is the delight of the holy King;	חֶדְוָתָא דְּמַלְכָּא קַדִּישָׁא. *Ḥedvata de'malka kaddisha.*
Prepare the meal of the King.	אַתְקִינוּ סְעוּדָתָא דְּמַלְכָּא. *Atkinu seudata de'malka.*
This is the meal of David, the Messiah King,	דָּא הִיא סְעוּדָתָא דְּדָוִד מַלְכָּא מְשִׁיחָא, *Da hi seudata de'David malka meshiḥa,*
And Abraham, Isaac, and Jacob come to join him in the meal [Zohar II:88a–b].	וְאַבְרָהָם, יִצְחָק וְיַעֲקֹב אַתְיָן לְסַעֲדָא בַּהֲדֵיהּ. *Ve'Avraham, Yitzḥak ve'Yaakov atyan lesaada ba'hadeh.*

נטילת ידיים

Washing of Hands

Before the *Melaveh Malkah* meal, the ritual washing of hands is done, and the following blessing recited:

בָּרוּךְ אַתָּה יְיָ, אֱלֹהֵינוּ מֶלֶךְ הָעוֹלָם, אֲשֶׁר קִדְּשָׁנוּ בְּמִצְוֹתָיו וְצִוָּנוּ עַל נְטִילַת יָדָיִם.

Barukh attah Adonai, Eloheinu melekh ha'olam, asher kiddshanu be'mitzvotav ve'tzivvanu al netilat yadayim.

Blessed are You, Lord our God, King of the universe, who has sanctified us with His commandments, and commanded us concerning the washing of the hands.

ברכת המוציא

Blessing over Bread

The bread is dipped in salt. At mealtimes, the table should always have a salt container on it, just as salt had to be on the holy altar of the Temple. Before breaking bread, the following blessing is recited:

בָּרוּךְ אַתָּה יְיָ, אֱלֹהֵינוּ מֶלֶךְ הָעוֹלָם, הַמּוֹצִיא לֶחֶם מִן הָאָרֶץ.

Barukh attah Adonai, Eloheinu melekh ha'olam, ha'motzi leḥem min ha'aretz.

Blessed are You, Lord our God, King of the universe, who brings forth bread from the earth.

Then, the Melaveh Malkah meal is held.

Zemirot *for the Departure of Shabbat*

Some people sing these *zemirot* right after Havdalah, while others sing them during the *Melaveh Malkah* meal.

במוצאי יום מנוחה
Be'Motzaei Yom Menuḥah

This *piyyut* first appears in the *Maḥzor Vitry,* and was written by Yaakov of Noy (or, as his name is given in the acrostic, Yaakov mi'Noy Ḥazak).

בְּמוֹצָאֵי יוֹם מְנוּחָה,
הַמְצֵא לְעַמְּךָ רְוָחָה.

Be'motzaei yom menuḥah,
hamtze le'ammkha revaḥah.

שְׁלַח תִּשְׁבִּי לְנֶאֱנָחָה,
וְנָס יָגוֹן וַאֲנָחָה.

Shlaḥ Tishbi le'ne'enaḥah,
ve'nas yagon va'anaḥah.

As the day of rest departs, grant Your people relief. Send [Elijah] the Tishbite to those groaning [under the weight of exile]; drive suffering and sighing away.

יָאֲתָה לְךָ, צוּרִי, לְקַבֵּץ עַם מְפֻזָּרִי,
Yaatah lekha, tzuri, lekabbetz am mefuzzari,
מִיַּד גּוֹי אַכְזָרִי אֲשֶׁר כָּרָה לִי שׁוּחָה.
Mi'yad goy akhzari asher karah li shuḥah.

It is fitting for You, my Creator, to gather my dispersed people from the grasp of an evil nation, who have dug a pit [of destruction].

עֵת דּוֹדִים תְּעוֹרֵר, אֵל, לְמַלֵּט עַם אֲשֶׁר שׁוֹאֵל,

Et dodim teorer, El, lemallet am asher shoel,

רְאוֹת טוּבְךָ בְּבוֹא גוֹאֵל, לְשֶׂה פְּזוּרָה נִדָּחָה.

Reot tuvkha be'vo goel, le'seh pzurah niddaḥah.

God, awaken a time of closeness. Rescue the nation that asks to see Your goodness, with the Redeemer's coming to the scattered, cast-off sheep.

קְרָא יֶשַׁע לְעַם נְדָבָה, אֵל דָּגוּל מֵרְבָבָה,

Kra yesha le'am nedavah, El dagul mi'revavah,

יְהִי הַשָּׁבוּעַ הַבָּא לָנוּ וּלְכָל יִשְׂרָאֵל

Yehi ha'shavua habba lanu ule'khol Yisrael

לִישׁוּעָה וְלִרְוָחָה.

li'yshuah veli'rvaḥah.

Announce salvation to a benevolent people. God, Supreme, encircled by countless angels, let this coming week bring redemption and relief.

בַּת צִיּוֹן הַשְּׁכוּלָה, אֲשֶׁר הִיא הַיּוֹם גְּעוּלָה,

Bat Tziyyon ha'shkhulah, asher ha'yom hi geulah,

מְהֵרָה תִּהְיֶה בְּעוּלָה, בְּאֵם הַבָּנִים שְׂמֵחָה.

Meherah tihyeh beulah, be'em ha'banim smeḥah.

Daughter of Zion, bereaved, and, today, despised—let her speedily be reunited [with God]—a rejoicing mother of her children.

מַעְיָנוֹת אֲזַי יְזוּבוּן,

Maayanot azay yezuvun,

וּפְדוּיֵי יְיָ עוֹד יְשׁוּבוּן,

u'fduyey Adonai od yeshuvun,

וּמֵי יֶשַׁע יִשְׁאָבוּן, וְהַצָּרָה נִשְׁכָּחָה.

U'mey yesha yishavun, veha'tzarah nishkaḥah.

Then the living springs will flow, and God's redeemed will return, and waters of deliverance will be drawn, and suffering will be forgotten.

נְחֵה עַמְּךָ כְּאָב רַחֲמָן,

Neḥeh ammkha ke'av raḥaman,

יְצַפְצְפוּ עַם לֹא אַלְמָן,

yetzaftzefu am lo alman,

Lead Your people like a compassionate father; [then] the nation that was not widowed will respond: "God's word is faithful;

You have kept Your promise."

דְּבַר יְיָ אֲשֶׁר נֶאֱמָן, בַּהֲקִימְךָ הַבְטָחָה.

Dvar Adonai asher neeman, ba'hakimkha havtaḥah.

And precious refugees, outrunning destruction, will freely burst out in song, without cries, without furor; no more bondage, no clamor.

וִידִידִים, פְּלֵיטֵי חֶרֶץ,

Vi'ydidim, pletei ḥeretz,

נְגִינָתָם יִפְצְחוּ בְמֶרֶץ,

neginatam yiftzeḥu ve'meretz,

בְּלִי צְוָחָה וּבְלִי פֶּרֶץ, אֵין יוֹצֵאת וְאֵין צְוָחָה.

Bli tzvaḥah u'vli peretz, ein yotzet ve'ein tzvaḥah.

Let this month complete the prophecy of [Moses,] the father of all seers, and let this household hear sounds of joy, voices of happiness.

יְהִי הַחֹדֶשׁ הַזֶּה כִּנְבוּאַת אֲבִי חוֹזֶה,

Yehi ha'ḥodesh ha'zeh ke'nevuat avi ḥozeh,

וְיִשָּׁמַע בְּבַיִת זֶה קוֹל שָׂשׂוֹן וְקוֹל שִׂמְחָה.

Ve'yishama be'vayit zeh kol sason ve'kol simḥah.

Almighty, fulfill our requests; Valiant One, effect our prayers. And He will send blessing and success to the work of our hands.

חָזָק יְמַלֵּא מִשְׁאֲלוֹתֵינוּ, אַמִּיץ יַעֲשֶׂה

Ḥazak yemalle mishaloteinu, ammitz yaaseh

בַּקָּשָׁתֵנוּ, וְהוּא יִשְׁלַח בְּמַעֲשֵׂה יָדֵינוּ

bakkashatenu, Ve'hu yishlaḥ be'maaseh yadeinu

בְּרָכָה וְהַצְלָחָה.

brakhah ve'hatzlaḥah.

As the day of rejoicing departs, let Your awesome Name perform deeds; send the Tishbite to the cherished nation—relief, rejoicing, and elation.

בְּמוֹצָאֵי יוֹם גִּילָה, שִׁמְךָ נוֹרָא עֲלִילָה,

Be'motzaei yom gilah, shimkha nora alilah,

שְׁלַח תִּשְׁבִּי לְעַם סְגֻלָּה, רֶוַח, שָׂשׂוֹן וַהֲנָחָה.

Shlaḥ Tishbi le'am sgullah, revaḥ, sason va'hanaḥah.

Then our lips will express joy and rapturous song. We implore You, God, deliver us. We implore You, God, grant us success.

קוֹל צָהֳלָה וְרִנָּה שְׂפָתֵינוּ אָז תְּרַנֵּנָה,
Kol tzahalah ve'rinnah sefateinu az terannenah,
אָנָּא, יְיָ, הוֹשִׁיעָה נָּא, אָנָּא, יְיָ, הַצְלִיחָה נָּא.
Anna, Adonai, hoshiah na, anna, Adonai, hatzliḥah na.

חדש ששוני

Ḥaddesh Sesoni

This *piyyut* also appears for the first time in the *Maḥzor Vitry,* its author evidently named Uri (as it appears in the initial letters of one of the phrases of this song); its verses are arranged in alphabetical order.

Renew my joy, please my God; bring Elijah the Prophet.

חַדֵּשׁ שְׂשׂוֹנִי, אֵל נָא, וְהָבִיא אֶת אֵלִיָּהוּ הַנָּבִיא.
Ḥaddesh sesoni, El na, ve'havi et Eliyahu ha'navi.

Give strength and courage to my weak hands; bless my work and my every labor.

אַמֵּץ וְחַזֵּק רִפְיוֹן יָדִי,
בָּרֵךְ מְלַאכְתִּי וְכָל מַעְבָּדִי,
Ammetz ve'ḥazzek rifyon yadi,
barekh melakhti ve'khol maabadi,

Recall, O my Redeemer, my poverty and distress; fulfill Your good word and encourage me.

גּוֹאֲלִי, זְכוֹר עָנְיִי וּמְרוּדִי,
דְּבָרְךָ הַטּוֹב הָקֵם לְעוֹדְדִי.
Goali, zkhor onyi u'mrudi,
devarkha ha'tov hakem leodedi.

Expedite, send swiftly, rejoicing my heart, Elijah the Prophet.

הָרֵץ וּשְׁלַח, וְשַׂמַּח לְבָבִי, אֶת אֵלִיָּהוּ הַנָּבִיא.
Haretz u'shlaḥ, ve'sammaḥ levavi, et Eliyahu ha'navi.

וָעֵד וְהָכֵן דֵּי סִפּוּקִי,
זַמֵּן מְזוֹנִי וְלֶחֶם חֻקִּי,

Vaed ve'hakhen dei sippuki,
zammen mezoni ve'leḥem ḥukki,

Gather and provide sufficient for my need; grant me food, my daily portion of bread.

חֲלֵב חֵיל גּוֹיִם חִישׁ לְהָנִיקִי,
טוּבְךָ תְּשַׂבַּע עוֹלְלַי וְיוֹנְקִי.

Ḥalev ḥeil goyim ḥish lehaniki,
tuvkha tesabba oleli ve'yonki.

Send me the milk [wealth] of the multitude of the nations to suck; Your goodness shall satisfy my baby and my child.

יָבֹא מְשִׁיחִי לְעִיר מוֹשָׁבִי, אֶת אֵלִיָּהוּ הַנָּבִיא.

Yavo meshiḥi le'ir moshavi, et Eliyahu ha'navi.

May my Messiah come to the city where I dwell, with Elijah the Prophet.

כּוֹנֵן לְעַם זוּ, צֳרִי צִיר לַחֲבוֹשׁ,
לֶחֶם לֶאֱכוֹל וּבֶגֶד לִלְבֹּשׁ,

Konen le'am zu, tzori tzir laḥavosh,
leḥem le'ekhol u'veged lilbosh,

Prepare balm for this people's pain, to bind their wounds, bread to eat and clothes to wear.

מְשַׂנְאַי יֶחֱזֶה, יֵרָא וְיֵבוֹשׁ,
נְוֵה הַר שֵׂעִיר בְּקָרוֹב תִּכְבֹּשׁ.

Mesanni yeḥezeh, yere ve'yevosh,
neveh har seir bekarov tikhbosh.

Let my enemies see, behold, and be ashamed; conquer soon the do main of Mount Se'ir.

שְׂשׂוֹנִי יִגְדַּל בִּרְאוֹת סְבִיבִי, אֶת אֵלִיָּהוּ הַנָּבִיא.

Sesoni yigdal bi'rot svivi, et Eliyahu ha'navi.

How great will be my joy when around me I see Elijah the Prophet.

עַמּוֹן וּמוֹאָב מְהֵרָה תְּכַלֶּה,
פְּדוּתְךָ לְעַמְּךָ בְּקָרוֹב תְּגַלֶּה,

Ammon u'Moav meherah tekhalleh,
pedutkha le'ammkha be'karov tegalleh,

Put a speedy end to the rule of Ammon and Moab; reveal Your redemptive power to Your people soon.

Zion shall You populate with this people; there shall we ascend, to the city of the great King;

You shall cause to dwell there, amidst a willing people, Elijah the Prophet.

צִיּוֹן תְּמַלֵּא מֵעַם אֵלֶּה,
קִרְיַת מֶלֶךְ רָב אָז נַעֲלֶה,

Tziyyon temalleh me'am elleh,
kiryat melekh rav az naaleh,

שַׁכֵּן תְּשַׁכֵּן בְּתוֹךְ עַם צְבִי
אֶת אֵלִיָּהוּ הַנָּבִיא.

Shakken teshakken be'tokh am tzvi
et Eliyahu ha'navi.

אגיל ואשמח
Agil ve'Esmaḥ

The author of this *piyyut*, as given in the initials of the stanzas, was named Eleazar. We know nothing about his identity, time, or place.

I will rejoice and celebrate with all my heart when I witness Your vengeance against my enemies. Bring the Redeemer to Zion. Let *Zemah* [the Redeemer] spring forth and bring Elijah the Prophet and King Messiah.

Then terror and dread will descend on the nations, their hearts will panic; when the One Nation goes up [to its land], successful in its quest.

אָגִיל וְאֶשְׂמַח בִּלְבָבִי,
Agil ve'esmaḥ bi'lvavi,
בִּרְאוֹתִי כִּי מֵאוֹיְבַי תָּרִיב רִיבִי,
Bi'roti ki me'oyvai tariv rivi,
וּלְצִיּוֹן גּוֹאֵל תָּבִיא. אִישׁ צֶמַח תַּצְמִיחַ,
Ule'TZiyyon goel tavi. Ish tzemaḥ tatzmiaḥ,
אֵלִיָּהוּ הַנָּבִיא וּמֶלֶךְ הַמָּשִׁיחַ.
Eliyahu ha'navi u'melekh ha'mashiaḥ.
לָכֵן בָּעַמִּים יַחַד תִּפּוֹל אֵימָה וָפַחַד,
Lakhen ba'ammim yaḥad tippol eyma va'faḥad,
לִבָּם יִפְחַד בְּעֵת יַעֲלֶה גּוֹי אֶחָד,
Libbam yifḥad be'et yaaleh goy eḥad,

[Bring] Elijah the Prophet and King Messiah.

וְאָרְחוֹתָיו יַצְלִיחַ,

Ve'orḥotav yatzliaḥ,

אֵלִיָּהוּ הַנָּבִיא וּמֶלֶךְ הַמָּשִׁיחַ.

Eliyahu ha'navi u'melekh ha'mashiaḥ.

The time draws near: from east to west he will arise, and slaughter great numbers in Aram, making war and battle, sounding the call to arms against his foes. [Bring] Elijah the Prophet and King Messiah.

עוֹד מִמִּזְרָח לְמַעֲרָב יֵעוֹר לַעֲשׂוֹת הֶרֶג רָב,

Od mi'mizraḥ le'maarav yeor laasot hereg rav,

בַּאֲרָם וַעֲרָב לַעֲרוֹךְ מִלְחָמָה וּקְרָב,

Ba'aram va'arav laarokh milḥamah u'krav,

עַל אוֹיְבָיו יַצְרִיחַ,

Al oyvav yatzriaḥ,

אֵלִיָּהוּ הַנָּבִיא וּמֶלֶךְ הַמָּשִׁיחַ.

Eliyahu ha'navi u'melekh ha'mashiaḥ.

Brazen kings of the earth—Yetur, Nafish, and Kedmah; Mishma and Dumah—flee to the south and the west, [before your devastation by] Elijah the Prophet and King Messiah.

זֵדִים מַלְכֵי אֲדָמָה, יְטוּר, נָפִישׁ וָקֵדְמָה,

Zedim malkhei adamah, Yetur, Nafish va'Kedmah,

מִשְׁמָע וְדוּמָה, נוּסוּ נֶגְבָּה וָיָמָּה,

Mishma ve'Dumah, nusu negbah ve'yammah,

אֲשֶׁר אֶתְכֶם יַבְרִיחַ,

Asher etkhem yavriaḥ,

אֵלִיָּהוּ הַנָּבִיא וּמֶלֶךְ הַמָּשִׁיחַ.

Eliyahu ha'navi u'melekh ha'mashiaḥ.

Sing out, humanity, for—timeless, resplendent—he comes forth with brilliant light [like the Temple menorah, with] stem, cups, and flowers. Let Redemption blossom on Mount Zion, with Elijah the Prophet and King Messiah.

רָנּוּ כָּל עֹבְרֵי אֹרַח, כִּי הִנֵּה רַעֲנָן אֶזְרָח,

Ronnu kol ovrei oraḥ, ki hinneh raanan ezraḥ,

אוֹרוֹ זָרַח, קָנֶה כַּפְתּוֹר וָפֶרַח,

Oro zaraḥ, kaneh kaftor va'feraḥ,

עַל הַר צִיּוֹן יַפְרִיחַ,

Al har Tziyyon yafriaḥ,

אֵלִיָּהוּ הַנָּבִיא וּמֶלֶךְ הַמָּשִׁיחַ.

Eliyahu ha'navi u'melekh ha'mashiaḥ.

אלהים יסעדנו

Elohim Yisadenu

The author of this *piyyut* is Avraham. Apart from his name, alluded to in the initials of the stanzas, we know nothing about him.

אֱלֹהִים יִסְעָדֵנוּ, בְּרָכָה בִּמְאוֹדֵנוּ,
Elohim yisadenu, brakhah bi'modenu,
וְזֶבֶד טוֹב יִזְבְּדֵנוּ, בְּכָל מִשְׁלַח יָדֵינוּ.
Ve'zeved tov yizbedenu; be'khol mishlaḥ yadeinu.

Support us, O God, send blessings on all we have, grant us a good portion in all to which we put our hands.

אֱלֹהִים יִסְעָדֵנוּ.
Elohim yisadenu.

Support us, O God.

בְּיוֹם רִאשׁוֹן לִמְלָאכָה, יְצַו אִתָּנוּ בְּרָכָה,
Be'yom rishon li'mlakha, yetzav ittanu brakhah,
וְיוֹם הַשֵּׁנִי כָּכָה, יַמְתִּיק אֶת סוֹדֵנוּ.
Ve'yom ha'sheni kakha, yamtik et sodenu.

On the first day of the working week may He ordain for us blessings; on the second let it be the same, may He make our counsel sweet.

אֱלֹהִים יִסְעָדֵנוּ.
Elohim yisadenu.

Support us, O God.

רַבֵּה צְבָאַי יִשְׁעִי, בַּשְּׁלִישִׁי וּבָרְבִיעִי,
Rabbeh tzvaei yishi, ba'shlishi uva'rvii,
בַּחֲמִישִׁי אַךְ לֹא בְעִי, יִשְׁלַח אֶת פּוֹדֵנוּ,
Ba'ḥamishi akh lo vei, yishlaḥ et podenu,

Increase my armies, [God of] my salvation, on the third [day] and the fourth; and on the fifth—without suffering—may He send us our redeemer.

אֱלֹהִים יִסְעָדֵנוּ.
Elohim yisadenu.

Support us, O God.

Prepare the food, get ready the meat. On the sixth day is the sacrifice—sanctified with lauds and praises over all our other desires.

הָכֵן טְבוֹחַ טֶבַח, בְּיוֹם הַשִּׁשִּׁי זֶבַח,
Hakhen tevoaḥ tevaḥ, beyom ha'shishi zevaḥ,
קוֹדֶשׁ הִלּוּל וָשֶׁבַח עַל כָּל מַחֲמַדֵּינוּ,
Kodesh hillul va'shevaḥ al kol maḥamaddeinu,

Support us, O God.

אֱלֹהִים יִסְעָדֵנוּ.
Elohim yisadenu.

We may treat ourselves with delicacies on our sacred day, and our couch is fresh, and night for us is light.

מַעֲדַנִּים לְנַפְשֵׁנוּ נִתֵּן בְּיוֹם קָדְשֵׁנוּ,
Maadanim le'nafshenu nitten be'yom kodshenu,
וְרַעֲנָנָה עַרְשֵׂנוּ, וְלַיְלָה אוֹר בַּעֲדֵנוּ.
Ve'raananah arsenu, ve'laylah or baadenu.

Support us, O God, send blessings on all we have, grant us a good portion in all to which we put our hands.

אֱלֹהִים יִסְעָדֵנוּ, בְּרָכָה בִּמְאוֹדֵנוּ,
Elohim yisadenu, brakhah bi'modenu,
וְזֶבֶד טוֹב יִזְבְּדֵנוּ, בְּכָל מִשְׁלַח יָדֵינוּ.
Ve'zeved tov yizbedenu be'khol mishlaḥ yadeinu.

אלי חיש גואלי
Eli Ḥish Goali

This *piyyut* was composed by Naḥman [ben Moshe]—possibly Rabbi Naḥman of Regensburg, cousin of Rabbi Judah he'Ḥassid.

Send my redeemer quickly, God, Your servant who brings me wisdom, who greets me, God, with Your good tidings,

אֵלִי, חִישׁ גּוֹאֲלִי, עַבְדְּךָ יַשְׂכִּילִי, מְבַשֵּׂר טוֹב אֵלִי,
Eli, ḥish goali, avdekha yaskili, mevasser tov Eli,

[whose name is] Elijah the Prophet.

אֶת אֵלִיָּהוּ הַנָּבִיא.
et Eliyahu ha'navi.

Beautiful upon the mountains are the footfalls of the messengers, sent by the mountains' Maker,

נָאווּ עַל הֶהָרִים שְׁלוּחֵי יוֹצֵר הָרִים,
וְרַגְלֵי הַמְבַשְּׂרִים,

Navu al he'harim shluḥei yotzer harim,
ve'raglei ha'mevassrim,

saying, "Return, O return!"

בֶּאֱמוֹר, שׁוּבִי, שׁוּבִי.

be'emor, Shuvi, shuvi.

Hide just for an instant; with every sickness and disease I shall smite your enemies,

חֲבִי כִּמְעַט רֶגַע, כָּל מַחֲלָה וְכָל נֶגַע,
אוֹיְבַיִךְ אֶפְגַּע,

Ḥavi khimat rega, kol maḥalah ve'khol nega,
oyvayikh efga,

the day of reckoning [is] in My heart.

יוֹם נָקָם בְּלִבִּי.

yom nakam be'libbi.

Your king shall surely come to you; for you are lovely utterly, My companion [is] before you,

מַלְכֵּךְ יָבֹא לָךְ, יָפָה אַתְּ כֻּלָּךְ,
וְרַעְיָתִי לְמוּלָךְ,

Malkekh yavo lakh, yafah at kullakh,
ve'raayati le'mulakh,

the Tishbite from Gilead.

גִּלְעָדִי הַתִּשְׁבִּי.

Giladi ha'Tishbi.

Sweetness falls from the lips of the dovelings, for the hour of her favor has come,

נוֹפֶת תִּטֹּפְנָה שִׂפְתֵי בְּנֵי יוֹנָה,
כִּי בָא עֵת לְחֶנְנָה,

Nofet tittofnah siftei vnei yonah,
ki va et le'ḥenenah,

Zion, fair and pleasing portion.

צִיּוֹן נַחֲלַת צְבִי.

Tziyyon naḥalat tzvi.

אדיר איום ונורא

Adir Ayom ve'Nora

This *piyyut* follows alphabetical order, and its author's name is unknown. Every third verse in the hymn begins with the name of God.

Majestic, mighty, awesome One,
in my trouble I call to You:

אַדִּיר אָיוֹם וְנוֹרָא, בַּצַּר לִי לְךָ אֶקְרָא,
Addir ayom ve'nora, ba'tzar li lekha ekra,

The Lord is with me, I have no fear.

יְיָ לִי לֹא אִירָא:
Adonai li lo ira.

Rebuild my Temple's broken walls, Exalted One, hasten the radiant [redeemer];

גְּדוֹר פִּרְצַת הֵיכָלִי, דָּגוּל, מַהֵר, חַכְלִילִי,
Gdor pirtzat heikhali, dagul, maher, ḥakhlili,

O Lord, surely You shall be my help.

יְיָ הֱיֵה עוֹזֵר לִי.
Adonai heyeh ozer li.

Truly it is You who are my hope,
for Your redemption do I wait,

הֵן אַתָּה תִּקְוָתִי, וְלִישׁוּעָתְךָ קִוִּיתִי,
Hen attah tikvati, veli'yshuatka kivviti,

O Lord, my strength and my salvation.

יְיָ עוֹז יְשׁוּעָתִי.
Adonai oz yeshuati.

Pure One, whose hands, alone, are clean, hear our prayer when we raise our hands,

זַךְ וּנְקִי כַּפַּיִם, חוֹן פּוֹרְשֵׂי כַּפַּיִם,
Zakh u'nki khappayim, ḥon porsei khappayim,

O Lord, patient and long-suffering.

יְיָ אֶרֶךְ אַפַּיִם.
Adonai erekh appayim.

טוּבְךָ תָּחִישׁ לְעַמֶּךָ,
יְהִי עָלֵינוּ כִּנְאֻמֶךָ,

Tuvkha taḥish le'ammekha,
yehi aleinu ki'numekha,

Send Your goodness to Your people swiftly, be to us as You have promised:

יְיָ עֲשֵׂה לְמַעַן שְׁמֶךָ.

Adonai aseh lemaan shmekha.

O Lord, do it for Your Name's sake.

כּוֹנֵן בֵּית מְכוֹנֶךָ, לְהַרְבֵּץ בּוֹ צֹאנֶךָ,

Konen beit mekhonekha, leharbetz bo tzonekha,

Build Your house in its true place and let Your flock find resting there,

יְיָ בְּאוֹר פָּנֶיךָ.

Adonai be'or panekha.

Lord, in the light of Your presence.

מִפַּחַד לְהַצִּילִי,
נַהֲלֵנִי לְצִיּוֹן קֹדֶשׁ גּוֹרָלִי,

Mi'paḥad lehatzili,
nahaleni le'Tziyyon kodesh gorali,

Rescue me from all I fear, lead me to my allotted place;

יְיָ שְׁמַע בְּקוֹלִי.

Adonai shma be'koli.

O Lord, hearken to my voice.

סְעוֹד וּסְמוֹךְ לְנִמְהָרִים, עֲזוֹר נָא אֶת הַנִּשְׁאָרִים,

Seod u'smokh le'nimharim, azor na et ha'nisharim,

The speedy succor and sustain, and help all those who have remained,

יְיָ יוֹצֵר הָרִים.

Adonai yotzer harim.

Lord, who formed the mountains.

פְּדֵה עַמְּךָ מֵעַזִּים, צֹאנְךָ מִיַּד גּוֹזְזִים,

Pdeh ammkha me'azzim, tzonekha mi'yad gozezim,

Preserve Your people from violence, Your flock from the hands of the shearers,

Lord who makes the lightning.

יְיָ עוֹשֶׂה חֲזִיזִים.

Adonai oseh ḥazizim.

Draw near the End, comforting, have pity on the people none pity,

קָרֵב קֵץ נֶחָמָה, רַחֵם אוֹם לֹא רֻחָמָה,

Karev ketz neḥamah, raḥem om lo ruḥamah,

Lord, Master of war.

יְיָ אִישׁ מִלְחָמָה.

Adonai ish milḥamah.

Dwell in our tents as You once did, and forever, God who brings us into being;

שְׁכוֹן כְּמֵאָז בְּאָהֳלֵנוּ,
תָּמִיד, אֵל מְחוֹלְלֵנוּ,

Shkhon keme'az be'oholeinu,
tamid, El meḥoleleinu,

O Lord, our King, who will save us.

יְיָ מַלְכֵּנוּ הוּא יוֹשִׁיעֵנוּ:

Adonai malkenu, hu yoshienu.

איש חסיד היה
Ish Ḥasid Hayah

This *piyyut* is written in alphabetical order, and its last verses contain the name of its author, Yishai ben Mordechai Ḥazak. It first appears in *Maḥzor Vitry,* and is based upon a story told in the name of Rabbenu Nissim ben Yaakov.

There once lived a pious man who lacked food and support.

אִישׁ חָסִיד הָיָה, בְּלִי מָזוֹן וּמִחְיָה,

Ish ḥasid haya, bli mazon u'miḥyah,

Ashamed, without clothing to wear, he stayed home [studying Torah],

בְּבֵיתוֹ עוֹסֵק מִלֵּבוּשׁ, וְאֵין בֶּגֶד לִלְבּוֹשׁ.

Be'veito osek mi'leivosh, ve'ein beged lilbosh.

גּוֹנֵן בַּחֲשׁוּבָה אִשָּׁה,
וְגַם בְּבָנִים חֲמִשָּׁה,

Gonen ba'ḥashuvah ishah,
ve'gam be'vanim ḥamishah.

Watched over by his praise-worthy wife and five children.

דִּבְּרָה לוֹ הָאִשָּׁה, יוֹתֵר אֵין לְהִתְיָאֲשָׁה,

Dibbrah lo ha'ishah, yoter ein lehityaasha,

We can no longer [afford to] despair," his wife told him,

הֲמִבְּלִי לֶחֶם לֶאֱכוֹל, בְּעֵרוֹם וּבְחוֹסֶר כֹּל,

Hami'bli leḥem leekhol, be'erom uve'ḥoser kol,

"Without bread to eat, without clothes—with nothing at all!

וְתוֹרָה מָצָאתָ כִּי יָגַעְתָּ, מַה נֹּאכַל מֵעַתָּה.

Ve'Torah matzata ki yagata, ma nokhal me'attah.

You have succeeded in Torah through your labors, but what can we eat from now on?

זָהִיר כְּבַר נָשׁוּק, הֲלֹא תֵצֵא לַשּׁוּק,

Zahir kvar nashuk, halo tetze la'shuk,

Cautiously, like an armored warrior, go to the market;

חַנּוּן וְרַחוּם בִּמְרוֹמָיו,
אוּלַי יִגְמְלֵנוּ בְּרַחֲמָיו.

Ḥannun ve'raḥum bi'mromav,
ulay yigmelenu be'raḥamav.

Perhaps the Gracious, Merciful One in Heaven will show us His compassion.

טוֹב, לְקוֹוָיו מַחֲסֶה, רְצוֹן יְרֵאָיו יַעֲשֶׂה.

Tov, le'kovav maḥaseh, retzon yereav yaaseh.

The Good One protects those relying on Him; He fulfills the desires of those who fear Him."

יָעַצְתְּ בְּדַעַת וּבְחָכְמָה,
עֲצָתֵךְ בְּלִי לְהַסְכִּימָה,

Yaatzt be'daat uve'ḥokhmah,
atzatekh bli lehaskimah,

"Your suggestion," [he answered,] "displays knowledge and wisdom, but I cannot concur;

כְּצֵאתִי לְבשֶׁת וְלִכְלִמָּה,
מִבְּלִי כְסוּת וְשַׂלְמָה,

Ke'tzeti le'voshet veli'khlimah,
mi'bli khsut ve'salmah,

I will be ridiculed if I leave without a garment [to cover myself],

לְאֵין בְּיָדִי לְפוּרְטָה, אֲפִילוּ שָׁוֶה פְּרוּטָה.

Le'ein be'yadi le'fortah, afilu shave prutah.

And empty-handed, without even a penny."

מִהֲרָה וְשָׁאֲלָה מִשְּׁכֵנִים,
מַלְבּוּשִׁים נָאִים, מְתֻקָּנִים,

Miharah ve'shaalah mi'shkhenim,
malbushim naim, metukkanim,

She rushed to borrow choice, tailored garments from the neighbors.

נִלְבַּשׁ וְהִשְׁלִיךְ יְהָבוֹ,
עַל יְיָ אֲשֶׁר אֲהֵבוֹ.

Nilbash ve'hishlikh yehavo,
al Adonai asher ahevo.

Outfitted, now, he cast his burden on his beloved God;

סָחוּ יְלָדָיו בְּפִלּוּלָם,
אַל יָשׁוּב דַּךְ נִכְלָם.

Saḥu yeladav be'fillulam,
al yashov dakh nikhlam.

His children voiced their prayers: "Let him not return broken and shamed."

עָבַר בַּשּׁוּק בְּסִבְרָתוֹ,
וְהִנֵּה אֵלִיָּהוּ הַנָּבִיא לִקְרָאתוֹ.

Avar ba'shuk be'sivrato,
ve'hinneh Eliyahu ha'navi likrato.

He walked through the market, trusting [in God,] and behold: Elijah the Prophet approached him.

פָּץ לוֹ הַמְּבַשֵּׂר, בֶּאֱמֶת הַיּוֹם תִּתְעַשֵּׁר.

Patz lo ha'mevasser, be'emet ha'yom titasher.

The heralder [of good tidings] avowed, "Indeed, today you'll become rich.

צַוֵּנִי בְּכָל כְּבוֹדְךָ, כִּי הִנְנִי עַבְדְּךָ.

Tzavveni be'khol kevodekha, ki ani avdekha.

Order me about imposingly, [as if] I were your servant.

Announce: 'Who wishes to purchase a servant without equal?' "

The pious man thought: "Can one tamper with [Divine] sentence? A servant sell his master?!"

[But Elijah] bestowed within him wisdom, and [the pious man behaved] as if he were Elijah's owner.

A merchant gladly bought him for eight hundred thousand gold pieces,

Asking, "What is your trade? If you are skilled in construction,

Make me a hall and castle—and then you'll be freed."

The first day on the job, [Elijah] worked with the laborers.

[Then] he cried out at midnight, "You, whose works are awesome, answer me!

קְרָא לְמִי בְדַעְתּוֹ, קְנוֹת עֶבֶד אֵין כְּמוֹתוֹ.

Kra le'mi ve'daato knot eved ein kmoto.

רָחַשׁ, אֵיךְ יְשַׁנֶּה דִּינוֹ,
עֶבֶד לִמְכּוֹר אֶת אֲדוֹנוֹ.

Raḥash, eikh yeshanneh dino,
eved limkor et adono.

שָׂת לוֹ חָכְמָתוֹ בְּקִרְבּוֹ,
וְהֶחֱזִיק בּוֹ כְּמוֹ רַבּוֹ.

Shat lo ḥokhmato be'kirbo,
ve'ḥehezik bo kmo rabbo.

תַּגָּר קְנָאוֹ בַּאֲהָבִים,
בִּשְׁמוֹנֶה מֵאוֹת אֶלֶף זְהוּבִים.

Taggar knao ba'ahavim,
bi'shmoneh meot elef zehuvim.

תְּבָעוֹ, מַה מְּלַאכְתֶּךָ,
אִם בְּבִנְיַן חָכְמָתֶךָ,

Tvao, ma melakhtekha,
im be'vinyan ḥokhmatekha,

תַּכְלִית טְרַקְלִין וּפַלְטְרִין, הֲרֵי אַתָּה בֶּן חוֹרִין.

Takhlit traklin u'falterin—harei attah ben ḥorin.

יוֹם רִאשׁוֹן בְּמִפְעָלִים, פָּעַל עִם פּוֹעֲלִים.

Yom rishon be'mifalim, paal im poalim.

שִׁוַּע בַּחֲצִי הַלַּיְלָה, עֲנֵנִי, נוֹרָא עֲלִילָה.

Shivva ba'ḥatzi ha'laila, Aneni, nora alilah.

I laid the plan and was sold as a slave; it was for Your honor, not mine.

Creator, Possessor of the world, You finish the building!

May my pleas awaken Your compassion, for my intention was worthy."

Angels of mercy from His high realms then began to build it;

The regal work force increased in numbers, and all the work was done.

Seeing that the effort was complete, the merchant was filled with joy;

[It was] replete with elegant towers, the work of peerless builders.

"Remember, now," [said Elijah,] "your words spoken yesterday.

יָזַמְתִּי וְנִמְכַּרְתִּי לְהַעֲבִידִי,
לִכְבוֹדְךָ וְלֹא לִכְבוֹדִי.

Yazamti ve'nimkarti lehaavidi,
li'khvodekha, ve'lo li'khvodi.

בּוֹרֵא עוֹלָם בְּקִנְיָן, הַשְׁלֵם זֶה הַבִּנְיָן.

Bore olam be'kinyan, hashlem zeh ha'binyan.

רַחֲמֶיךָ יִכְמְרוּ בַּחֲנִינָתִי,
כִּי לְטוֹבָה כַּוָּנָתִי.

Raḥamekha yikhmeru ba'ḥaninati,
ki le'tovah kavvanati.

מַלְאֲכֵי רַחֲמִים מִמְּעוֹנָתוֹ
אָז הֵחֵלּוּ לִבְנוֹתוֹ,

Malakhei raḥamim mi'meonato
az heḥelu livnoto,

רַבּוּ בְּנֵי הַמְּלוּכָה,
וַתִּשְׁלַם כָּל הַמְּלָאכָה.

Rabbu bnei ha'melukhah,
va'tishlam kol ha'mlakhah.

דָּץ הַסּוֹחֵר בִּרְאוֹתוֹ כִּי נִגְמְרָה מְלַאכְתּוֹ,

Datz ha'soḥer bi'roto ki nigmerah melakhto,

כְּלוּלַת מִגְדָּלִים נָאִים, לְפִי עִנְיַן הַבַּנָּאִים.

Klulat migdalim naim, le'fi inyan ha'bannaim.

יִזָּכֵר לְךָ עַתָּה אֶתְמוֹל אֲשֶׁר דִּבַּרְתָּ.

Yizzakher lekha attah etmol asher dibbarta.

Give me my freedom—complete, unrestricted—as you said."

חָפְשֵׁנִי בְּוַדַּאי וּבְבֵרוּר,
כְּנַמְתָּ לְעִנְיַן שִׁחְרוּר.

Ḥofsheni be'vaddai uve'verur,
ke'namta le'inyan shiḥrur.

He earnestly fulfilled his promise, and the man of truth vanished.

זֶה קִיְּמוֹ בֶּאֱמֶת, וּפָרַח לוֹ אִישׁ הָאֱמֶת.

Zeh kiyyemo be'emet, u'faraḥ lo ish ha'emet.

אמר יי ליעקב
Amar Adonai le'Yaakov

This *pizmon* is alphabetically arranged, each verse being based upon a verse from Scripture alluding to the patriarch Jacob.

God said to Jacob,

אָמַר יְיָ לְיַעֲקֹב,

Amar Adonai le'Yaakov,

Chorus:
"Have no fear, Jacob, My servant!"

[פִּזְמוֹן]
אַל תִּירָא עַבְדִּי יַעֲקֹב.

Al tira avdi Yaakov.

God chose Jacob,

בָּחַר יְיָ בְּיַעֲקֹב,

Baḥar Adonai be'Yaakov,

[Chorus]

[פִּזְמוֹן]

God has redeemed Jacob,

גָּאַל יְיָ אֶת יַעֲקֹב,

Gaal Adonai et Yaakov,

[Chorus]

[פִּזְמוֹן]

A star will arise from Jacob,

דָּ֫רַךְ כּוֹכָב מִיַּעֲקֹב,

Darakh kokhav mi'Yaakov,

[Chorus] [פִּזְמוֹן]

Before long, Jacob will take root,

הַבָּאִים יַשְׁרֵשׁ יַעֲקֹב,

Ha'baim yashresh Yaakov,

[Chorus] [פִּזְמוֹן]

A ruler will descend from Jacob,

וְיֵרְדְּ מִיַּעֲקֹב,

Va'yerd mi'Yaakov,

[Chorus] [פִּזְמוֹן]

Remember [to fulfill] this for Jacob,

זְכֹר זֹאת לְיַעֲקֹב,

Zekhor zot le'Yaakov,

[Chorus] [פִּזְמוֹן]

Joyful deliverances for Jacob,

חֶדְוַת יְשׁוּעוֹת יַעֲקֹב,

Ḥedvat yeshuot Yaakov,

[Chorus] [פִּזְמוֹן]

How goodly are your tents, Jacob,

טוֹבוּ אֹהָלֶיךָ יַעֲקֹב,

Tovu ohalekha Yaakov,

[Chorus] [פִּזְמוֹן]

They will teach Your precepts to Jacob,

יוֹרוּ מִשְׁפָּטֶיךָ לְיַעֲקֹב,

Yoru mishpatekha le'Yakov,

[Chorus] [פִּזְמוֹן]

For there is no sorcery in Jacob,

[Chorus]

He has seen no evil in Jacob,

[Chorus]

Who can count Jacob's descendants?

[Chorus]

God swore to Jacob,

[Chorus]

Forgive, please, the sin of Jacob,

[Chorus]

Free Jacob from bondage, now,

[Chorus]

God will liberate Jacob,

[Chorus]

כִּי לֹא נַחַשׁ בְּיַעֲקֹב,

Ki lo naḥash be'Yaakov,

[פִּזְמוֹן]

לֹא הִבִּיט אָוֶן בְּיַעֲקֹב,

Lo hibbit aven be'Yaakov,

[פִּזְמוֹן]

מִי מָנָה עֲפַר יַעֲקֹב,

Mi manah afar Yaakov,

[פִּזְמוֹן]

נִשְׁבַּע יְיָ לְיַעֲקֹב,

Nishba Adonai le'Yaakov,

[פִּזְמוֹן]

סְלַח נָא לַעֲוֹן יַעֲקֹב,

Slaḥ na la'avon Yaakov,

[פִּזְמוֹן]

עַתָּה הָשֵׁב שְׁבוּת יַעֲקֹב,

Attah hashev shvut Yaakov,

[פִּזְמוֹן]

פָּדָה יְיָ אֶת יַעֲקֹב,

Padah Adonai et Yaakov,

[פִּזְמוֹן]

Command Jacob's release,

צַוֵּה יְשׁוּעוֹת יַעֲקֹב,

Tzaveh yeshuot Yaakov,

[Chorus]

[פִּזְמוֹן]

The voice [of supplication] is Jacob's voice,

קוֹל קוֹל יַעֲקֹב,

Kol kol Yaakov,

[Chorus]

[פִּזְמוֹן]

Sing out with joy, Jacob, [for the coming Redemption,]

רָנִּי וְשִׂמְחִי לְיַעֲקֹב,

Roni ve'simḥi le'Yaakov,

[Chorus]

[פִּזְמוֹן]

God will restore Jacob's glory,

שָׁב יְיָ אֶת שְׁבוּת יַעֲקֹב,

Shav Adonai et shvut Yaakov,

[Chorus]

[פִּזְמוֹן]

Give truth to Jacob,

תִּתֵּן אֱמֶת לְיַעֲקֹב,

Titten emet le'Yaakov,

[פִּזְמוֹן]

[Chorus]

אליהו הנביא

Eliyahu ha'Navi

This is an alphabetical *pizmon* of unknown authorship.

Chorus:
Elijah the Prophet, Elijah the Tishbite, Elijah the Gileadite—let him come speedily with Messiah, son of David.

[פִּזְמוֹן]

אֵלִיָּהוּ הַנָּבִיא, אֵלִיָּהוּ הַתִּשְׁבִּי, אֵלִיָּהוּ הַגִּלְעָדִי,
בִּמְהֵרָה יָבֹא אֵלֵינוּ עִם מָשִׁיחַ בֶּן דָּוִד.

Eliyahu ha'navi, Eliyahu ha'Tishbi, Eliyahu ha'Giladi,
bi'mherah yavo eleinu im Mashiaḥ ben David.

A man who was zealous for God's Name. A man who was pledged [a covenant of] peace by Yekutiel [Moses]. A man who [prayed and] atoned for the children of Israel.

אִישׁ אֲשֶׁר קִנֵּא לְשֵׁם הָאֵל,
Ish asher kinne le'shem ha'El,
אִישׁ בֻּשַּׂר שָׁלוֹם עַל יַד יְקוּתִיאֵל,
Ish bussar shalom al yad Yekutiel,
אִישׁ גָּשׁ וַיְכַפֵּר עַל בְּנֵי יִשְׂרָאֵל.
Ish gash va'yekhapper al bnei Yisrael.

[Chorus]

[פִּזְמוֹן]

A man whose eyes witnessed twelve generations. A man described as "hirsute" in appearance. A man wearing a leather sheath over his thighs.

אִישׁ דּוֹרוֹת שְׁנֵים עָשָׂר רָאוּ עֵינָיו,
Ish dorot shneim asar ra'u eynav,
אִישׁ הַנִּקְרָא בַּעַל שֵׂעָר בְּסִמָּנָיו,
Ish ha'nikra baal sear be'simmanav,
אִישׁ וְאֵזוֹר עוֹר אָזוּר בְּמָתְנָיו.
Ish ve'ezor or azur be'motnav.

[Chorus]

[פִּזְמוֹן]

A man who stormed against sun-worshipers. A man who hastened and took an oath to forestall rains from the sky. A man who halted dew and rainfall for three years.

אִישׁ זָעַף עַל עוֹבְדֵי חַמָּנִים,
Ish zaaf al ovdei ḥammanim,
אִישׁ חָשׁ וְנִשְׁבַּע מִהְיוֹת גִּשְׁמֵי מְעוֹנִים,
Ish ḥash ve'nishba mi'hyot gishmey meonim,
אִישׁ טַל וּמָטָר עָצַר שָׁלֹשׁ שָׁנִים.
Ish tal u'matar atzar shalosh shanim.

[Chorus]

[פִּזְמוֹן]

A man who set out to find solace. A man to whom the ravens brought food, and did not perish in the grave. A man on whose behalf the vessel [of flour] and pitcher [of oil] were blessed.

אִישׁ יָצָא לִמְצֹא לְנַפְשׁוֹ נַחַת,
Ish yatza limtzo le'nafsho naḥat,
אִישׁ כִּלְכְּלוּהוּ הָעוֹרְבִים וְלֹא מֵת לַשַּׁחַת,
Ish kilkeluhu ha'orvim ve'lo met la'shaḥat,
אִישׁ לְמַעֲנוֹ נִתְבָּרְכוּ כַּד וְצַפַּחַת.
Ish le'maano nitbarkhu kad ve'tzappaḥat.

[Chorus]

[פִּזְמוֹן]

A man to whose admonitions they harkened fervently. A man who was answered with fire from lofty heavens. A man after whom they proclaimed: "The Lord is [the only] God!"

אִישׁ מוּסָרָיו הִקְשִׁיבוּ כְּמֵהִים,
Ish musarav hikshivu kmehim,
אִישׁ נַעֲנָה בָּאֵשׁ מִשְּׁמֵי גְבוֹהִים,
Ish naanah ba'esh mi'shemey gvohim,
אִישׁ סָחוּ אַחֲרָיו, יְיָ הוּא הָאֱלֹהִים!
Ish saḥu aḥarav, Adonai hu ha'Elohim!

[Chorus]

[פִּזְמוֹן]

A man destined to be sent from the highest firmament [to announce the Redemption]. A man appointed to report all good tidings. A man—a faithful

אִישׁ עָתִיד לְהִשְׁתַּלֵּחַ מִשְּׁמֵי עֲרָבוֹת,
Ish atid le'hishtalleaḥ mi'shmei aravot,
אִישׁ פָּקִיד עַל כָּל בְּשׂוֹרוֹת טוֹבוֹת,
Ish pakid al kol bsorot tovot,

אִישׁ צִיר נֶאֱמָן לְהָשִׁיב לֵב בָּנִים עַל אֲבוֹת.

Ish tzir neeman lehashiv lev banim al avot.

messenger—who turns the hearts of children back to their parents.

[פִּזְמוֹן]

[Chorus]

אִישׁ קָרָא, קַנֹּא קִנֵּאתִי לַיהֹוָה בְּתִפְאָרָה,

Ish kara, Kanno kinneti l'Adonai be'tifarah,

אִישׁ רָכַב עַל סוּסֵי אֵשׁ בִּסְעָרָה,

Ish rakhav al susei esh bi'se'arah,

אִישׁ שֶׁלֹּא טָעַם טַעַם מִיתָה וּקְבוּרָה.

Ish she'lo taam taam mitah u'kvurah.

A man declaring majestically: "I have been zealous on God's behalf." A man riding fiery stallions, [ascending] in a whirlwind. A man who never tasted death and burial.

[פִּזְמוֹן]

[Chorus]

אִישׁ תִּשְׁבִּי תַּצִּילֵנוּ מִפִּי אֲרָיוֹת,

Ish tishbi tatzilenu mi'pi arayot,

יְבַשְּׂרֵנוּ בְּשׂוֹרוֹת טוֹבוֹת,

Yevassrenu besorot tovot,

יְשַׂמְּחֵנוּ בָּנִים עַל אָבוֹת,

Yesammḥenu banim al avot,

בְּמוֹצָאֵי שַׁבָּתוֹת.

Be'motzaei Shabbatot.

A man called "Tishbite": Save us from the jaws of lions. Let us hear from you glad tidings. Let us rejoice together, sons and fathers, on Sabbaths' ends.

[פִּזְמוֹן]

[Chorus]

אִישׁ תִּשְׁבִּי עַל שְׁמוֹ נִקְרָא,

Ish Tishbi al shmo nikra,

תַּצְלִיחֵנוּ עַל יָדוֹ בַּתּוֹרָה,

Tatzliḥenu al yado ba'Torah,

תַּשְׁמִיעֵנוּ מִפִּיו בְּשׂוֹרָה טוֹבָה בִּמְהֵרָה,

Tashmienu mi'piv bsorah tovah bi'mherah,

A man with [the designation] "Tishbite" appended to his name: May we succeed in Torah in his merit. May we speedily hear good news from his lips. Bring us out from darkness to light.

תּוֹצִיאֵנוּ מֵאֲפֵלָה לְאוֹרָה.

Totzienu me'afelah le'orah.

[פִּזְמוֹן]

[Chorus]

אַשְׁרֵי מִי שֶׁרָאָה פָּנָיו בַּחֲלוֹם,

Ashrei mi she'raah panav ba'ḥalom,

אַשְׁרֵי מִי שֶׁנָּתַן לוֹ שָׁלוֹם

Ashrei mi she'natan lo shalom

וְהֶחֱזִיר לוֹ שָׁלוֹם,

Ve'heḥezir lo shalom,

יְיָ יְבָרֵךְ אֶת עַמּוֹ בַשָּׁלוֹם.

Adonai yevarekh et ammo va'shalom.

Happy is he who saw his face in a dream. Happy is the one who welcomes him with "Peace," and to whom he responds, "Peace." May God bless His people with Peace.

[פִּזְמוֹן]

[Chorus]

Grace after Meals

Introduction to the Blessing after Meals

The Blessing after Meals (*Birkat ha'Mazon*) is required by the Torah itself, based upon the verse "When you have eaten and are satiated, you shall bless the Lord Your God for the good land which He has given you" (Deuteronomy 8:10).

Here we give thanks for what we have enjoyed from the world that God has given us. Like all blessings of thanksgiving, the Blessing after Meals expresses a very basic emotion: the acknowledgment of kindness. This feeling is general, and even goes beyond the human realm, for animals, too, recognize the kindness done to them by their benefactors ("The ox knows its owner, and the donkey its master's crib" [Isaiah 1:3]). The sages commented that this is how Abraham would bring his visitors closer to the service of God: when they thanked him for the food they had eaten in his home, he would tell them that they ought also to acknowledge the source of all goodness.

Preparations

Before reciting the Blessing after Meals, it is a widespread custom to leave a piece of bread on the table, so that the table is not bare. Many people wear the same clothes they wear during their prayers, as a sign of the importance of this Blessing. In many places, people are careful during weekdays (and in some places on Shabbat as well) to remove or cover any knives on the table; the table is a kind of altar, and it is inappropriate for destructive iron tools to be on it.

Before the Blessing itself, a psalm is recited. This is done to imbue the meal with spiritual content. In the words of the sages, "A meal without words of Torah is considered as offerings of the dead" (*Pirkei Avot* 3:3). On weekdays, Psalm 137 is recited, which mentions the mourners of Zion, following the sages' counsel that one remember the destruction of the Temple during the course of a meal. On Shabbat and festivals, Psalm 126 is read, which speaks of the return to Zion.

Many people take care, in keeping with the words of the Mishnah and the Talmud, to perform *mayim aḥaronim,* washing the tips of the fingers before the Blessing after Meals. This water must then be removed from the table.

There are some people who, before the Blessing—as before the performance of any other mitzvah—recite, "I am ready and prepared to perform the positive commandment of Blessing after Meals, as is written: 'When you have eaten and are satiated, you shall bless the Lord your God for the good Land which He has given you.'" Some add: "For the sake of the unification of the Holy One, blessed be He, and His Shekhinah, hidden and concealed in the name of all Israel."

Zimmun

The *Zimmun* is an invitation to the Blessing after Meals, said whenever at least three men have eaten together (or three women, when eating by themselves). The obligation of *Zimmun* is a very ancient one, already mentioned in the Mishnah (*Berakhot* 7:1); some medieval authorities treat it as a Torah-based obligation, constituting an integral part of the Blessing.

The Talmud derives the institution of *Zimmun* from the verse "Magnify the Lord with me, and let us exalt His name together" (Psalms 34:4). This indicates the special significance attached to giving thanks to God publicly.

The Zohar states that there are two sides present in the act of eating: on the one hand, the aspect of the Shekhinah and of holiness, and, on the other hand, the bodily, physical side. Eating may be commandment-oriented, and thus be a matter of holiness, or it may be directed toward bodily enjoyment alone. Thus, one recites the *Zimmun* in order to invite the Shekhinah, as it were, to participate in the blessing. There is a special *Zimmun* formulation for wedding ceremonies (see page 187). The Seven Marriage Blessings (*Sheva Brakhot*) (see page 197) are also recited, when there is a quorum of ten present, both at the wedding feast and during the week following the wedding.

Overview

In its present form, the Blessing after Meals consists of five units: three blessings that are ancient and very basic (*Ha'Zan*—"He who provides sustenance"; *Ha'Aretz*—"For the Land"; *Boneh Yerushalayim*—"He who rebuilds Jerusalem"), which the sages of the Talmud (*Berakhot* 28b) related to the verse "When you shall eat and be satiated, you shall bless the Lord your God for the good Land which He has given you"; a fourth blessing added in mishnaic times (*Ha'Tov veha'Meitiv*—"He who is good and does good"); and an additional section (*Ha'Raḥaman*—"The Merciful One"), containing various phrases of praise and petition that were added during the Geonic period and later.

Birkat Ha'Zan—He Who Provides Sustenance

The opening blessing is a very general one, whose composition is attributed by the Talmud to Moses, written when Israel was still in the wilderness and sustained by manna from Heaven. Its main element is praise of God, who provides food for all living creatures, including us. It also includes a request that we never lack food.

Birkat Ha'Aretz—The Blessing for the Land

The second blessing connects our gratitude for the food we have eaten with the gift of the Land of Israel to the Jewish people. To this we add various other biblical phrases of praise for the Land, which acknowledge its superiority and express our rejoicing in it. According to rabbinic tradition, this blessing was introduced by Joshua following the conquest of the Land. We also mention other gifts given specifically to Israel: the Exodus from Egypt, circumcision, Torah, life, and food; each acquires special significance and meaning in the context of this blessing. Since this blessing is one of praise, on Ḥanukkah and Purim one adds here the passage *Al ha'Nissim* ("For the Miracles").

Boneh Yerushalayim—He Who Rebuilds Jerusalem

The essence of this blessing—which, according to tradition, was instituted by King David and his son Solomon—is prayer and petition for the Holy City and the Temple, as well as for the sustenance and well-being of Israel. We ask to receive our livelihood from God's hand in a good way, without needing loans or gifts from others.

Our sages (*Berakhot* 48b) found an allusion to this blessing, as they did for the first two blessings, in the verse "When you shall eat … you shall bless…." They read the words "the good" in this verse as alluding to Jerusalem and the Temple, based on the words "this good mountain and the Lebanon" (Deuteronomy 3:25). The point is that the gift of the Land of Israel as such is incomplete if it is merely the land; in order for it to be "the good Land," it needs to achieve the highest level of perfection possible for it—namely, the building of the Temple surrounded by the Holy City, and complete

Jewish sovereignty. When the Temple was standing, this blessing was expressed somewhat differently, referring to the Shekhinah residing forever within the Temple and in Jerusalem; after the destruction of the Temple, it was rephrased.

Since this blessing speaks of the perfection of spiritual levels, beyond food and the Land, it is also the appropriate moment to thank God for other good gifts that involve spiritual perfection—the Shabbat and festivals. On Shabbat, we add to this blessing the paragraph *Retzeh* ("Merit us and strengthen us"), which contains petitions related to the central theme of the blessing, with particular emphasis upon Shabbat. Similarly, on festivals and new months—days marked with joy, in which special sacrifices were offered in the Temple—we add *Yaaleh ve'Yavo* ("May there ascend"), in which we ask God to remember Israel, Jerusalem, and the Temple.

Ha'Tov veha'Meitiv—He Who Is Good and Does Good

According to tradition, this section was introduced after the abolition of the edicts made against Israel in wake of the Bar Kokhba revolt, especially when the Jews were finally permitted to bury the victims of that war, whose bodies had been left unburied for many years. This section includes general words of praise to God for His goodness and mercy to us. It was connected to the *Boneh Yerushalayim* blessing because, according to the Jerusalem Talmud, once the city of Betar was destroyed, the people of Israel will not be fully restored until the time of the Redemption.

This blessing essentially repeats the idea that God does good with us, and that we need to thank Him and to pray for future mercies.

Ha'Raḥaman—The Merciful One

The petitionary phrases beginning with *Ha'Raḥaman*—"The Merciful One"—are not part of the basic text of the Blessing, but were added from the time of the Talmud and the

Geonim onwards. Their text varies considerably among different communities, because they were added in various times and places, and such praises and prayers are not rigidly fixed. In any event, the predominant custom is that ten paragraphs beginning with *Ha'Raḥaman* should be recited regularly, ten being a perfect and sacred number. At the meal in honor of a circumcision, it is customary to add a number of special *Ha'Raḥaman* petitions.

Conclusion of the Blessing

After *Ha'Raḥaman*, it is customary to end the Blessing after Meals with the phrase *Oseh Shalom bi'Mromav* ("He Who Makes Peace on High"), and other verses that praise God and His kindness to all His creatures. This custom is an ancient one, already mentioned in early Siddurim.

The Blessing after Meals

שיר המעלות

A Song of Ascents (Psalm 126)

The following psalm [Psalm 126] is read before the Blessing after Meals is recited:

שִׁיר הַמַּעֲלוֹת. בְּשׁוּב יְיָ אֶת שִׁיבַת צִיּוֹן הָיִינוּ כְּחֹלְמִים. אָז יִמָּלֵא

Shir ha'maalot. Be'shuv Adonai et shivat Tziyyon, hayinu ke'ḥolmim. Az yimmale

שְׂחוֹק פִּינוּ, וּלְשׁוֹנֵנוּ רִנָּה, אָז יֹאמְרוּ בַגּוֹיִם: הִגְדִּיל יְיָ לַעֲשׂוֹת עִם אֵלֶּה.

sḥok pinu, u'lshonenu rinnah, Az yomru va'goyim: Higdil Adonai laasot im elleh,

הִגְדִּיל יְיָ לַעֲשׂוֹת עִמָּנוּ, הָיִינוּ שְׂמֵחִים. שׁוּבָה יְיָ אֶת שְׁבִיתֵנוּ

Higdil Adonai laasot immanu, hayinu smeḥim. Shuvah Adonai et shvitenu

כַּאֲפִיקִים בַּנֶּגֶב. הַזֹּרְעִים בְּדִמְעָה בְּרִנָּה יִקְצֹרוּ. הָלוֹךְ יֵלֵךְ וּבָכֹה

ka'afikim ba'negev. Ha'zorim be'dimah be'rinnah yiktzoru. Halokh yelekh u'vakhoh

נֹשֵׂא מֶשֶׁךְ הַזָּרַע, בֹּא יָבֹא בְרִנָּה נֹשֵׂא אֲלֻמֹּתָיו.

nose meshekh ha'zara, bo yavo ve'rinnah nose' alummotav.

זימון

Zimmun

(For the special *Zimmun* texts for a wedding feast see p. 187.)

When blessing with a quorum of three or more, the *Zimmun* leader begins:

רַבּוֹתַי, נְבָרֵךְ!

Rabbotai, nevarekh!

Those who join the *Zimmun* reply:

יְהִי שֵׁם יְיָ מְבֹרָךְ מֵעַתָּה וְעַד עוֹלָם.

Yehi shem Adonai mevorakh me'attah ve'ad olam.

The leader then repeats:

יְהִי שֵׁם יְיָ מְבֹרָךְ מֵעַתָּה וְעַד עוֹלָם.

Yehi shem Adonai mevorakh me'attah ve'ad olam.

And continues:

בִּרְשׁוּת מָרָנָן וְרַבָּנָן וְרַבּוֹתַי נְבָרֵךְ (בעשרה: אֱלֹהֵינוּ) שֶׁאָכַלְנוּ מִשֶּׁלּוֹ.

Bi'rshut maranan ve'rabbanan ve'rabbotai, nevarekh
(in a quorum of ten: *Eloheinu) she'akhalnu mi'shelo.*

Those present then say:

בָּרוּךְ (בעשרה: אֱלֹהֵינוּ) שֶׁאָכַלְנוּ מִשֶּׁלּוֹ וּבְטוּבוֹ חָיִינוּ.

*Barukh (*in ten: *Eloheinu) she'akhalnu me'shelo uve'tuvo ḥayinu.*

The *Zimmun* leader repeats:

בָּרוּךְ (בעשרה: אֱלֹהֵינוּ) שֶׁאָכַלְנוּ מִשֶּׁלּוֹ וּבְטוּבוֹ חָיִינוּ.

*Barukh (*in ten: *Eloheinu) she'akhalnu me'shelo uve'tuvo ḥayinu.*

And adds:

בָּרוּךְ הוּא וּבָרוּךְ שְׁמוֹ.

Barukh hu u'varukh shmo.

זימון

Zimmun for a Wedding Meal

In a wedding feast, the *Zimmun* leader begins as usual,
and after the words *me'attah ve'ad olam*, adds:

דְּוַי הָסֵר וְגַם חָרוֹן, וְאָז אִלֵּם בְּשִׁיר יָרוֹן.

Dvai haser ve'gam ḥaron, ve'az illem be'shir yaron,

נְחֵנוּ בְּמַעְגְּלֵי צֶדֶק, שְׁעֵה בִּרְכַּת בְּנֵי יְשׁוּרוּן, בְּנֵי אַהֲרֹן.

Neḥenu be'maaglei tzedek, she'eh birkat bnei Yeshurun, bnei Aharon.

בִּרְשׁוּת מָרָנָן וְרַבָּנָן וְרַבּוֹתַי,

Birshut maranan ve'rabbanan ve'rabbotai,

נְבָרֵךְ אֱלֹהֵינוּ שֶׁהַשִּׂמְחָה בִּמְעוֹנוֹ וְשֶׁאָכַלְנוּ מִשֶּׁלּוֹ.

Nevarekh Eloheinu she'hasimḥah bi'mono veshe'akhalnu mi'shelo.

Those present reply:

בָּרוּךְ אֱלֹהֵינוּ שֶׁהַשִּׂמְחָה בִּמְעוֹנוֹ,

Barukh Eloheinu she'hasimḥah bi'mono,

וְשֶׁאָכַלְנוּ מִשֶּׁלּוֹ וּבְטוּבוֹ חָיִינוּ.

Veshe'akhalnu mi'shelo uve'tuvo ḥayinu.

The *Zimmun* leader repeats:

בָּרוּךְ אֱלֹהֵינוּ שֶׁהַשִּׂמְחָה בִּמְעוֹנוֹ, וְשֶׁאָכַלְנוּ מִשֶּׁלּוֹ וּבְטוּבוֹ חָיִינוּ.

Barukh Eloheinu sheha'simḥah bi'mono, veshe'akhalnu mi'shelo uve'tuvo ḥayinu.

And adds:

בָּרוּךְ הוּא וּבָרוּךְ שְׁמוֹ.

Barukh hu u'varukh shmo.

ברכת המזון
The Blessing

ברכת הזן
He Who Provides Sustenance

בָּרוּךְ אַתָּה יְיָ, אֱלֹהֵינוּ מֶלֶךְ הָעוֹלָם, הַזָּן אֶת הָעוֹלָם כֻּלּוֹ בְּטוּבוֹ,
Barukh attah Adonai, Eloheinu melekh ha'olam, ha'zan et ha'olam kullo be'tuvo,
בְּחֵן בְּחֶסֶד וּבְרַחֲמִים. הוּא נוֹתֵן לֶחֶם לְכָל בָּשָׂר, כִּי לְעוֹלָם חַסְדּוֹ.
be'ḥen, be'ḥesed uve'raḥamim. Hu noten leḥem le'khol basar, ki le'olam ḥasdo,
וּבְטוּבוֹ הַגָּדוֹל תָּמִיד לֹא חָסַר לָנוּ וְאַל יֶחְסַר לָנוּ מָזוֹן לְעוֹלָם וָעֶד.
uv'tuvo ha'gadol tamid lo ḥasar lanu, ve'al yeḥsar lanu mazon le'olam va'ed;
בַּעֲבוּר שְׁמוֹ הַגָּדוֹל, כִּי הוּא אֵל זָן, וּמְפַרְנֵס לַכֹּל, וּמֵטִיב לַכֹּל,
ba'avur shmo ha'gadol, ki hu El zan, u'mefarnes la'kol, u'meitiv la'kol,
וּמֵכִין מָזוֹן לְכָל בְּרִיּוֹתָיו אֲשֶׁר בָּרָא (כָּאָמוּר: פּוֹתֵחַ אֶת יָדֶךָ
u'mekhin mazon le'khol briyyotav asher bara (ka'amur: poteaḥ et yadekha
וּמַשְׂבִּיעַ לְכָל חַי רָצוֹן). בָּרוּךְ אַתָּה יְיָ, הַזָּן אֶת הַכֹּל.
u'masbia le'khol ḥai ratzon). Barukh attah Adonai, ha'zan et ha'kol.

ברכת הארץ
The Blessing for the Land

נוֹדֶה לְּךָ יְיָ אֱלֹהֵינוּ עַל שֶׁהִנְחַלְתָּ לַאֲבוֹתֵינוּ אֶרֶץ חֶמְדָּה טוֹבָה
Nodeh lekha Adonai Eloheinu, al she'hinḥalta la'avoteinu eretz ḥemdah tovah
וּרְחָבָה, וְעַל שֶׁהוֹצֵאתָנוּ יְיָ אֱלֹהֵינוּ מֵאֶרֶץ מִצְרַיִם, וּפְדִיתָנוּ מִבֵּית
u'reḥavah, ve'al she'hotzetanu Adonai Eloheinu me'eretz Mitzrayim u'fditanu mi'beit

עֲבָדִים, וְעַל בְּרִיתְךָ שֶׁחָתַמְתָּ בִּבְשָׂרֵנוּ, וְעַל תּוֹרָתְךָ שֶׁלִּמַּדְתָּנוּ, וְעַל
avadim, ve'al britkha she'ḥatamta bi'vsarenu, ve'al toratkha she'limmadtanu, ve'al
חֻקֶּיךָ שֶׁהוֹדַעְתָּנוּ, וְעַל חַיִּים חֵן וָחֶסֶד שֶׁחוֹנַנְתָּנוּ, וְעַל אֲכִילַת
ḥukkekha she'hodatanu, ve'al ḥayyim, ḥen va'ḥesed she'ḥonantanu, ve'al akhilat
מָזוֹן שָׁאַתָּה זָן וּמְפַרְנֵס אוֹתָנוּ תָּמִיד, בְּכָל יוֹם וּבְכָל עֵת וּבְכָל שָׁעָה.
mazon she'attah zan u'mefarnes otanu tamid, be'khol yom uve'khol et uve'khol shaah.

On Ḥanukkah and Purim, one adds:

וְעַל הַנִּסִּים וְעַל הַפֻּרְקָן וְעַל הַגְּבוּרוֹת וְעַל הַתְּשׁוּעוֹת וְעַל הַנִּפְלָאוֹת וְעַל
Ve'al ha'nissim ve'al ha'purkan ve'al ha'gvurot ve'al ha'tshuot ve'al ha'niflaot ve'al
הַנֶּחָמוֹת וְעַל הַמִּלְחָמוֹת שֶׁעָשִׂיתָ לַאֲבוֹתֵינוּ בַּיָּמִים הָהֵם בַּזְּמַן הַזֶּה.
ha'neḥamot ve'al ha'milḥamot she'asita la'avoteinu ba'yamim ha'hem, ba'zman ha'zeh.

For Ḥanukkah:

בִּימֵי מַתִּתְיָהוּ בֶּן יוֹחָנָן כֹּהֵן גָּדוֹל חַשְׁמוֹנָאִי וּבָנָיו, כְּשֶׁעָמְדָה
Bi'ymei Mattityahu ben Yoḥanan kohen gadol Ḥashmonai u'vanav, keshe'amdah
מַלְכוּת יָוָן הָרְשָׁעָה עַל עַמְּךָ יִשְׂרָאֵל לְהַשְׁכִּיחָם תּוֹרָתֶךָ וּלְהַעֲבִירָם
malkhut Yavan ha'reshaa al ammkha Yisrael le'hashkiḥam toratekha ule'haaviram
מֵחֻקֵּי רְצוֹנֶךָ, וְאַתָּה בְּרַחֲמֶיךָ הָרַבִּים עָמַדְתָּ לָהֶם בְּעֵת
me'ḥukkei retzonekha, ve'attah be'raḥamekha ha'rabbim amadta lahem be'et
צָרָתָם, רַבְתָּ אֶת רִיבָם, דַּנְתָּ אֶת דִּינָם, נָקַמְתָּ אֶת נִקְמָתָם, מָסַרְתָּ גִבּוֹרִים
tzaratam, ravta et rivam, danta et dinam, nakamta et nikmatam, masarta gibborim
בְּיַד חַלָּשִׁים, וְרַבִּים בְּיַד מְעַטִּים, וּטְמֵאִים בְּיַד טְהוֹרִים, וּרְשָׁעִים
be'yad ḥallashim, ve'rabbim be'yad me'attim, u'tmeim be'yad tehorim, u'rshaim
בְּיַד צַדִּיקִים, וְזֵדִים בְּיַד עוֹסְקֵי תוֹרָתֶךָ. וּלְךָ עָשִׂיתָ שֵׁם גָּדוֹל
be'yad tzaddikim, ve'zedim be'yad oskei toratekha. U'lekha asita shem gadol
וְקָדוֹשׁ בְּעוֹלָמֶךָ, וּלְעַמְּךָ יִשְׂרָאֵל עָשִׂיתָ תְּשׁוּעָה גְדוֹלָה וּפֻרְקָן
ve'kadosh be'olamekha, ule'ammkha Yisrael asita tshuah gdolah u'furkan

כְּהַיּוֹם הַזֶּה. וְאַחַר כָּךְ בָּאוּ בָנֶיךָ לִדְבִיר בֵּיתֶךָ, וּפִנּוּ אֶת הֵיכָלֶךָ,

keba'yom ha'zeh. Ve'aḥar kakh ba'u vanekha li'dvir beitekha, u'finu et heikhalekha,

וְטִהֲרוּ אֶת מִקְדָּשֶׁךָ, וְהִדְלִיקוּ נֵרוֹת בְּחַצְרוֹת קָדְשֶׁךָ, וְקָבְעוּ שְׁמוֹנַת

ve'tiharu et mikdashekha, ve'hidliku nerot be'ḥatzrot kodshekha, ve'kavu shmonat

יְמֵי חֲנֻכָּה אֵלּוּ לְהוֹדוֹת וּלְהַלֵּל לְשִׁמְךָ הַגָּדוֹל.

yemei Ḥanukkah ellu lehodot u'lehallel le'shimkha ha'gadol.

For Purim:

בִּימֵי מָרְדְּכַי וְאֶסְתֵּר בְּשׁוּשַׁן הַבִּירָה, כְּשֶׁעָמַד עֲלֵיהֶם הָמָן

Bi'ymei Mordechai ve'Esther be'Shushan ha'birah, kshe'amad aleihem Haman

הָרָשָׁע, בִּקֵּשׁ לְהַשְׁמִיד לַהֲרֹג וּלְאַבֵּד אֶת כָּל הַיְּהוּדִים, מִנַּעַר וְעַד

ha'rasha bikkesh lehashmid, laharog u'le'abbed et kol ha'yehudim, mi'naar ve'ad

זָקֵן, טַף וְנָשִׁים, בְּיוֹם אֶחָד, בִּשְׁלֹשָׁה עָשָׂר לְחֹדֶשׁ שְׁנֵים עָשָׂר הוּא חֹדֶשׁ

zaken, taf ve'nashim be'yom eḥad, bi'shloshah asar le'ḥodesh shneim asar hu ḥodesh

אֲדָר, וּשְׁלָלָם לָבוֹז. וְאַתָּה בְּרַחֲמֶיךָ הָרַבִּים הֵפַרְתָּ אֶת עֲצָתוֹ, וְקִלְקַלְתָּ

Adar, u'shlalam lavoz, ve'attah be'raḥamekha ha'rabbim hefarta et atzato, ve'kilkalta

אֶת מַחֲשַׁבְתּוֹ, וַהֲשֵׁבוֹתָ לּוֹ גְּמוּלוֹ בְּרֹאשׁוֹ, וְתָלוּ אוֹתוֹ וְאֶת בָּנָיו עַל הָעֵץ.

et maḥashavto, ve'hashevota lo gmulo ve'rosho, ve'talu oto ve'et banav al ha'etz

(End of the special Ḥanukkah and Purim addition)

וְעַל הַכֹּל יְיָ אֱלֹהֵינוּ אֲנַחְנוּ מוֹדִים לָךְ וּמְבָרְכִים אוֹתָךְ, יִתְבָּרַךְ

ve'al ha'kol Adonai Eloheinu anaḥnu modim lakh u'mevarkhim otakh, yitbarakh

שִׁמְךָ בְּפִי כָּל חַי תָּמִיד לְעוֹלָם וָעֶד. כַּכָּתוּב: וְאָכַלְתָּ וְשָׂבָעְתָּ וּבֵרַכְתָּ

shimkha be'fi kol ḥai tamid le'olam va'ed, ka'katuv: ve'akhalta ve'savata u'verakhta

אֶת יְיָ אֱלֹהֶיךָ עַל הָאָרֶץ הַטֹּבָה אֲשֶׁר נָתַן לָךְ.

et Adonai Eloheikha al ha'aretz ha'tovah asher natan lakh.

בָּרוּךְ אַתָּה יְיָ עַל הָאָרֶץ וְעַל הַמָּזוֹן.

Barukh attah Adonai al ha'aretz ve'al ha'mazon.

בונה ירושלים

He Who Rebuilds Jerusalem

רַחֵם נָא יְיָ אֱלֹהֵינוּ עַל יִשְׂרָאֵל עַמֶּךָ, וְעַל יְרוּשָׁלַיִם עִירֶךָ, וְעַל

Raḥem na Adonai Eloheinu al Yisrael ammekha ve'al Yerushalayim irekha, ve'al

צִיּוֹן מִשְׁכַּן כְּבוֹדֶךָ, וְעַל מַלְכוּת בֵּית דָּוִד מְשִׁיחֶךָ, וְעַל הַבַּיִת

Tziyyon mishkan kvodekha, ve'al malkhut beit David meshiḥekha, ve'al ha'bayit

הַגָּדוֹל וְהַקָּדוֹשׁ שֶׁנִּקְרָא שִׁמְךָ עָלָיו. אֱלֹהֵינוּ, אָבִינוּ, רְעֵנוּ, זוּנֵנוּ,

ha'gadol veha'kadosh she'nikra shimkha alav. Eloheinu, avinu, re'enu, zunenu,

פַּרְנְסֵנוּ וְכַלְכְּלֵנוּ וְהַרְוִיחֵנוּ, וְהַרְוַח לָנוּ יְיָ אֱלֹהֵינוּ מְהֵרָה

parnesenu ve'khalkelenu ve'harviḥenu ve'harvaḥ lanu, Adoni Eloheinu, meherah

מִכָּל צָרוֹתֵינוּ. וְנָא אַל תַּצְרִיכֵנוּ יְיָ אֱלֹהֵינוּ לֹא לִידֵי מַתְּנַת בָּשָׂר

mi'kol tzaroteinu, ve'na al tatzrikhenu, Adonai Eloheinu, lo li'ydei matnat basar

וָדָם וְלֹא לִידֵי הַלְוָאָתָם, כִּי אִם לְיָדְךָ הַמְּלֵאָה, הַפְּתוּחָה, הַקְּדוֹשָׁה

va'dam ve'lo li'ydei halvaatam, ki im le'yadkha ha'mleah, ha'ptuḥah, ha'kdoshah

וְהָרְחָבָה, שֶׁלֹּא נֵבוֹשׁ וְלֹא נִכָּלֵם לְעוֹלָם וָעֶד.

veha'reḥavah, she'lo nevosh ve'lo nikkalem le'olam va'ed.

On Shabbat, one adds:

רְצֵה וְהַחֲלִיצֵנוּ, יְיָ אֱלֹהֵינוּ, בְּמִצְוֹתֶיךָ, וּבְמִצְוַת יוֹם הַשְּׁבִיעִי,

Retzeh ve'haḥalitzenu, Adonai Eloheinu, be'mitzvotekha, uve'mitzvat yom ha'shvii,

הַשַּׁבָּת הַגָּדוֹל וְהַקָּדוֹשׁ הַזֶּה. כִּי יוֹם זֶה גָּדוֹל וְקָדוֹשׁ הוּא לְפָנֶיךָ

ha'Shabbat ha'gadol veha'kadosh ha'zeh. Ki yom zeh gadol ve'kadosh hu lefanekha

לִשְׁבָּת בּוֹ וְלָנוּחַ בּוֹ בְּאַהֲבָה כְּמִצְוַת רְצוֹנֶךָ. וּבִרְצוֹנְךָ הָנִיחַ

lishbot bo ve'lanuaḥ bo be'ahavah ke'mitzvat retzonekha. Uvi'rtzonkha haniaḥ

לָנוּ, יְיָ אֱלֹהֵינוּ, שֶׁלֹּא תְהֵא צָרָה וְיָגוֹן וַאֲנָחָה בְּיוֹם מְנוּחָתֵנוּ,

lanu, Adonai Eloheinu, she'lo tehe tzara ve'yagon va'anaḥah be'yom menuḥatenu,

וְהַרְאֵנוּ, יְיָ אֱלֹהֵינוּ, בְּנֶחָמַת צִיּוֹן עִירֶךָ, וּבְבִנְיַן יְרוּשָׁלַיִם

ve'harenu, Adonai Eloheinu, be'neḥamat Tziyyon irekha, uve'vinyan Yerushalayim

עִיר קָדְשֶׁךָ, כִּי אַתָּה הוּא בַּעַל הַיְשׁוּעוֹת וּבַעַל הַנֶּחָמוֹת.

ir kodshekha, ki attah hu baal ha'yeshuot u'vaal ha'neḥamot.

(End of the Shabbat addition)

On Rosh Ḥodesh, festival days, and Ḥol ha'Moed, one adds this *Ya'aleh ve'Yavo* blessing:

אֱלֹהֵינוּ וֵאלֹהֵי אֲבוֹתֵינוּ, יַעֲלֶה וְיָבֹא וְיַגִּיעַ, וְיֵרָאֶה וְיֵרָצֶה

Eloheinu v'Elohei avoteinu, yaaleh ve'yavo ve'yagia, ve'yeraeh ve'yeratzeh

וְיִשָּׁמַע, וְיִפָּקֵד וְיִזָּכֵר, זִכְרוֹנֵנוּ וּפִקְדוֹנֵנוּ וְזִכְרוֹן אֲבוֹתֵינוּ,

ve'yishama, ve'yippaked ve'yizzakher, zikhronenu u'fikdonenu ve'zikhron avoteinu

וְזִכְרוֹן מָשִׁיחַ בֶּן דָּוִד עַבְדֶּךָ, וְזִכְרוֹן יְרוּשָׁלַיִם עִיר קָדְשֶׁךָ,

ve'zikhron mashiaḥ ben David avdekha, ve'zikhron Yerushalayim ir kodshekha

וְזִכְרוֹן כָּל עַמְּךָ בֵּית יִשְׂרָאֵל לְפָנֶיךָ, לִפְלֵיטָה, לְטוֹבָה, לְחֵן וּלְחֶסֶד

ve'zikhron kol ammkha beit Yisrael lefanekha li'fleitah, le'tovah, le'ḥen ule'ḥesed

וּלְרַחֲמִים, לְחַיִּים (טוֹבִים) וּלְשָׁלוֹם בְּיוֹם

ule'raḥamim, le'ḥayyim (tovim) ule'shalom, be'yom

On Rosh Ḥodesh:

רֹאשׁ הַחֹדֶשׁ הַזֶּה.

rosh ha'ḥodesh

On Pesaḥ:

חַג הַמַּצּוֹת

ḥag ha'matzot

On Shavuot:

חַג הַשָּׁבֻעוֹת

ḥag ha'shavuot

On Sukkot:

חַג הַסֻּכּוֹת

ḥag ha'sukkot

On Shmini Atzeret and Simḥat Torah:

שְׁמִינִי חַג הָעֲצֶרֶת

shmini ḥag ha'atzeret

On Rosh ha'Shanah:

הַזִּכָּרוֹן

ha'zikkaron

For Children who eat on Yom Kippur:

הַכִּפּוּרִים

ha'kippurim

הַזֶּה. זָכְרֵנוּ יְיָ אֱלֹהֵינוּ בּוֹ לְטוֹבָה, וּפָקְדֵנוּ בוֹ לִבְרָכָה, וְהוֹשִׁיעֵנוּ
ha'zeh Zokhrenu, Adonai Eloheinu, bo le'tovah, u'fokdenu vo li'vrakah, ve'hoshienu
בוֹ לְחַיִּים טוֹבִים. וּבִדְבַר יְשׁוּעָה וְרַחֲמִים חוּס וְחָנֵּנוּ וְרַחֵם עָלֵינוּ
vo le'ḥayyim tovim. Uvi'dvar yeshuah ve'raḥamim ḥus ve'ḥonenu ve'raḥem aleinu
וְהוֹשִׁיעֵנוּ, כִּי אֵלֶיךָ עֵינֵינוּ, כִּי אֵל מֶלֶךְ חַנּוּן וְרַחוּם אָתָּה.
ve'hoshienu, ki elekha eyneynu, ki El melekh ḥannun ve'raḥum attah.

(End of the *Ya'aleh ve'Yavo* addition)

וּבְנֵה יְרוּשָׁלַיִם עִיר הַקֹּדֶשׁ בִּמְהֵרָה בְיָמֵינוּ. בָּרוּךְ אַתָּה יְיָ,
U'vneh Yerushalayim ir ha'kodesh be'mherah ve'yameynu. Barukh attah Adonai,
בּוֹנֵה בְרַחֲמָיו יְרוּשָׁלָיִם, אָמֵן.
boneh ve'raḥamav Yerushalayim, Amen.

הטוב והמטיב

He Who Is Good and Does Good

בָּרוּךְ אַתָּה יְיָ, אֱלֹהֵינוּ מֶלֶךְ הָעוֹלָם, הָאֵל אָבִינוּ, מַלְכֵּנוּ, אַדִּירֵנוּ,
Barukh attah Adonai, Eloheinu melekh ha'olam, ha'El avinu, malkenu, addirenu,
בּוֹרְאֵנוּ, גּוֹאֲלֵנוּ, יוֹצְרֵנוּ, קְדוֹשֵׁנוּ, קְדוֹשׁ יַעֲקֹב, רוֹעֵנוּ, רוֹעֵה יִשְׂרָאֵל, הַמֶּלֶךְ
borenu, goalenu, yotzrenu, Kdoshenu, kdosh Yaakov, roenu, roeh Yisrael, ha'melekh
הַטּוֹב וְהַמֵּטִיב לַכֹּל, שֶׁבְּכָל יוֹם וָיוֹם הוּא הֵטִיב, הוּא מֵטִיב, הוּא יֵיטִיב לָנוּ,
ha'tov veha'meitiv la'kol, shebe'khol yom va'yom hu heitiv, hu meitiv, hu yeytiv lanu,
הוּא גְמָלָנוּ, הוּא גוֹמְלֵנוּ, הוּא יִגְמְלֵנוּ לָעַד, לְחֵן וּלְחֶסֶד וּלְרַחֲמִים וּלְרֶוַח,
hu gmalanu, hu gomlenu, hu yigmelenu la'ad, le'ḥen ul'ḥesed ul'raḥamim ul'revaḥ,
הַצָּלָה וְהַצְלָחָה, בְּרָכָה וִישׁוּעָה, נֶחָמָה, פַּרְנָסָה וְכַלְכָּלָה,
hatzalah ve'hatzlaḥah, brakhah vi'yshuah, neḥamah, parnasah ve'khalkalah,
וְרַחֲמִים וְחַיִּים וְשָׁלוֹם וְכָל טוֹב, וּמִכָּל טוּב לְעוֹלָם אַל יְחַסְּרֵנוּ.
ve'raḥamim ve'ḥayyim ve'shalom ve'khol tov, umi'kol tuv le'olam al yeḥasrenu.

הרחמן

The Merciful One

הָרַחֲמָן הוּא יִמְלֹךְ עָלֵינוּ לְעוֹלָם וָעֶד.

Ha'Raḥaman hu yimlokh aleinu le'olam va'ed.

הָרַחֲמָן הוּא יִתְבָּרַךְ בַּשָּׁמַיִם וּבָאָרֶץ.

Ha'Raḥaman hu yitbarakh ba'shamayim uva'aretz.

הָרַחֲמָן הוּא יִשְׁתַּבַּח לְדוֹר דּוֹרִים, וְיִתְפָּאַר בָּנוּ לָעַד וּלְנֵצַח נְצָחִים,

Ha'Raḥaman hu yishtabbaḥ le'dor dorim, ve'yitpaar banu la'ad ule'netzaḥ netzaḥim,

וְיִתְהַדַּר בָּנוּ לָעַד וּלְעוֹלְמֵי עוֹלָמִים. הָרַחֲמָן הוּא יְפַרְנְסֵנוּ בְּכָבוֹד.

ve'yithaddar banu la'ad ule'olmey olamim. Ha'Raḥaman hu yefarnesenu be'khavod.

הָרַחֲמָן הוּא יִשְׁבֹּר עֹל גָּלוּת מֵעַל צַוָּארֵנוּ, וְהוּא יוֹלִיכֵנוּ קוֹמְמִיּוּת

Ha'Raḥaman hu yishbor ol galut me'al tzavarenu, ve'hu yolikhenu komemiyut

לְאַרְצֵנוּ. הָרַחֲמָן הוּא יִשְׁלַח לָנוּ בְּרָכָה מְרֻבָּה בַּבַּיִת הַזֶּה, וְעַל

le'artzenu. Ha'Raḥaman hu yishlaḥ lanu brakhah merubah ba'bayit ha'zeh, ve'al

שֻׁלְחָן זֶה שֶׁאָכַלְנוּ עָלָיו. הָרַחֲמָן הוּא יִשְׁלַח לָנוּ אֶת אֵלִיָּהוּ הַנָּבִיא

shulḥan zeh she'akhalnu alav. Ha'Raḥaman hu yishlaḥ lanu et Eliyahu ha'navi,

זָכוּר לַטּוֹב, וִיבַשֶּׂר לָנוּ בְּשׂוֹרוֹת טוֹבוֹת, יְשׁוּעוֹת וְנֶחָמוֹת.

zakhur la'tov, vi'yvasser lanu bsorot tovot, yeshuot ve'neḥamot.

One who eats at other people's table says:

הָרַחֲמָן הוּא יְבָרֵךְ אֶת (אָבִי מוֹרִי) בַּעַל הַבַּיִת הַזֶּה, וְאֶת (אִמִּי מוֹרָתִי)

Ha'Raḥaman hu yevarekh et (avi mori) ba'al ha'bayit ha'zeh, ve'et (immi morati)

בַּעֲלַת הַבַּיִת הַזֶּה, אוֹתָם וְאֶת בֵּיתָם וְאֶת זַרְעָם וְאֶת כָּל אֲשֶׁר לָהֶם,

ba'alat ha'bayit ha'zeh, otam ve'et beytam ve'et zaram ve'et kol asher lahem,

One who eats at one's own table says:

הָרַחֲמָן הוּא יְבָרֵךְ (אֶת אָבִי מוֹרִי וְאֶת אִמִּי מוֹרָתִי), אוֹתִי (וְאֶת

Ha'Raḥaman hu yevarekh (et avi mori ve'et immi morati,) oti (ve'et

A married woman says:

וְאֶת בַּעְלִי,

Ve'et ba'li,

A married man says:

וְאֶת אִשְׁתִּי,

Ve'et ishti,

Both add:

וְאֶת זַרְעִי וְאֶת כָּל אֲשֶׁר לִי),

ve'et zar'i ve'et kol asher li),

אוֹתָנוּ וְאֶת כָּל אֲשֶׁר לָנוּ, כְּמוֹ שֶׁנִּתְבָּרְכוּ אֲבוֹתֵינוּ, אַבְרָהָם יִצְחָק וְיַעֲקֹב,

otanu ve'et kol asher lanu, kmo she'nitbarkhu avoteinu, Avraham, Yitzhak ve'Yaakov,

בַּכֹּל מִכֹּל כֹּל, כֵּן יְבָרֵךְ אוֹתָנוּ כֻּלָּנוּ יַחַד בִּבְרָכָה שְׁלֵמָה, וְנֹאמַר אָמֵן.

ba'kol mi'kol kol, ken yevarekh otanu kullanu yaḥad bi'vrakha shlema, ve'nomar Amen.

בַּמָּרוֹם יְלַמְּדוּ עֲלֵיהֶם וְעָלֵינוּ זְכוּת שֶׁתְּהֵא לְמִשְׁמֶרֶת שָׁלוֹם, וְנִשָּׂא

Ba'marom yelammdu aleihem ve'aleinu zkhut she'tehe le'mishmeret shalom, ve'nissa

בְרָכָה מֵאֵת יְיָ, וּצְדָקָה מֵאֱלֹהֵי יִשְׁעֵנוּ, וְנִמְצָא חֵן וְשֵׂכֶל טוֹב

vrakha me'et Adonai, u'tzdaka m'Elohei yishenu, ve'nimtza ḥen ve'sekhel tov

בְּעֵינֵי אֱלֹהִים וְאָדָם.

be'eyney Elohim ve'adam.

The Guest's Blessing:

יְהִי רָצוֹן שֶׁלֹּא יֵבוֹשׁ בַּעַל הַבַּיִת בָּעוֹלָם הַזֶּה, וְלֹא יִכָּלֵם לָעוֹלָם הַבָּא,

Yehi ratzon she'lo yevosh baal ha'bayit ba'olam ha'zeh, ve'lo yikkalem le'olam ha'ba,

וְיִצְלַח מְאֹד בְּכָל נְכָסָיו, וְיִהְיוּ נְכָסָיו וּנְכָסֵינוּ מֻצְלָחִים

ve'yitzlaḥ meod be'khol nekhasav, ve'yihyu nekhasav u'nekhaseinu mutzlaḥim

וּקְרוֹבִים לָעִיר. וְאַל יִשְׁלֹט שָׂטָן לֹא בְּמַעֲשֵׂה יָדָיו וְלֹא בְּמַעֲשֵׂה יָדֵינוּ,

u'krovim la'ir. Ve'al yishlot satan lo be'maaseh yadav ve'lo be'maaseh yadeinu,

וְאַל יִזְדַּקֵּק לֹא לְפָנָיו וְלֹא לְפָנֵינוּ שׁוּם דְּבַר הִרְהוּר חֵטְא וַעֲבֵירָה וְעָוֹן,

ve'al yizdakkek lo lefanav ve'lo lefaneinu shum dvar hirhur ḥet va'avera ve'avon,

מֵעַתָּה וְעַד עוֹלָם.

me'attah ve'ad olam.

For Shabbat:

הָרַחֲמָן הוּא יַנְחִילֵנוּ יוֹם שֶׁכֻּלּוֹ שַׁבָּת וּמְנוּחָה לְחַיֵּי הָעוֹלָמִים.

Ha'Raḥaman hu yanḥilenu yom she'kullo Shabbat u'mnuḥah le'ḥayey ha'olamim.

For Rosh Ḥodesh:

הָרַחֲמָן הוּא יְחַדֵּשׁ עָלֵינוּ אֶת הַחֹדֶשׁ הַזֶּה לְטוֹבָה וְלִבְרָכָה.

Ha'Raḥaman hu yeḥaddesh aleinu et ha'ḥodesh ha'zeh le'tovah ve'livrakhah.

For Festival Days:

הָרַחֲמָן הוּא יַנְחִילֵנוּ יוֹם שֶׁכֻּלּוֹ טוֹב (לְיוֹם שֶׁכֻּלּוֹ אָרוּךְ, לְיוֹם

Ha'Raḥaman hu yanḥilenu yom she'kullo tov (le'yom she'kullo arokh, le'yom

שֶׁצַּדִּיקִים יוֹשְׁבִין וְעַטְרוֹתֵיהֶם בְּרָאשֵׁיהֶם וְנֶהֱנִין מִזִּיו הַשְּׁכִינָה,

she'tzaddikim yoshvin ve'atroteihem be'rasheihem, ve'nehenin mi'ziv ha'Shkhinah,

וִיהִי חֶלְקֵנוּ עִמָּהֶם).

vi'yhi ḥelkenu immahem).

For Rosh ha'Shanah:

הָרַחֲמָן הוּא יְחַדֵּשׁ עָלֵינוּ אֶת הַשָּׁנָה הַזֹּאת לְטוֹבָה וְלִבְרָכָה.

Ha'Raḥaman hu yeḥaddesh aleinu et ha'shanah ha'zot le'tovah ve'livrakhah.

For Sukkot:

הָרַחֲמָן הוּא יָקִים לָנוּ אֶת סֻכַּת דָּוִד הַנּוֹפָלֶת.

Ha'Raḥaman hu yakim lanu et sukkat David ha'nofalet.

הָרַחֲמָן הוּא יְזַכֵּנוּ לִימוֹת הַמָּשִׁיחַ וּלְחַיֵּי הָעוֹלָם הַבָּא.

Ha'Raḥaman, hu yezakkenu li'ymot ha'mashiaḥ ule'ḥayyey ha'olam ha'ba.

מַגְדִּיל (בשבת ובכל יום שיש בו מוסף אומרים: מִגְדּוֹל) יְשׁוּעוֹת מַלְכּוֹ וְעֹשֶׂה חֶסֶד

Magdil (On Shabbat and on all other days in which the *Musaf* prayer is recited, one says instead: *Migdol*) *yeshuot malko, ve'oseh ḥesed*

לִמְשִׁיחוֹ, לְדָוִד וּלְזַרְעוֹ עַד עוֹלָם.

li'mshiḥo, le'David ule'zaro ad olam,

עֹשֶׂה שָׁלוֹם בִּמְרוֹמָיו הוּא יַעֲשֶׂה שָׁלוֹם עָלֵינוּ וְעַל כָּל יִשְׂרָאֵל וְאִמְרוּ אָמֵן.

Oseh shalom bi'mromav hu yaaseh shalom aleinu ve'al kol Yisrael, ve'imru amen.

יְראוּ אֶת יְיָ קְדוֹשָׁיו, כִּי אֵין מַחְסוֹר לִירֵאָיו. כְּפִירִים רָשׁוּ וְרָעֵבוּ, וְדוֹרְשֵׁי

Yiru et Adonai kdoshav, ki ein maḥsor li'yreav. Kfirim rashu ve'raevu, ve'dorshei

יְיָ לֹא יַחְסְרוּ כָל טוֹב. הוֹדוּ לַיְיָ כִּי טוֹב, כִּי לְעוֹלָם חַסְדּוֹ. פּוֹתֵחַ אֶת יָדֶךָ,

Adonai lo yaḥseru khol tov. Hodu l'Adonai ki tov, ki le'olam ḥasdo. Poteaḥ et yadekha,

וּמַשְׂבִּיעַ לְכָל חַי רָצוֹן. בָּרוּךְ הַגֶּבֶר אֲשֶׁר יִבְטַח בַּייָ, וְהָיָה יְיָ

u'masbia le'khol ḥai ratzon. Barukh ha'gever asher yivtaḥ b'Adonai, ve'hayah Adonai

מִבְטַחוֹ. נַעַר הָיִיתִי גַּם זָקַנְתִּי, וְלֹא רָאִיתִי צַדִּיק נֶעֱזָב וְזַרְעוֹ מְבַקֶּשׁ

mivtaḥo. Naar hayiti gam zakanti, ve'lo raiti tzaddik ne'ezavw ve'zaro mevakkesh

לָחֶם. יְיָ עֹז לְעַמּוֹ יִתֵּן, יְיָ יְבָרֵךְ אֶת עַמּוֹ בַשָּׁלוֹם.

laḥem. Adonai oz le'ammo yitten, Adonai yevarekh et ammo ba'shalom.

שבע ברכות

The Seven Marriage Blessings (Sheva Brakhot)

At a wedding feast meal, in which there is a quorum of ten,
one now adds the seven marriage blessings:

1. בָּרוּךְ אַתָּה יְיָ, אֱלֹהֵינוּ מֶלֶךְ הָעוֹלָם, שֶׁהַכֹּל בָּרָא לִכְבוֹדוֹ.

1. *Barukh attah Adonai, Eloheinu melekh ha'olam, she'hakkol bara li'khvodo.*

2. בָּרוּךְ אַתָּה יְיָ, אֱלֹהֵינוּ מֶלֶךְ הָעוֹלָם, יוֹצֵר הָאָדָם.

2. *Barukh attah Adonai, Eloheinu melekh ha'olam, yotzer ha'adam.*

3. בָּרוּךְ אַתָּה יְיָ, אֱלֹהֵינוּ מֶלֶךְ הָעוֹלָם, אֲשֶׁר יָצַר אֶת הָאָדָם בְּצַלְמוֹ,

3. Barukh attah Adonai, Eloheinu melekh ha'olam, asher yatzar et ha'adam be'tzalmo,

בְּצֶלֶם דְּמוּת תַּבְנִיתוֹ, וְהִתְקִין לוֹ מִמֶּנּוּ בִּנְיַן עֲדֵי עַד.

be'tzelem demut tavnito, ve'hitkin lo mimmenu binyan adei ad.

בָּרוּךְ אַתָּה יְיָ, יוֹצֵר הָאָדָם.

Barukh attah Adonai, yotzer ha'adam.

4. שׂוֹשׂ תָּשִׂישׂ וְתָגֵל הָעֲקָרָה בְּקִבּוּץ בָּנֶיהָ לְתוֹכָהּ בְּשִׂמְחָה.

4. Sos tasis ve'tagel ha'akarah, be'kibbutz banehah le'tokhah be'simḥah.

בָּרוּךְ אַתָּה יְיָ, מְשַׂמֵּחַ צִיּוֹן בְּבָנֶיהָ.

Barukh attah Adonai, mesammeaḥ Tziyyon be'vanehah.

5. שַׂמֵּחַ תְּשַׂמַּח רֵעִים הָאֲהוּבִים כְּשַׂמֵּחֲךָ יְצִירְךָ בְּגַן עֵדֶן מִקֶּדֶם.

5. Sammeaḥ tesammaḥ reim ha'ahuvim, ke'sameḥakha yetzirkha be'gan eden mi'kedem.

בָּרוּךְ אַתָּה יְיָ, מְשַׂמֵּחַ חָתָן וְכַלָּה.

Barukh attah Adonai, mesammeaḥ ḥatan ve'khallah.

6. בָּרוּךְ אַתָּה יְיָ, אֱלֹהֵינוּ מֶלֶךְ הָעוֹלָם, אֲשֶׁר בָּרָא שָׂשׂוֹן וְשִׂמְחָה, חָתָן

6. Barukh attah Adonai, Eloheinu melekh ha'olam, asher bara sason ve'simḥah, ḥatan

וְכַלָּה, גִּילָה, רִנָּה, דִּיצָה וְחֶדְוָה, אַהֲבָה וְאַחֲוָה וְשָׁלוֹם וְרֵעוּת.

ve'khallah, gilah, rinnah, ditzah ve'ḥedvah, ahavah ve'aḥavah, ve'shalom ve'reut.

מְהֵרָה יְיָ אֱלֹהֵינוּ יִשָּׁמַע בְּעָרֵי יְהוּדָה וּבְחוּצוֹת יְרוּשָׁלָיִם, קוֹל שָׂשׂוֹן

Meherah Adonai Eloheinu yishama be'arei Yehudah uve'ḥutzot Yerushalayim, kol sason

וְקוֹל שִׂמְחָה, קוֹל חָתָן וְקוֹל כַּלָּה, קוֹל מִצְהֲלוֹת חֲתָנִים מֵחֻפָּתָם וּנְעָרִים

ve'kol simḥah, kol ḥatan ve'kol kallah, kol mitzhalot ḥatanim me'ḥuppatam u'ne'arim

מִמִּשְׁתֵּה נְגִינָתָם. בָּרוּךְ אַתָּה יְיָ, מְשַׂמֵּחַ חָתָן עִם הַכַּלָּה.

mi'mishteh neginatam. Barukh attah Adonai, mesammeaḥ ḥatan im ha'kallah.

Then the *Zimmun* leader says:

7. בָּרוּךְ אַתָּה יְיָ, אֱלֹהֵינוּ מֶלֶךְ הָעוֹלָם, בּוֹרֵא פְּרִי הַגָּפֶן.

7. Barukh attah Adonai, Eloheinu melekh ha'olam, bore' pri ha'gafen.

The Blessing after Meals, Translation and Commentary

A Song of Ascents (Psalm 126)

A Song of Ascents. When the Lord returns the exiles of Zion, we will have been like dreamers. Then our mouth will be filled with laughter, and our tongue with songs of joy; then will they say among the nations, "The Lord has done great things for these." The Lord has done great things for us; we were joyful. Lord, return our exiles as streams in the desert. Those who sow in tears will reap with songs of joy. He goes along weeping, carrying the bag of seeds; he will surely return with songs of joy, carrying his sheaves.

Commentary

This is one of the Songs of Ascent (Psalms 120–134), which were sung on the steps (*maalot;* literally, "ascents") of the Temple, and mentioned in the Mishnah's description (*Sukkah* 5:4) of the Temple celebration of Sukkot.

When the Lord returns the exiles of Zion, we will have been like dreamers: The literal meaning is that when we return to Zion, it will seem unreal to us, like the wonder of a dream. But the sages understood the exact opposite: that at the time of redemption, we will understand that now, at the time of exile, we were "like dreamers." The exile will have been no more than an extended sleep of the soul of the people, a kind of nightmare from which the people of Israel will awake.

Then our mouth will be filled with laughter: The sages say that a Jew's mouth should not be filled with laughter until the return from Zion. Only then will a Jew be able to rejoice wholeheartedly.

Lord, return our exiles as streams in the desert: Like dry stream beds in the desert that suddenly fill up with water and with life, on a day when everything seems dry and parched.

Those who sow in tears: Who anticipate and labor for the return to Zion, with grave doubts that their labor will have been in vain—**will reap with songs of joy:** "Those who sow in tears" are the people.

He goes along weeping, carrying the bag of seed: The one who sows in sorrow, who cannot believe that any good will come from his work; **he will surely return with songs of joy, carrying his sheaves:** He himself will return at harvest time with song, when the hidden blessing becomes evident.

Zimmun

When blessing with a quorum of three or more, the *Zimmun* Leader begins:

Friends, let us say the Blessings!

Those who join the *Zimmun* reply:

May the Name of the Lord be blessed from now and to all eternity.

The *Zimmun* leader repeats:

May the Name of the Lord be blessed from now and to all eternity. With your permission, friends, let us bless Him (in a quorum of ten: our God) of whose bounty we have eaten.

Those present then say:

Blessed be He (in ten: our God) of whose bounty we have eaten, and by whose goodness we live.

The *Zimmun* leader repeats:

Blessed be He (in ten: our God) of whose bounty we have eaten, and by whose goodness we live.

And adds:

May He be blessed, and His Name be blessed.

Commentary

Of whose bounty we have eaten: This is, in effect, the essence and root of the blessing: thanks to the Almighty, that everything is essentially His. As the verse says, "For all things come from You, and of Your own we have given You" (1 Chronicles 29:14).

And by whose goodness we live: That is, our lives are conducted with His goodness and mercy.

Zimmun for a Wedding Meal

In a wedding feast, after the *Zimmun* leader says, "May the Name of the Lord be blessed from now and to all eternity," he adds:

Remove from us suffering and anger, and then the mute will burst forth in song; guide us in the path of righteousness; accept the blessing of the sons of Jeshurun, [of] the children of Aaron. With your permission, (masters and) friends, let us bless our God in whose Abode there is joy, of whose bounty we have eaten.

Those present reply:

Blessed be our God in whose Abode there is joy, of whose bounty we have eaten, and through whose goodness we live.

The *Zimmun* leader repeats:

Blessed be our God in whose Abode there is joy, of whose bounty we have eaten, and through whose goodness we live.

And adds:

May He be blessed, and His Name be blessed.

This special *Zimmun* is written in rhyme.

Remove from us suffering and anger: A time of great joy is a suitable occasion to ask for the full joy of the Redemption, for that time when there will no longer be any pain or anger.

And then the mute will burst forth in song: This is one of the descriptions of the Redemption (Isaiah 35:6).

Guide us in the path of righteousness: In the words of King David, "He directs me in the paths of righteousness for the sake of His name" (Psalm 23:3).

Accept the blessing of the sons of Jeshurun, of the children of Aaron: This refers to the blessing by which the priests (*cohanim,* the sons of Aaron) bless Israel (the sons of Jeshurun), as they are commanded, "And I shall place my name on the children of Israel, and I will bless them" (Numbers 6:27). It is customary to ask a *cohen* to lead the *Zimmun* (if one is present). This, then, is a request that the blessing of the *cohen*, which is that of all those gathered, be acceptable to God.

The Blessing

Birkat Ha'Zan—He Who Provides Sustenance

Blessed are You, Lord our God, King of the universe, who, in His goodness, provides sustenance for the entire world, with grace, with kindness and with mercy. He gives food to all flesh, for His kindness is everlasting. Through His great goodness to us continuously we do not lack food and may we never lack food, for the sake of His great Name. For He, benevolent God, provides nourishment and sustenance for all, does good to all, and prepares food for all His creatures whom He has created, (as it is said:

"You open Your hand and satisfy the desire of every living thing" [Psalms 145:16]). Blessed are You Lord, who provides food for all.

Commentary

With grace, with kindness and with mercy: This is how our food is given to us: through the goodness and mercies of God, in a manner of grace (freely), and with kindness and compassion.

He gives food to all flesh, for His kindness is everlasting: In the words of the psalmist (Psalms 136:25), which speak not only of food, but also of the satisfaction of all the needs of every living creature.

He ... provides nourishment and sustenance for all, does good to all: Medieval exegetes explained that "nourishment" refers to food, "sustenance" refers to all other needs, and "does good" refers to other aspects of goodness and blessing.

As it is said: "You open Your hand and satisfy the desire of every living thing" (Psalms 145:16): In some communities, it is the custom to stretch forth the palms of both hands upon reciting this verse, as a sign of receiving blessing.

Birkat Ha'Aretz—The Blessing for the Land

We offer thanks to You, Lord our God, for having given as a heritage to our ancestors a precious, good, and spacious land; for having brought us out, Lord our God, from the land of Egypt and redeemed us from the house of bondage; for Your covenant which You have sealed in our flesh; for Your Torah which You have taught us; for Your statutes which You have made known to us; for the life, favor, and kindness which You have graciously bestowed upon us; and for the food we eat with which You constantly nourish and sustain us every day, at all times, and at every hour.

Commentary

A precious ... land: One that everyone desires and covets. This term is used in the Bible to refer to the Land of Israel (as in Jeremiah 3:19 and elsewhere).

Good and spacious: As in the words of the verse "a good and spacious land" (Exodus 3:8)." This blessing of thanksgiving also includes thanks for other favors that the Lord has conferred upon us.

For having brought us out ... from the land of Egypt: Mentioned in every thanksgiving and on every occasion, as it is the beginning and essence of the coming into being of the people.

We also give thanks for Your covenant which You have sealed in our flesh: That is, the covenant of circumcision, which is the first covenant and sign of the first gift that God gave to our ancestors. Thereafter, **we give thanks for Your Torah**, the written Torah, **and for Your statutes,** in the oral law and in the tradition.

For life, favor, and kindness ... and for the food we eat ... every day, at all times, and at every hour: Some people objected to this formulation because of the redundancy in its wording. Others, however, argued that in every day there are four periods, corresponding to the changes between day and night; others suggested that time refers to one of the seasons of the year; still others said that time does not refer to any specific, clearly defined period of time, but rather to a certain mode of life, as stated in Ecclesiastes 3:8, "a time for war and a time for peace…" and so on.

On Hanukkah and Purim, one adds:

And [we thank You] for the miracles, for the redemption, for the mighty deeds, for the saving acts, and for the wonders, and for the consolations and for the battles which You have wrought for our ancestors in those days, at this time.

For Ḥanukkah:

In the days of Matityahu, the son of Yoḥanan the High Priest, the Hasmonean and his sons, when the wicked [Hellenic] government rose up against Your people Israel to make them forget Your Torah and violate the decrees of Your will. But You, in Your abounding mercies, stood by them in the time of their distress. You waged their battles, defended their rights, and avenged the wrong done to them. You delivered the mighty into the hands of the weak, the many into the hands of the few, the impure into the hands of the pure, the wicked into the hands of the righteous, and the wanton sinners into the hands of those who occupy themselves with Your Torah. You made a great and holy name for Yourself in Your world, and effected a great deliverance and redemption for Your people to this very day. Then Your children entered the shrine of Your House, cleansed Your Temple, purified Your Sanctuary, kindled lights in Your holy courtyards, and instituted these eight days of Ḥanukkah to give thanks and praise to Your great Name.

For Purim:

In the days of Mordechai and Esther, in Shushan the capital, when the wicked Haman rose up against them, and sought to destroy, slaughter, and annihilate all the Jews, young and old, infants and women, in one day, on the thirteenth day of the twelfth month, the month of Adar, and to take their spoil for plunder. But You, in Your abounding mercies foiled his counsel, and frustrated his intention, and caused the evil he planned to recoil on his own head, and they hanged him and his sons upon the gallows.

(End of the Ḥanukkah and Purim addition)

For all this, Lord our God, we give thanks to You and bless You. May Your Name be blessed by the mouth of every living being, constantly and forever. As it is written: "When you have eaten and are satiated, you shall bless the Lord your God for the good land which He has given you" (Deuteronomy 8:10). Blessed are You, Lord, for the land and for the sustenance.

Commentary

For all this: So far, we have spoken about various specific things for which we give thanks. Now we add and include all those things that have not been mentioned yet.

As it is written: "And when you have eaten and are satiated, you shall bless the Lord your God for the good land which He has given you": At this point, the text returns to the main theme of the blessing, so as to conclude with it, as in the final phrase, "for the land and for the sustenance."

Some people are accustomed, following the Kabbalah, to add a drop of water to the cup of wine of *Zimmun* while saying the word *et* (the connective in the phrase "the Lord your God"), a custom supported by halakhah as well. The idea, according to Kabbalah, is to sweeten the judgment (symbolized by wine) with mercies (symbolized by water). This custom also reflects the love and praise of the Land of Israel, for which this blessing was instituted, by showing that its wine is so good and powerful that it needs to be mixed with water.

Blessed are You, Lord, for the land and for the sustenance: The Talmud [*Berakhot* 49a] comments that we do not ordinarily conclude a blessing with two different subjects; however, in this case there is a logical connection between the two—the land that brings forth sustenance.

Boneh Yerushalayim— He Who Rebuilds Jerusalem

Have mercy, Lord our God, upon Israel Your people, upon Jerusalem Your city, upon Zion the abode of Your glory, upon the kingship of the house of David Your anointed, and upon the great and holy House over which Your Name was proclaimed. Our God, our Father, our Shepherd, nourish us, sustain us, feed us, and provide us with plenty; and speedily, Lord our God, grant us relief from all our afflictions. Lord our God, please do not make us dependent upon the gifts of mortal men nor upon their loans, but only upon Your full, open, holy, and generous hand, that we may never be shamed or disgraced.

Commentary

Have mercy ... upon Israel Your people—in all their concerns and troubles; **upon Jerusalem Your city**—that it be rebuilt and restored to its full glory; **upon the kingship of the house of David Your anointed**—a prayer for the restoration of the

Davidic monarchy and the coming of the Messiah; **and upon the great and holy House,** the Temple, **over which Your name was proclaimed,** as the Temple is called the House of the Lord.

Our God, our Father—in any formula of petitionary prayer, whenever there are supplications, we refer to God as a father who has mercy on His children; **our shepherd**—as in the verse "shepherd of Israel" (Psalms 80:2), God being the leader and the one who provides for all the needs of His people Israel.

Provide us with plenty—that is, give us abundantly, so that the gift of food and sustenance also be with a full and open hand, and **grant us relief from all our afflictions.**

Do not make us dependent upon the gifts of mortal men—so that we not be forced to receive our sustenance through means of charity or generosity; **nor upon their loans, but only upon Your full, open … hand**—we ask for a livelihood that will come from the hand of the Lord, who has many gifts, without limitation. Some have commented that these words entail a paradox, intended to emphasize the uniqueness of God's gifts: a human hand cannot be both full and open; but these limitations apply only to human beings, not to God, who can do everything simultaneously.

That we may never be shamed or disgraced—while gifts of human beings may be consumed with a certain feeling of shame and disgrace.

On Shabbat, one adds:

May it please You, Lord our God, to strengthen us through Your mitzvot, and through the mitzvah of the Seventh Day, this great and holy Shabbat. For this day is great and holy before You, to refrain from work and to rest thereon with love, in accordance with the commandment of Your will. In Your good will, Lord our God, bestow upon us tranquility, that there will be no distress, sadness, or sorrow on the day of our rest. Lord our God, let us see the consolation of Zion Your city, and the rebuilding of Jerusalem Your holy city, for You are the Master of deliverance and the Master of consolation.

Commentary

May it please You—here we ask that God be pleased with us, **to strengthen us,** that He give us relief and freedom (the Hebrew ***haḥalitzenu*** comes from the same root as *ḥilutz atzamot:* strengthening of bones) **through your mitzvot**—in general, **and through the mitzvah of the Seventh Day, this great and holy Shabbat** in particular.

For this day is great and holy before You, to refrain from work and to rest thereon—because it is a day of holiness, we can also feel rest and relief; **with love**, of God to us and of ourselves to God; **in accordance with the commandment of Your will**, as You wished us to do on the Shabbat, out of that very same love.

In Your good will ... bestow upon us tranquility—for this, through the manifestation of Your will and Your mercies, give us rest.

Let us see—from here, the blessing turns to a more general emphasis: that precisely on the day of rest and calmness of soul, it is appropriate to mention those things that we are still lacking for the wholeness of our souls; **the consolation of Zion Your city, and the rebuilding of Jerusalem Your holy city**—for there is no comfort, rest, or joy, save through complete salvation.

On Rosh Ḥodesh, festival days, and *Ḥol ha'Moed*, one adds this *Ya'aleh ve'Yavo* blessing:

Our God and God of our fathers, may there ascend, come, and reach, be seen, accepted, and heard, recalled and remembered before You, the remembrance and recollection of us, the remembrance of our fathers, the remembrance of Messiah the son of David Your servant, the remembrance of Jerusalem Your holy city, and the remembrance of all Your people the House of Israel, for deliverance, well-being, grace, kindness, mercy, good life, and peace, on this day of

On Rosh Ḥodesh:	On Pesaḥ:	On Shavuot:	On Sukkot:
Rosh Ḥodesh.	Festival of Matzot.	Festival of Shavuot.	Festival of Sukkot.

On Rosh ha'Shanah: | On Shmini Atzeret and Simḥat Torah: | For Children who eat on Yom Kippur:

Remembrance. | Shmini Atzeret, the Festival. | Day of Atonement.

Remember us on this [day], Lord our God, for good; be mindful of us on this [day] for blessing; help us on this [day] for good life. With the promise of deliverance and compassion, spare us and be gracious to us; have mercy upon us and deliver us; for our eyes are directed to You, for You, God, are a gracious and merciful King.

Commentary

May there ascend, come, and reach ...—all these words are petitions, asking that the memory of Israel come before the Lord. They are written in a kind of progression: **ascend**—that our prayers reach Heaven, and not remain as mere utterings; **come**—to the suitable place; **and reach**—God; **be seen**—before Him; **accepted**—that the Lord accept our prayer; **and heard**—that the content of this petition be heard; **recalled**—that is, be felt; **and remembered ... the remembrance and recollection of us**—the word *pikkadon* (recollection) has the connotation of memory, but it also gives the sense of dealing with something concrete, like a deposit that is kept until it is time for it to be returned to its owner; **the remembrance of our fathers**—upon whose merits we rely; **the remembrance of Messiah the son of David Your servant**—that is, when the time of redemption comes, in which the Davidic Messiah will be revealed; **the remembrance of Jerusalem**—which will also be redeemed then; **and the remembrance of all Your people the House of Israel**—who will be redeemed along with it.

All these should be remembered, first of all, for **deliverance**—from troubles and sufferings; but even more than that, for much **well-being**—beyond the salvation itself; **grace, kindness, mercy**—even though we may not be deserving of it, our redemption should nevertheless come in fullness.

Remember us ... for good; be mindful of us ... for blessing—that is great, and adds to the good; and **with the promise of deliverance and compassion,**

spare us and be gracious to us ... for our eyes are directed to You—and we are unable to look up to, or to rely upon, anyone or anything else; **for You ... are a gracious and merciful King**—and we look forward to Your mercies, even if we do not deserve them.

(Conclusion of the third blessing)

And rebuild Jerusalem the holy city speedily in our days. Blessed are You Lord, who in His mercy rebuilds Jerusalem. Amen.

Commentary

And rebuild Jerusalem the holy city—this conclusion is the quintessence of this blessing, for Jerusalem symbolizes the very essence of Israel; **speedily in our days**—what is speedy in God's terms may be a very long period of time from our perspective; therefore, whenever there is a petition that something be done speedily, there is always added emphasis that this be in our days, and not according to the Divine calculation.

Who in His mercy rebuilds Jerusalem: Some medieval authorities (i.e., the *Kolbo* and others) questioned this phrase, noting that it states explicitly in the Bible that Jerusalem will be built by justice alone (e.g., Isaiah 1:27). Rabbi Shlomo Luria (the *Maharshal*), however, explains that here we ask not only for the rebuilding of Jerusalem, but also that it grow and be far more beautiful than in ancient times, and the realization of this hope depends upon God's mercies alone.

Who in His mercy [*be'raḥamav*] rebuilds: According to kabbalistic sources, this is the precise way in which this phrase should be said, and not just "in mercy" (*be'raḥamim*), for there are different levels to the attribute of mercy, and this refers to Divine mercy.

Jerusalem: Metaphorically and kabbalistically, Jerusalem symbolizes the attribute of *Malkhut* (Kingdom) and the Shekhinah (Divine Presence). For this reason, it serves as a suitable and all-inclusive ending to all the requests mentioned in this blessing, whose concern is returning the Congregation of Israel from Exile. The Congregation of Israel is *Malkhut*, and its rebuilding consists of setting up the Davidic kingdom and rebuilding the Land of Israel.

Amen: There are differing halakhic opinions and differing customs, down to our own day, as to under what circumstances one may answer "Amen" to one's own blessing. However, in this particular case there is universal agreement that one does say "Amen" at this point. This amen serves as a sign that here the main section of the Blessing after Meals, which is a Torah-based commandment, ends, and that what follows are rabbinic additions. Some say that this amen was instituted because of the halakhic ruling according to which laborers hired on a daily basis are obligated to recite only the first three blessings of the Blessing after Meals; and this amen is a reminder that this is where their blessing ends.

Ha'Tov veha'Meitiv—
He Who Is Good and Does Good

Blessed are You, Lord our God, King of the universe, benevolent God, our Father, our King, our Strength, our Creator, our Redeemer, our Maker, our Holy One, the Holy One of Jacob, our Shepherd, the Shepherd of Israel, the King who is good and does good to all, each and every day. He has done good for us, He does good for us, and He will do good for us; He has bestowed, He bestows, and He will forever bestow upon us grace, kindness, and mercy, relief, salvation, and success, blessing and deliverance, consolation, livelihood, and sustenance, compassion, life, peace, and all goodness; and may He never cause us to lack any good.

Commentary

Our Strength, our Creator, our Redeemer ...—this list of praises is arranged according to the first letters of the Hebrew alphabet; **our Holy One, the Holy One of Jacob**—this is based upon the verse "the Holy One of Jacob" (Isaiah 29:23); **our**

Shepherd—as in the verse "the Shepherd of Israel" (Psalms 80:2); **the King who is good**—in essence; **and does good**—to His creatures.

He has bestowed grace, kindness, and mercy—the bestowal mentioned here means giving out of kindness, and not—as the Hebrew verb *gml* used here often means—the repaying of favors; therefore, this is followed by a list of various kinds of rewards and acts of kindness; **and may He never cause us to lack any good**—as in the verse "those who seek the Lord never lack any good thing" (Psalms 34:11).

The Jerusalem Talmud observes that this blessing includes three phrases referring to God as king, three phrases referring to His goodness, and three phrases referring to His bestowing ("He has bestowed, He bestows, and He will forever bestow"). Some commentators explain this repetition as corresponding to three worlds: our world, the world of the spheres (the planets), and the world of the angels, all of which are dependent upon God's mercy and goodness.

Ha'Raḥaman—The Merciful One

May the Merciful One reign over us forever and ever. May the Merciful One be blessed in heaven and on earth. May the Merciful One be praised for all generations, and pride Himself in us forever and all eternity, and glorify Himself in us forever and ever.

Commentary

May the Merciful One be praised for all generations, and pride Himself in us forever—that is, apart from God's Splendor itself, we pray that His splendor and glory be upon us and for our sake, as in the verse "His majesty is upon Israel, and his power is in the heavens" (Psalms 68:35).

May the Merciful One provide our livelihood with honor. May the Merciful One break the yoke of exile from our neck, and may He lead us upright to our land.

Commentary

Break the yoke of exile from our neck—in other versions: the yoke of the nations. **Upright**—that is, in an upright position, freely and openly.

May the Merciful One send abundant blessing into this house and upon this table at which we have eaten. May the Merciful One send us Elijah the prophet—may he be remembered for good—and let him bring us good tidings, deliverance, and consolation.

Commentary

Send us Elijah the prophet—as it is said, "Behold, I send you Elijah the prophet, before the coming of the great and terrible day of the Lord. And he will turn the hearts of the parents to their children, and the heart of the children to their fathers" (Malachi 3:23–24); since the prophet Elijah is the messenger who will bring the tidings of the Messiah and of the great day of the Lord, as well as **good tidings, deliverance, and consolation** concerning the approaching Redemption.

One who eats at other people's table says:

May the Merciful One bless (Here one mentions one's parents, spouse, and children, as appropriate.) (my father, my teacher,) the master of this house, and (my mother, my teacher,) the mistress of this house; them, their household, their children, and all that is theirs;

One who eats at one's own table says:

May the Merciful One bless me (and my father, my teacher, and mother, my teacher,

A married man says:	A married woman says:
my wife,	my husband,

my descendants, and all that is mine),

us, and all that is ours, just as He blessed our forefathers, Abraham, Isaac, and Jacob, "in all things, by all things, with all things" (Cf. Genesis 24:1; 27:33; 33:11; see *Bava Batra* 17a).

Commentary

Just as he blessed our forefathers, Abraham, Isaac, and Jacob, "in all things, by all things, with all things": The blessing of all alludes to a complete, perfect blessing, which, because it includes everything that a person may desire, incorporates the feeling of fulfillment of all needs and wishes. For this reason, it is interpreted as referring to life in the world to come, where there is a feeling of wholeness and peace, and where there is neither want nor desire.

Furthermore, it is said that God gave the patriarchs so much goodness that even in this world, they felt a taste of the World to Come. Indeed, we find the expression *kol* (all), which includes all the good in the world, mentioned in relation to each one of the patriarchs. Concerning Abraham, we read, "And the Lord had blessed Abraham in **all**" (Genesis 24:1); about Isaac, it says, "And he brought it to me, and I ate of **all**" (Genesis 27:33); and of Jacob, "For God has dealt graciously with me, and I have **all**" (Genesis 33:11).

So may He bless all of us together [the children of the Covenant] with a perfect blessing, and let us say, Amen.

Commentary

All of us together is a further petition, beyond the blessing itself, that we be united, and that the blessing devolve upon all. **With a perfect blessing**—namely, this blessing, which includes every possible kind of goodness. **And let us say, Amen**—to this perfect blessing.

From heaven, may there be invoked upon him and upon us such merit which will bring enduring peace.

Commentary

From heaven, may there be invoked upon him and upon us such merit: Invoking merit is required in situations where there is judgment and law. Here, we pray on behalf of the owner of the house and the other participants in the meal, that they be found deserving before the heavenly court. **Which will bring enduring peace**—that this merit be such that blessing and peace will be preserved for them also in the future.

May we receive blessing from the Lord and kindness from God our deliverer, and may we find grace and good understanding in the eyes of God and man.

The Guest's Blessing:

May it be God's will that the master of this house not be shamed in this world, and will not be disgraced in the world to come, and be highly successful in all his property, "and may his, and our, property be valuable and close to the city, and may the Evil One not have power over his, and our, deeds, and may there not occur, neither to him nor to us, any thought of sin, transgression, or iniquity, from now and forever more."

Commentary

The Guest's Blessing: According to some ancient liturgies, this is the only *ha'Rahaman* formula recited after the Blessing after Meals, and it is mentioned already in the Talmud.

For Shabbat:

May the Merciful One let us inherit that day which will be all Shabbat and rest for life everlasting.

Commentary

May the Merciful One let us inherit that day which will be all Shabbat and rest for life everlasting: It is stated in the Talmud that this world corresponds to the six days of Creation, while the life of the world to come is the time of rest, which is **all Shabbat.** This is a "day" not in the literal sense, but rather in the more general sense: a period that, as stated here, will be **for eternal life.** Since, as said above, Shabbat is a taste of the world to come, we pray that we also merit to reach the day that is all Shabbat.

For Rosh Ḥodesh:

May the Merciful One renew for us this month for good and for blessing.

For Festival Days:

May the Merciful One let us inherit that day which is all good (a day which is entirely long, in which the righteous ones sit, crowns on their heads, and delight in the light of the Shekhinah, and may our lot be with them.)

Commentary

May the Merciful One let us inherit that day which is all good: In this world, the Festival days (in Hebrew, *Yamim Tovim;* literally: "good days") are only a small portion of the entire year, while the eternal day of the world to come is entirely good, with no mixture of evil or trouble at all. Some also add the following: **a day which is entirely long**—as this day of the life of the world to come is, in fact, beyond the limitations of time, and therefore it continues indefinitely; in which the righteous ones sit, crowns on their heads, and delight in the light of the Shekhinah—this is an ornate, poetic description of receiving the gift of Divine light, based upon the words of the prophets.

For Rosh ha'Shanah:

May the Merciful One renew for us this year for good and for blessing.

For Sukkot:

May the Merciful One restore for us the fallen sukkah of David.

May the Merciful One grant us the privilege of reaching the days of the Messiah and the life of the world to come.

Commentary

The days of the Messiah are the time that follows the coming of the Messiah. According to Maimonides and others, this period is in many respects a continuation of the normal course of life, but with peace and great abundance, which will enable everyone to engage in what is truly important—knowledge of the Lord.

The world to come is the subsequent period, during which there will be a change in the nature of the physical world and its transformation into a different reality.

He gives great deliverance (On Shabbat and on all other days in which the *Musaf* prayer is recited, one says instead: He is a tower of deliverance—[2 Samuel 22:51]) to His king, and bestows kindness upon His annointed, to David and his descendants forever (Psalms 18:51).

Commentary

He gives great deliverance (in Hebrew: *magdil*) / **He is a tower of deliverance** (In Hebrew: *migdol*) **to His king:** The distinction between the verse recited on weekdays and that said on Shabbat and festivals is a very ancient one. It is based on the two readings of the concluding verse of the Song of David (Psalms 18:51 and 2 Samuel 22:51). The linguistic difference between the two forms corresponds to the distinction between weekdays and Shabbat and Festival days. Magdil (He gives great) is a verb, referring to ongoing activity of change and enhancement, taking place during the weekdays, while migdol ("tower") is a noun, alluding to a greatness that exists fully, as is the case in the holy days.

He who makes peace in His heavens, may He make peace for us and for all Israel; and say, Amen.

Commentary

He who makes peace in His heavens (Job 25:2) means that all of the Divine forces unite completely to fulfill His will. **May He make peace for us and for all Israel:** This sentence concludes the Blessing after Meals, just as it does every *Amidah* prayer, for the blessing of peace is the most elevated blessing, which gives sense and meaning to all other blessings.

Fear the Lord, you His holy ones, for those who fear Him suffer no want. Young lions are in need and go hungry, but those who seek the Lord shall not lack any good [Psalms 34:10-11]. Give thanks to the Lord, for He is good, for His kindness is everlasting [Psalms 136:1]. You open Your hand and satisfy the desire of every living thing [Psalms 145:16]. Blessed is the man who trusts in the Lord, and the Lord will be his security [Jeremiah 17:7].

I was a youth and also have aged, and have not seen a righteous man forsaken, with his children begging for bread [Psalms 37:25]. The Lord will give strength to His people; the Lord will bless His people with peace [Psalms 29:11].

If one recites *Zimmun* over a cup of wine, the *Zimmun* leader now says the blessing over wine, and drinks the wine from the cup.

The Seven Marriage Blessings (Sheva Brakhot)

At a feast in honor of bride and groom, held during the seven days of feasting, the special wedding blessings are recited at the end of the Blessing after Meals. The blessings for the wedding as such are only six in number, but the blessing over wine is always added as a seventh blessing.

These blessings are already mentioned and discussed in the Talmud [*Ketubot* 8a]. They contain blessing and praise for the union of man and woman, which is a sequel to the act of creating Adam and Eve in the Garden of Eden. They also compare this union to the connection between God and the people of Israel. These blessings, then, praise God for the creation of man and of woman, as well as petition for the future of the newly married couple. They also constitute a prayer for joy and redemption for the Congregation of Israel.

Blessed are You, Lord our God, King of the universe, who has created all things for His glory.

Commentary

Who has created all things for His glory—and the marriage, and the home that is being created, too, derive their significance from the fact that they contain, and should contain, praise and glory to God, the Creator of man and woman.

Blessed are You, Lord our God, King of the universe, Creator of man.

Commentary

Creator of man—in the present tense, because a new, complete human is now being created out of this partnership of marriage, as is said, "Male and female He created them.… and He called their name Adam" (Genesis 1:27; 5:2).

Blessed are You, Lord our God, King of the universe, who created man in His image, in the image [of His] likeness [He fashioned] his form, and prepared for him from his own self an everlasting edifice. Blessed are You, Lord, Creator of man.

Commentary

Who created man in His image: In the Creation of the world, as it says, "and He created man in His own image, in the image of God He created him" (Genesis 1:27). This refers to the unique intelligence and to the faculty of free choice that were given to human beings.

In the image [of His] likeness [He fashioned] his form: Kabbalistic commentaries dwell at length upon the meaning of these three phrases in relation to God. However, these verses may be understood in the literal sense as referring to the image and form of man, which encompasses a unique spiritual dimension, as well as man's physical form.

And prepared for him—as described in the creation of woman from Adam's rib (Genesis 2:21-22), **an everlasting edifice**—this, both in the literal sense, that the union of man and woman brings into existence the future generations, and in the spiritual sense, that by means of the united service and elevation, a perfect edifice, which lasts forever, is created.

May the barren one [Jerusalem] rejoice and be happy at the ingathering of her children to her midst in joy. Blessed are You, Lord, who gladdens Zion with her children.

Commentary

May the barren one ... rejoice and be happy—refers to Jerusalem in the period of Exile, which the prophet compares to a childless woman. This blessing, then, is the prayer for **the ingathering of her children to her midst in joy**—that is, to the ingathering of exiles to Jerusalem, which symbolizes the Congregation of Israel. The prophets also compare the connection between God and the Congregation of Israel, and between God and Jerusalem, to the connection between man and woman.

Grant abundant joy to these loving friends, as You bestowed gladness upon Your created being in the Garden of Eden of old. Blessed are You, Lord, who gladdens the groom and bride.

Commentary

Loving friends—the couple who are marrying now. **As You bestowed gladness upon Your created being in the Garden of Eden:** According to the Midrash, God served as best man to Adam. Others interpret this as both a request and a wish: just as Adam had only Eve, who was all his world and the sole source of his joy, so should these partners rejoice in one another, as if there were no one else in the world.

Blessed are You, Lord our God, King of the universe, who created joy and happiness, groom and bride, gladness, jubilation, cheer and delight, love, friendship, harmony, and fellowship. Lord our God, let there speedily be heard in the cities of Judah and in the streets of Jerusalem the sound of joy and the sound of happiness, the sound of a groom and the sound of a bride, the sound of exultation of grooms from under their bridal canopy and youths from their joyous banquets. Blessed are You, Lord, who gladdens the groom with the bride.

Then the *Zimmun* leader says:

Blessed are You, Lord our God, King of the universe, who creates the fruit of the vine.

Commentary

Who created joy and happiness: This is a blessing of praise and thanksgiving to God for creating joy and love in general, in all their richness and variety, and the joy of bride and groom in particular. To this blessing is added a prayer for the appearance of perfect joy, with the coming of the redeemer.

Who gladdens the groom with the bride: The conclusion of the preceding blessing reads, "who gladdens the groom and bride"—that is, each one on his/her own—while here, there is a higher praise to the Almighty for making the two happy with one another, and together.